Emergency Manoeuver Training

Controlling Your Airplane During A Crisis

Rich Stowell
Master Flight Instructor

Australian Edition

Emergency Manoeuvre Training
Australian Edition

© 2024 PilotTrain Aviation Publishing

ISBN   978-0-6455298-6-9
Edition   First

First published in the United States by Rich Stowell.

Published by:
PilotTrain Aviation Publishing
PO Box 2044
Newnham TAS 7248
PTD-18
www.pilottrain.com.au

Disclaimer
All rights reserved. No part of this book may be reproduced in any form without the publisher's permission, except as permitted by law. While every precaution has been taken in the preparation of this book, the publisher and Rich Stowell assume no responsibility for errors or omissions. No liability is assumed for damages resulting from the use of information contained herein.

Acknowledgements
Special thanks to Anderson Aviation Australia Pty Ltd for their support in making this title available in Australia.

Erratum and Addendum
This book follows the latest rules and regulations; however, the aviation industry is volatile, and rules can change rapidly.

PilotTrain publishes updates via free downloadable PDFs on their website for changes issued post-publication.

Dedication

To my best friend, Jan Evans.

About The Author

Rich Stowell received his private pilot's certificate in January, 1984, from Burnside-Ott Aviation Training Center. In September, 1987, Stowell left his engineering career behind to become Chief Aerobatic Pilot at CP Aviation in Santa Paula, California. He became a Certified Flight Instructor nine months later.

While at CP Aviation, Stowell turned an existing emergency manoeuvres course into the renowned EMT®—Emergency Manoeuvre Training—Program. The Program and Stowell's teaching techniques have been featured in several aviation magazines, including *Flying*, *Private Pilot*, *Sport Pilot*, *Hot Kits & Homebuilts*, and *AOPA Pilot*.

Stowell has provided more than 8,500 hours of emergency manoeuvre, spin, aerobatic, and tailwheel instruction. He has been a frequent lecturer at the annual EAA conventions at Oshkosh, Wisconsin, and Lakeland, Florida, as well as a contributing editor for *Aviation Safety* and *Flight Training* magazines. Stowell wrote, associate produced, and hosted several critically acclaimed educational videos on emergency manoeuvre training, stall/spin awareness, and basic aerobatics. His first book, *PARE®—The Emergency Spin Recovery Procedure*, based on the PARE® acronym he developed as part of the EMT® Program, was published in 1991; his third book, *The Light Airplane Pilot's Guide to STALL/SPIN AWARENESS*, was published in 2007.

Stowell is a member of the Society of Aviation and Flight Educators, the International Aerobatic Club, the Experimental Aircraft Association, and the Aircraft Owners and Pilots Association. He is a FAASTeam Lead Representative, and is active as a speaker at safety programs across the country. He also holds a Bachelor's degree in Mechanical Engineering from Rensselaer Polytechnic Institute in Troy, New York.

For his contributions to aviation safety and education, Stowell received the FAA/Industry National Flight Instructor of the Year Award in 2006 and the IAC President's Award in 1994.

Acknowledgments

Wow! Little did I know that it would take seven years to complete this project. But then, that's how long it took for my own experience to evolve to the point where I could present these topics in a reasonably comprehensive, easily readable form. Of course, none of this would have been possible without the assistance of a host of other people. So, let me gratefully acknowledge...

Clay Phelps and **CP Aviation**, for giving me tremendous latitude in the development and promotion of the EMT° Program.

Sammy Mason and **Tony LeVier**, for their support and wisdom in the early days of the Program's development.

Jim Campbell of *US Aviator* magazine, for his on-going media support of our Program in particular, and of spin and aerobatic training in general.

Greg Smith and **Margie Carbonell-Smith**, for their years of encouragement and friendship. Thanks, Greg, for your detailed review of the manuscript as well as for providing the front cover photos and the author mug shot!

Dan Matejczyk, for thoroughly critiquing the text from several viewpoints: engineer, competition aerobatic pilot, general aviation pilot.

Martin Lin of Marlin Designs, for generating the illustrations used in this book.

Gene Beliveau, **Bob Phelps**, and **Jim Taylor**, for reviewing the manuscript.

My **EMT° Students**, for teaching me about the student-instructor interrelationship in the training environment.

Jan Evans, for typing and editing earlier iterations of the manuscript. Thanks, too, for persevering through my sometimes difficult metamorphosis from engineer to flight instructor, from instructor to writer.

Portions of this book have appeared in articles written by the author for *Plane & Pilot* and *Flight Training* magazines.

Disclaimer

This book is intended to be a teaching tool for emergency manoeuvre and other unusual attitude training programs. The information presented herein is as accurate, complete, and authoritative as possible. However, there may be errors and omissions, both typographical and in content.

This book should be used as a general guide only and not as the ultimate source of aeronautical principles or procedures. It is designed to complement and supplement other aviation texts and formal flight instruction. For additional reference materials and recommended reading, refer to the Bibliography.

Stalls, spins, inverted flight, and other unusual attitudes, whether intentional or unintentional, may be life threatening. The information presented herein is not a substitute for actual flight training or for proficiency in the manoeuvres and techniques described. The author and publisher strongly recommend that you receive hands-on flight training only from qualified flight instructors experienced in the procedures outlined herein, using only approved, well maintained, and properly loaded airplanes with appropriate safety equipment—including parachutes—before attempting any of the manoeuvres described in this text.

The author and the publisher shall not be liable or responsible to any person or entity with respect to any loss or damage caused or alleged to be caused directly or indirectly by the information contained in this book. This text is not a substitute for common sense or the exercise of good judgment.

Nothing in this text supersedes any regulatory material or operational documents issued by aviation regulators or certified operators.

As stated in the Civil Aviation Safety Regulations, Part 91, Section 91.215, Paragraph (2):

The pilot in command of the aircraft:

(a) has final authority over:

(i) the aircraft; and:

(ii) the maintenance of discipline by all persons on the aircraft; and

(b) must ensure:

(i) the safety of persons on the aircraft; and

(ii) the safety of cargo on the aircraft; and

(iii) the safe operation of the aircraft during the flight.

Table Of Contents

About The Author v

Acknowledgments vi

Disclaimer vii

Emergency Manoeuvre Training 1

Basic Aerodynamics 5
    Steady Flight 9
    Important Ratios 13

Roll, Yaw, and Pitch 15
    Roll 16
    Yaw 16
    Pitch 17
    Secondary Roll Effects 17
    Secondary Yaw Effects 18
    Secondary Pitch Effects 23

Pitch and Power 25
    Energy Management 26
    The Power Curve 32

Curved Flight 37
    Forces in Turns 39
    G-Loads 40
    The V-g Diagram 43
    Helpful Hints 47
    Shallow Turns 48
    Medium Turns 48
    Steep Turns 48
    Climbing & Descending Turns 49
    Skidding Turns 50
    Slipping Turns 51
    Turn/Roll Combinations 52
    Spirals 52

Final Thoughts 53

Stalls 55

Flying the V-g Diagram 59
Aerodynamic Cues 63
Mechanical Cues 65
Physiological Cues 66
Approach-To-Landing Stall 68
Departure Stall 68
Under-The-Bottom Stall 68
Over-The-Top Stall 69
Prolonged Stall 69
Deep Stall 69
Tail Stall 70
Stall Speed vs. C.G. 71
Flaps 72
Final Thoughts 72

Spins 73

Spin Dynamics 74
Incipient 77
Developed 77
Recovery 78
Inertia Effects 78
Wing Design 79
Fuselage Design 80
Tail Design 81
Pilot-Controlled Variables 82
Power 82
Ailerons 83
Flaps 84
Rudder 84
Elevator 86
Procedure vs. Technique 87
Accelerated Spin 87
Transition Spin 87

Cross-Over Spin	88
Pilot-Induced Flat Spin	89

Overbanked 93

Roll Dynamics	95
V-p & V-g Diagrams	97
Power	99
Push	99
Roll	99
Managing The Airspeed	100
In The Pattern	101
Invisible Tornadoes	102
Aircraft Configuration Effects	103
Atmospheric Effects	103
Separation	104
Elevation	104
Be Prepared	106

Control Failures 109

Ailerons	109
Rudder	110
Elevator	111
Flaps	114
Flutter	115

Glides 117

Weight	118
Wind	119
Turning Flight	120
Airplane Configuration	123
Judging Glide Distance	124
The Glide Envelope	128

Powerplant Failures 131

Power Loss	131
Speed	133
Spot	135

> Set-up 139
>
> Loss Of Power Control 140

Off-Airport Landings 143

> Engine Restart 143
>
> Evaluating Your Options 145
>
> Flying the Approach 148
>
> The Touchdown 151

The Pilot In Command 153

> Situational Awareness 154
>
> Judgment 155
>
> Hazardous Attitudes 156
>
> Stressors 157
>
> See And Be Seen 161
>
> It's Up To You 162

Appendix 1—For More Information 165

Appendix 2—EMT® Program Syllabus 167

Bibliography 171

1

Emergency Manoeuvre Training

"it is possible to fly without motors, but not without knowledge and skill."

—Wilbur Wright

This profound thought was conveyed in a letter to the pioneering glider designer, Octave Chanute, years before the Wright Brothers' historic first powered flight. It reveals the essence of becoming a proficient pilot. In a life that holds few guarantees, pilots are guaranteed one inescapable truth: every takeoff will be followed by a landing. Determining exactly where, when, what condition, and in what attitude the airplane will return to the Earth is the most challenging part of learning to fly. Compared to now, early aviators were handicapped with unreliable powerplants. To compensate for deficiencies inherent in their equipment, they had to master the art of flying; it simply was a matter of survival. Fortunately, they didn't have the additional burden of dealing with a complex web of structured airspace, massive regulations, and sophisticated equipment.

Even though greater system reliability has reduced the likelihood of an unscheduled landing, today's pilots must be adept at traversing an intricate airspace system. They must be able to communicate effectively on the radio. They must be familiar with an array of instruments, bells, whistles, and other gadgets bristling from the instrument panel, as well as a variety of other requirements. The broad scope of experience needed for modern aviation, however, often detracts from time spent perfecting the sole operation that's a matter of life or death in the air: **FLYING THE AIRPLANE**!

General aviation has undoubtedly benefited from technological advances over the years, but the fundamental relationship between pilot and airplane remains unchanged. We can modify Mr. Wright's statement, in fact, to fit today's complex flight environment without diminishing the significance of its message:

"It's possible to fly without motors, radios, VOR, GPS, sectional charts, control towers, and Class E airspace, but not without knowledge and skill."

Nowhere are knowledge and skill more important than during an in-flight crisis; sadly, nowhere are weaknesses in these areas more evident, either. The responsibility for surviving an in-flight emergency rests squarely on the pilot's shoulders. The probability of successfully recognising and dealing with in-flight problems ultimately boils down to one, and only one action: flying the airplane. More often than not, those who habitually do the right things enjoy long and happy flying careers; those who do the wrong things, don't. An all-too-common accident report bears this out:

The aircraft lost power on takeoff a few hundred feet above the ground. Witnesses said the airplane entered a steep turn at low airspeed when it suddenly descended out of control [or rolled inverted and crashed, or entered a spin].

All that's missing is a date, time, place, type of aircraft, and number of occupants on board. What's not addressed, though, are questions like, why do such similar accidents continue to occur? how come these accidents don't discriminate between experienced and novice pilots? and what's going on in the cockpit?

A loss of power does not, in and of itself, cause an airplane to descend out of control. It's the pilot's reaction to an engine failure, or any other emergency for that matter, that determines the ensuing course of events. Pilot error, which is cited as a primary factor in most accidents, results from three elements influencing the pilot: distraction, faulty perceptions, and inappropriate control inputs.

What basic knowledge and skill components are missing in flight training that influence a pilot's reactions in favor of an accident? Simply, a lot of pilots learn to fly within a bubble that is much smaller than the airplane's operating envelope. Gray areas left in primary training often multiply as pilots are exposed to a wider assortment of in-flight situations. This can lead to self-doubt about one's flying abilities, which fosters confusion, an increasing lack of confidence, and apprehension at the controls. To drive home the importance of sharp flying skills, let's simulate the classic stall/spin accident during a base-to-final turn.

Assume we're flying a left-hand pattern, close to the ground, in a strong wind, at an unfamiliar airport (multiple distractions). As we begin our turn from base to final, the airplane overshoots the runway centerline. Our normal range of experience and comfort level preclude us from increasing the angle of bank any further to correct back to the centerline (faulty perception), particularly close to the ground (distraction). Instead, we elect to skid our way onto final approach using the rudder (inappropriate input).

We're trying to turn with the rudder (inappropriate input) only because we're close to the ground in a critical configuration (distractions). The rudder doesn't turn the airplane; it YAWS it. Its primary function is to cancel yaw, keeping the airplane in coordinated flight and safeguarding against spinning. But now here we are intentionally misapplying the rudder. We're actually teasing the airplane with precisely what it needs to spin (inappropriate input).

The rudder input slices the nose downward, through the horizon. In our straight-and-level experience, the elevator appears to hold our nose "up" (faulty perception), so we respond with back elevator pressure (inappropriate input). Unfortunately, back elevator neither holds us up, nor can it stop the yaw generated by the rudder. Back elevator pressure absolutely, positively, always pulls us closer to critical angle of attack and a stall. Even though it's not our intention to stall with excessive rudder applied a few hundred feet above the ground, we are nevertheless configuring the airplane for this eventuality.

Compounding matters, the rudder input causes the outside wing to travel faster than the inside wing; hence, it experiences more Lift, rolling us farther into the turn. We didn't want to increase our bank in the first place, so we respond now by applying opposite aileron. Given our proximity to critical angle of attack, this input is inappropriate. In fact, deflecting the ailerons at this stage could initiate a stall earlier than usual and could aggravate stall characteristics.

We've forgotten about the runway, the turn, and the strong wind by now. Our attention turns to the developing unusual attitude and the odd movements seen over the nose (new distractions). Figuring our corrective actions mustn't be strong enough (faulty perceptions), we vigorously apply more of everything (inappropriate inputs). The airplane, obeying our every command, suddenly snaps into a spin.

Pilots certainly don't intend to spin in the traffic pattern, yet those who have did so by unwittingly duplicating the inputs required to spin. The chain of events leading to the classic stall/spin accident center around miscommunication between the pilot and the airplane. Much of the confusion stems from our normal flight experience, which represents a limited snapshot of a much larger, more dynamic picture.

For instance, at what point do our normal perceptions become erroneous in a skidding turn? Twenty degrees of bank, maybe less. How much yaw does it take to excite the spin? A glance at the slip/skid ball reveals, amazingly, that it's resting JUST A HALF A BALL OUT FROM THE CENTER! Any excess yaw at the wrong time can excite Autorotation. Without acute situational awareness, a good understanding of aerodynamics, and proper stick-and-rudder skills, how can we ever know with certainty where the edge of our operating envelope really is?

Exposing pilots to the full 360 degrees of roll, yaw, and pitch possible in an airplane is not a new concept. The first formally-recognised, all-attitude training program began in the U.S. in 1917 as the Army Air Service's, "Basic Battle Acrobacy and Trick Flying" course. Inspired by aerial combat as World War I raged on, the week-long syllabus went like this: Monday, Stalls; Tuesday, Spins; Wednesday, Loops; Thursday, Chandelles; Friday, Barrel Rolls.

Unfortunately, as the title of this early unusual attitudes course demonstrates, anything beyond normal, straight and level flight was considered "aerobatics", "trick flying", or "stunting". The benefits of aerobatic training have often been overshadowed by the stunt pilot stigma perpetuated since the early days of aviation. As a result of this negative connotation—coupled with the lack of specific guidelines for the conduct of such training—many pilots are reluctant to incorporate aerobatics into their aviation education. Emergency manoeuvre training, on the other hand, draws on the positive aspects of aerobatics, but it tailors them specifically to the straight-and-level pilot. Packaged as a separate class of instruction, emergency manoeuvre training forms a natural bridge between normal and aerobatic training.

NORMAL TRAINING	EMERGENCY MANOEUVRE TRAINING	AEROBATIC TRAINING
• PRIMARY • INSTRUMENT • COMMERCIAL & CFI • TYPE RATINGS	• STALL/SPIN AWARENESS • UNUSUAL ATTITUDES • SAFETY COURSES • CONFIDENCE COURSES • EMT® PROGRAM	• BASIC • ADVANCED • COMPETITION • AIRSHOW • MOVIE & STUNT FLYING

Figure 1-1: Bridging the Training Gap

The emergency manoeuvre training philosophy addresses the gray areas left in normal flight training. Several topics fall under this umbrella of specialised instruction, including the fundamentals of flight; stall/spin awareness; recoveries from inverted attitudes; control failures, powerplant failures, and off-airport landings; and critical manoeuvres such as turns, slips, skids, and glides. In its broadest sense, emergency manoeuvre training attempts to improve pilot proficiency and confidence in all flight attitudes. It strives to develop pilot awareness, recognition, and avoidance of steps that can lead to an unusual attitude. Emergency manoeuvre training also instills the instinctive responses needed to cope with in-flight emergencies.

Seeds for a cohesive emergency manoeuvre training philosophy were planted in 1984 when Tony LeVier, former Lockheed Chief Test Pilot, established a non-profit organisation called Safe Action in Flight Emergencies (S.A.F.E.). The primary goal of the organisation was to foster spin and unusual attitude training through scholarships used to defray some of the training's cost.

Scholarship recipients, however, needed access to schools that could accommodate this specialised training. To start, LeVier turned to his longtime friend, Sammy Mason—a renowned flight instructor, author, and test pilot. Mason designed a five hour package offered by Aerobatic Safety Unlimited (ASU), in Santa Paula, California. By 1985, ASU was teaching S.A.F.E. students under the banner, "Emergency Manoeuvre Training Course". Soon thereafter, two other California-based aerobatic schools joined in, earning S.A.F.E. approval for similar programs.

In 1987, CP Aviation, Inc. (also in Santa Paula) took over ASU's training operation. The medley of courses once offered by ASU subsequently underwent extensive revision. The "Emergency Manoeuvre Training Course", for example, was considered still too much like aerobatic training—students learned Loops, Immelmanns, Hammerheads, Snap Rolls, Vertical Reversements, Split-S's, and Inverted Spins in the first five hours. The premise behind emergency manoeuvre training, however, called for a stronger emphasis on more non-aerobatic elements up front; thus evolved the EMT®—Emergency Manoeuvre Training—Program.

Armed with the EMT Program, CP Aviation stepped to the forefront of the now burgeoning emergency manoeuvre training movement. The rapid and widespread success of this particular program soon lead to a string of magazine articles appearing in major aviation publications. A series of critically-acclaimed videotapes produced by Precision Productions Aviation Videos ensued. The impact of the EMT Program, combined with its magazine articles, videos, and companion seminars, certainly helped to inject the emergency manoeuvre training philosophy into the mainstream of general aviation.

Emergency manoeuvre training terminology is now common language in general aviation. The annual "Directory of Aerobatic Schools" published by the International Aerobatic Club, for example, lists many facilities offering training under the specific headings "Emergency Manoeuvres" and "Emergency Manoeuvre Training". Other flight schools and organisations have adopted similar language and offer comparable services to their students. Even major airlines have begun to incorporate unusual attitude recoveries into their simulator training programs (disguised under such innocuous labels as "Advanced Manoeuvre Training" and "Selected Event Training").

Like the first all-attitude course in 1917, emergency manoeuvre training hones basic VFR flying skills. It highlights the impact our control inputs have on flight, emphasising that airplanes only respond to these inputs, not to what we hope will happen, or to what we think will happen. We learn to appreciate, therefore, how the controls really work, what our role is in the flight process, and how to interact properly with the airplane. Integrating these elements and concentrating on flight from the pilot's perspective is what emergency manoeuvre training is all about.

2
Basic Aerodynamics

Airplanes are governed by immutable aerodynamic principles. Regardless of the number of engines, the location of the wings, or the design of the tail feathers (or canards), airplanes respond to changes in Lift, Drag, angle of attack, and stability. This chapter offers a review of the fundamentals of flight, which form the backbone for the emergency strategies developed in later chapters.

For this review, let's assume the role of "flying machine designer". We're not interested in solving complex aerodynamic formulas, or trying to understand philosophical theories; we want to fly like the majestic eagles soaring high overhead. To do so, we must supply enough force to suspend our airplane above the ground. This lifting force is generated using principles discovered hundreds of years earlier by Daniel Bernoulli and Sir Isaac Newton. They could only imagine the wonders of powered flight, but we're fortunate enough to be able to experience it!

According to Bernoulli, the total pressure exerted by an airstream is the sum of static pressure and dynamic pressure ($H = p + q$). Total pressure, however, must remain constant; so, a drop in static pressure causes the dynamic pressure to rise to maintain the same total. Likewise, a rise in static pressure causes a drop in dynamic pressure. Many combinations of static and dynamic pressures are possible, as long as they add up to the same total. This is analogous to making change for one hundred dollar bills using different combinations of fives and tens.

Newton determined that the magnitude of a force acting on an object depends on its mass and its rate of change in velocity (the classic equation, $F = m \times a$). Newton also theorised that every action is accompanied by an equal but opposite reaction. To illustrate the latter point, imagine wading chest-high in a river. The flowing water does not willingly alter its course around your body. It tries to force you downstream, which you must resist to remain in one place.

We can harness the potential in Bernoulli's and Newton's principles by moving specially designed wings through the air. For example, let's test these principles on a section of planks taken from a nearby barn door. Like the constriction in a Venturi tube, placing this rough airfoil into a wind tunnel causes the air to accelerate when flowing around it. Aligned with the airstream, this symmetrical airfoil speeds up the air equally along the top and bottom surfaces. No local imbalance of static and dynamic pressures is created; therefore, no net lifting action occurs from Bernoulli's principle. Newton's principle has no effect either, since the airstream is deflected equally around the wing.

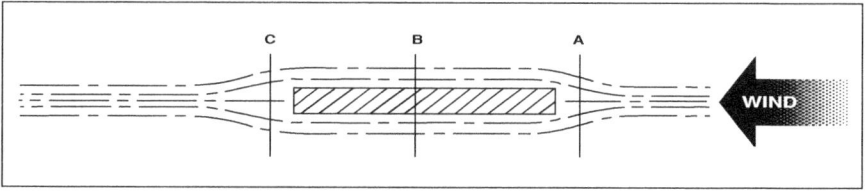

Figure 2-1: Airflow around Rough Airfoil at Zero Angle of Attack

Notice what happens, though, when we tilt the wing a little: the path from A to C becomes slightly longer on the top than on the bottom. Air traversing the upper surface now is accelerated more than the air flowing along the bottom. Consequently, the upper surface experiences a net rise in dynamic pressure with a commensurate drop in static pressure. The reduced static pressure pulls the wing upward, buoyed up further by the higher static pressure along the wing's bottom. Air flowing along the bottom now also impinges on the surface and is deflected downward and rearward. Accordingly, our wing is pushed upward and rearward through an equal-but-opposite reaction to the air.

As a result of these air pressure and direction changes, airflow in the vicinity of the wing experiences a net deflection downward, appropriately called **DOWNWASH**. The total aerodynamic force thus generated happens to be tilted slightly aft. It's more convenient, though, to relate aerodynamic forces to the free airstream. The component perpendicular to the free airstream wind is the beneficial lifting force—Lift—that we're seeking. The small, parallel component pointing aft, on the other hand, serves no practical purpose. This wasted force—Drag—is an unfortunate penalty indelibly linked to our attempt to obtain Lift.

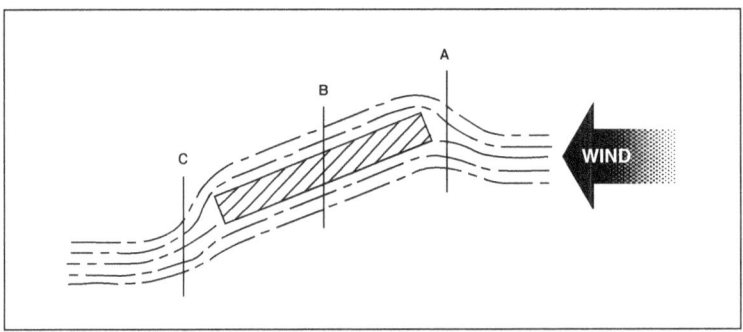

Figure 2-2: Airflow around Rough Airfoil at Small Angle of Attack

We're ecstatic, nonetheless. Our barn door-wing is flying! Through more testing, we find several factors that influence the magnitude of the forces generated: the speed and density of the airstream; the degree of tilt; and the wing's shape, profile, and surface area. Above a certain tilt angle, we also witness the airflow suddenly tearing away from the wing's upper surface.

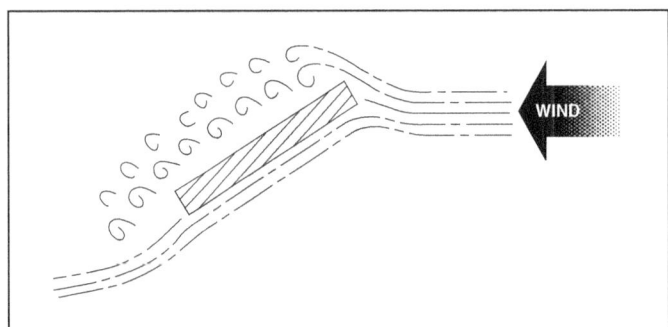

Figure 2-3: Airflow around Rough Airfoil at Large Angle of Attack

Let's now incorporate some pertinent aerodynamic nomenclature into our vocabulary:

LEADING EDGE is the upwind edge of the wing. **TRAILING EDGE** is the downwind edge of the wing. **CHORD** is an imaginary straight line connecting the leading and trailing edges. **AIRFOIL** refers to the shape of the wing from leading to trailing edge.

RELATIVE WIND is the free-airstream wind acting on the wing. It always points opposite to the wing's direction of movement.

ANGLE OF ATTACK (AOA) is the degree of tilt between the wing's chord line and the relative wind. **CRITICAL ANGLE OF ATTACK** is the maximum degree of tilt that maintains smooth airflow over the wing. Above this angle, airflow separates from the wing's surface.

AIRSPEED is the actual speed of the relative wind flowing over the wing. Indicated airspeed is an instrument reading uncorrected for altitude, position, and installation errors. In general, airspeed indicators manufactured after the mid-to-late 1970's display indicated airspeed. (Note: indicated airspeed errors tend to be larger at lower speeds, especially with the flaps down.)

Unlike indicated airspeed, calibrated airspeed is an instrument reading already corrected for position and installation errors. Airspeed indicators manufactured prior to the mid-70's usually show calibrated airspeed. Calibrated airspeed values should be used whenever computing V-speeds and other aerodynamic relationships. For example, a recommended approach speed of 1.3Vso means 1.3 times the **CALIBRATED**, power-off stall speed in the landing configuration. In newer airplanes, be sure to convert indicated airspeed into calibrated airspeed (using the correction table provided in the airplane's flight manual), perform the calculation, then convert the calibrated airspeed back into the corresponding indicated airspeed—the speed you'll observe on the airspeed indicator.

STALL is the turbulent separation of air from the wing occurring above critical angle of attack.

LIFT is the net force acting perpendicular to the relative wind resulting from Bernoulli's and Newton's principles ($L = C_l \times q \times S$). Ultimately, it's Lift that allows us to fly.

DRAG is the net force acting parallel to the relative wind resulting from Bernoulli's and Newton's principles ($D = C_d \times q \times S$). Nothing in nature is free, and Drag is the price we pay to have Lift. The total Drag force retarding the airplane's progress, though, is actually made up of two components: Induced and Parasite.

Induced Drag is the adverse by-product of the lifting process, and downwash is its telltale sign. So are wingtip vortices. Parasite Drag, on the other hand, results simply from moving the airplane through the air. It's composed of form and surface friction drag, air leakage losses, and interference drag at the junctions of the various parts of the airplane (such as where the wing meets the fuselage). Induced Drag dominates during high angle of attack/low speed flight, whereas Parasite Drag dominates during low angle of attack/high speed flight.

MOMENT is the product of an applied force times its distance from a pivot point ($M = F \times d$). To appreciate the significance of this relationship, perform this simple experiment on any swinging door: With the door almost closed, place your thumb one-half inch from the hinged end and push the door open. Try again, now pushing the door open with your thumb one-half inch from the free end. You must push harder to open the door near its hinge (smaller distance = larger force). But farther from the hinge, the door opens effortlessly (larger distance = smaller force). Aerodynamic moments work the same way. As we'll see, moments not only make our airplane stable, but they also make it easily manoeuvrable.

Further testing of the barn door-wing reveals the impracticality of such an inefficient shape. It'll fly, but only at high airspeed. Lots of horsepower is needed to overcome the high Drag, and it has a narrow range of angles of attack prior to the stall. After testing several streamlined shapes, we settle on the half-teardrop cross-section. Placed in an airstream at moderate angles of attack, this efficient shape has a relatively wide band of usable angles of attack prior to the stall. It doesn't require excessive airspeeds, nor huge powerplants to fly. As a result, it's commonly used on many light airplanes.

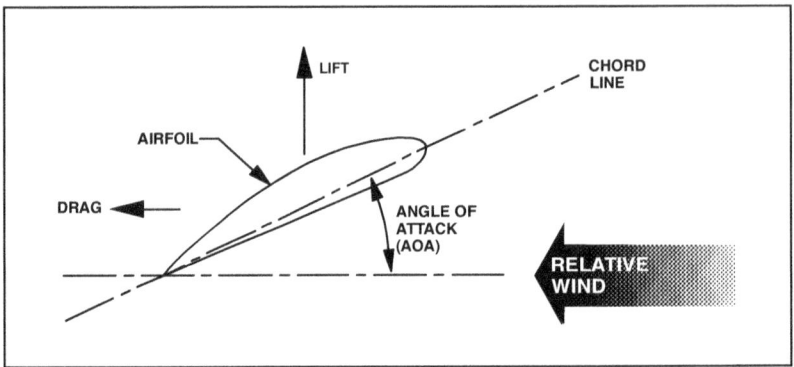

Figure 2-4: Streamlined Airfoil

Our tests reveal that different shapes provide different degrees of Lift and Drag. They also have different ranges of available angles of attack preceding the stall. We can represent the relative efficiency of different shapes graphically by plotting coefficients of Lift and Drag as a function of angle of attack. These graphs allow us to match performance characteristics with the airplane's intended mission, or to analyse the characteristics of a given airfoil.

Figure 2-5 reveals the personality of a typical wing. The coefficient of Lift increases steadily, reaches a maximum value at the critical angle of attack, then decreases rapidly thereafter. The coefficient of Drag, however, always increases as angle of attack increases, rising sharply beyond critical angle of attack. Let's summarise some key points represented in Figure 2-5:

1. Coefficients of Lift and Drag are **INDEPENDENT OF AIRSPEED**;

2. Critical angle of attack is a fixed value, **INDEPENDENT OF AIRSPEED AND ATTITUDE**;

3. Wings still generate Lift above critical angle of attack, but in decreasing proportions compared to Drag.

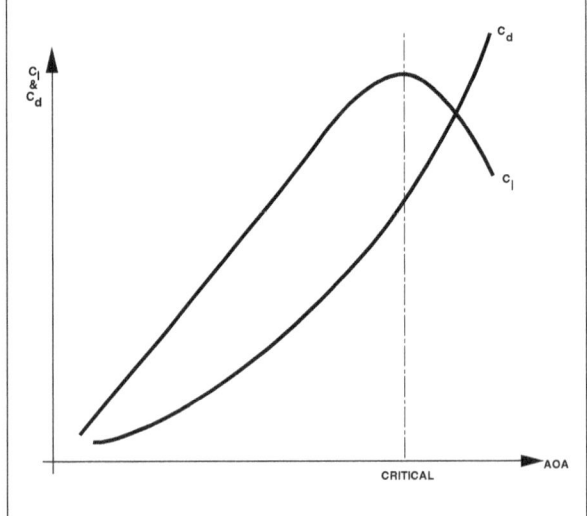

Figure 2-5: Coefficients of Lift and Drag vs. Angle of Attack

Steady Flight

Now that we understand our wing a little better, let's assemble the rest of our airplane, starting with the cockpit area mounted under the wing. Two important design considerations are manoeuvrability and stability. We want to control our airplane easily (it should be manoeuvrable) without it getting beyond our control (it should be stable). The more manoeuvrable we make the airplane, the less stable it will be, and vice versa. We must continually strike a balance between forces and moments acting on the airplane.

Most general aviation flight operations involve steady flight conditions. Stabilised climbs, descents, most traffic pattern operations, cruise flight, and flight in Instrument Meteorological Conditions (IMC) have one thing in common: balanced forces and moments. In level flight at a constant airspeed, for instance, all forces acting on the airplane cancel each other. All moments cancel each other as well. The airplane is perfectly balanced, as if suspended by a string.

Weight is the primary nemesis of flight. We must contend with this relentless force in order to fly. Recalling Newton's formula, total Weight equals the mass of the airplane times the acceleration of gravity (W = m x g). Weight always acts in a direction pointing toward the Earth's center, regardless of aircraft attitude. The airplane's pivot point—its **CENTER OF GRAVITY** (c.g.)—represents the point through which the Weight of the airplane is assumed to be concentrated, and around which the airplane rotates. From a practical standpoint, the c.g. varies with the location and weight of passengers, baggage, and fuel.

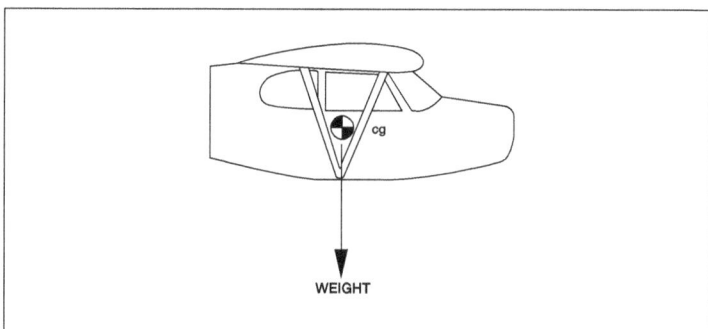

Figure 2-6: Aircraft Weight Concentrated at the Center of Gravity

Lift is our answer to Weight. The wing must generate enough Lift to offset the airplane's Weight; otherwise we'll accelerate earthward. For simplicity, total Lift is often assumed to be concentrated at a single point on the wing—its **CENTER OF PRESSURE** (c.p.)—which is analogous to the airplane's center of gravity. Center of pressure, however, varies with angle of attack. It slides forward, toward the leading edge, as angle of attack increases; rearward, toward the trailing edge, as angle of attack decreases.

Unfortunately, generating Lift also introduces the inevitable Drag penalty. Without a counter-force balancing Drag, the airplane will lose altitude like a glider. An engine-driven propeller provides this force—Thrust—by changing the velocity of air moving through it. Although Thrust is the force developed by a spinning propeller, Power is the common measure of performance for reciprocating engines. Power is actually Thrust moving forward at some speed (P = T x V). Operationally, Power output corresponds directly to fuel flow; thus, it provides more meaningful information to the pilot than Thrust. Nevertheless, it's Thrust that balances us in steady flight.

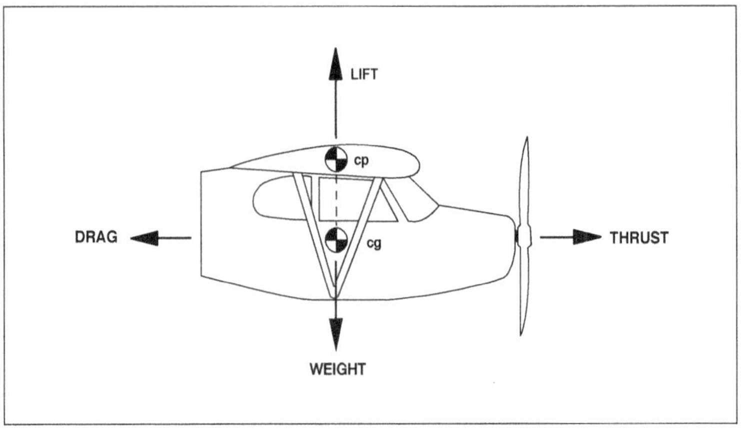

Figure 2-7: The Four Forces of Flight

Lift equals Weight, Thrust equals Drag; we're balanced in level flight. Moments, on the other hand, only balance when these forces act along straight lines passing through the center of gravity. For example, if the center of pressure is located directly above the center of gravity, Lift does not rotate the airplane around the c.g. If they're not aligned, a moment is created: Lift balances Weight, but it also pivots the airplane around its c.g.

Let's focus on Lift and examine the pitching moments resulting from different center of gravity locations. Imagine a paper model of our airplane pinned through the c.g. to a table so it can pivot like a seesaw. A piece of string attached to the c.p. represents our Lift vector. No moment is generated when the center of gravity and the center of pressure are aligned. Pulling on the string doesn't pivot the airplane (Figure 2-8a). Now move the c.g. aft—behind the c.p. Stick the pin through the c.g. and pull on the string. The airplane pitches to a higher angle of attack (Figure 2-8b). Now slide the c.g. forward—ahead of the c.p.—and pin it down. Pulling on the string pitches the airplane to a lower angle of attack (Figure 2-8c).

The relationship between center of gravity and center of pressure is critical for stability. Whenever the c.g. slides behind the c.p., Lift creates a moment that pitches the airplane toward high angles of attack, high Drag, and stalled flight. When the c.g. slides ahead of the c.p., Lift pitches the airplane toward lower angles of attack, away from stalled flight. The latter is more desirable; hence let's establish an aft c.g. limit that's ahead of the wing's forward-most c.p. point.

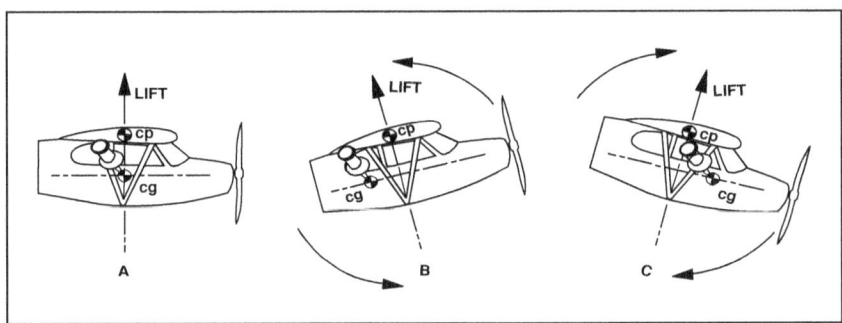

Figure 2-8: How C.G. & C.P. Locations Affect Pitch Stability

If the center of gravity moves too far forward, however, our yet-to-be-designed pitch control may not be able to raise the nose enough for a good landing. Consequently, we must also set a forward c.g. limit based on control effectiveness. We're starting to shape the airplane's operating envelope. The c.g. range thus defined makes our airplane "nose-heavy". We now have to find a way to balance the airplane's inherent forward pitching tendency.

Let's add a small stabilising wing—the **HORIZONTAL STABILISER**—to our airplane. Its job is to counter the main wing's nose-down pitching moment. Locating this surface aft of the c.g. means that it must produce a small downward force, called Negative Lift. We now have a large Lift force, close to the c.g., trying to pitch the nose forward, and a small force, far from the c.g., trying to pitch the nose back. The resulting moments cancel. In addition, placing the horizontal stabiliser within the downwash of our main wing helps it generate the necessary Negative Lift.

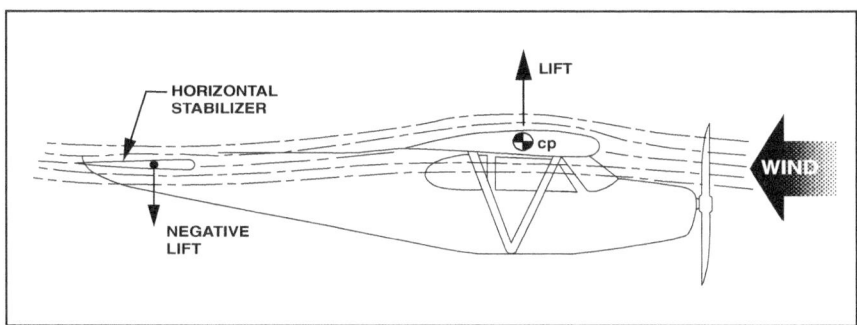

Figure 2-9: Stabilising the Aircraft in Pitch

Now that the moments finally balance, it's time to recheck our force balance: Thrust still equals Drag in steady, level flight. But Lift must now equal airplane Weight plus the Negative Lift generated by the horizontal stabiliser. Negative Lift is counterproductive to lifting the airplane skyward. Locating the horizontal stabiliser as far aft as practical minimises the adverse impact of this downward tail force. It's often convenient to treat the Negative Lift simply as added Weight, which then allows us to say Lift-equals-Weight in steady flight.

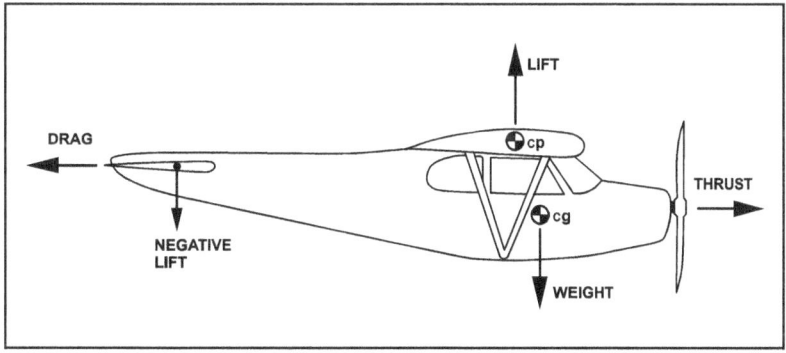

Figure 2-10: Balancing the Forces of Flight

As with pitch stability, our airplane should be stable about its center of gravity during sideslip conditions. Sideslip occurs when the relative wind does not point directly from the nose to the tail, but rather is skewed at an angle. The fuselage is wide at the nose for the engine, it's wide under the wing for pilots, passengers, and baggage, and it tapers off to support the small, horizontal stabiliser. The fuselage is streamlined, resembling a wing when viewed from the top. It shouldn't come as a surprise, then, that wind contacting the fuselage from the side causes it to behave like a wing.

Let's place our airplane back in the wind tunnel, canted slightly from the relative wind to simulate a sideslip. Acting like a wing with a positive angle of attack, the fuselage now develops its own Lift force. The center of pressure of our sideslipping fuselage, however, is well forward of the c.g. limits established for pitch stability. The resulting moment rotates the airplane's nose away from the relative wind. Inherently, our airplane would rather fly sideways!

Although that might be an interesting ride, it's better to keep our nose pointed into the wind. Increasing the amount of side surface area well aft of the c.g. stabilises the airplane during sideslips by generating a restoring force and moment. This is our **VERTICAL STABILISER**. Properly designed, it counters sideslip by swinging the nose back into the relative wind, just like the tail of a weathervane and the feathers on an arrow weathercock them into the wind.

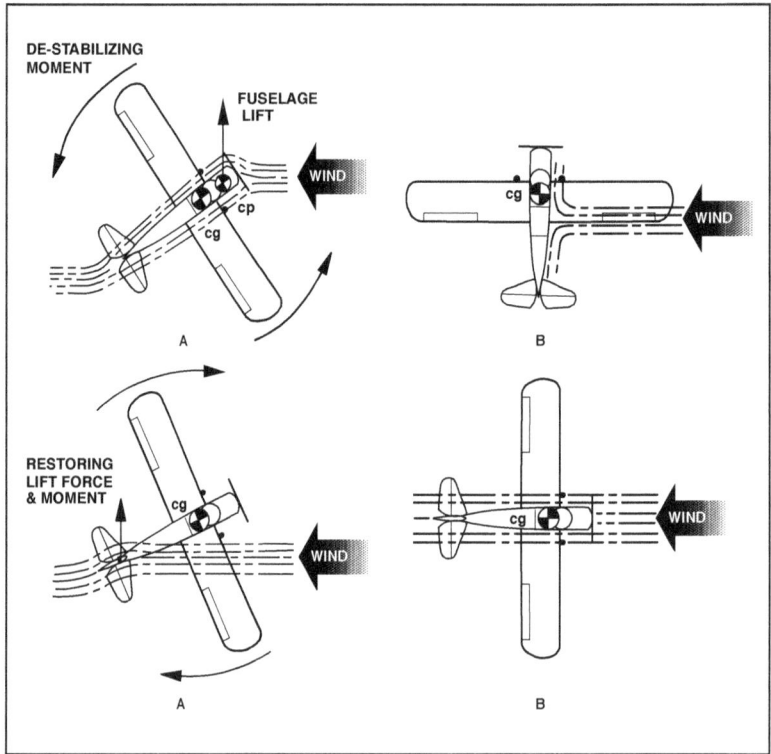

Figure 2-11: Creating Yaw Stability with the Vertical Stabiliser

All we need now are some flight controls. Let's install a throttle to control the engine's output. Let's also add movable surfaces to control motion around the three flight axes. Locating these as far as possible from the c.g. maximises the moments generated when they're deflected into the wind. The **ELEVATOR** is attached to the end of the horizontal stabiliser; it controls **PITCH**. The **RUDDER** is attached to the end of the vertical stabiliser; it controls sideslip, or **YAW**. The **AILERONS** are attached near each wingtip; they move differentially (one up/one down) to control **ROLL**. Oh, and let's add some wheels for smoother takeoffs and landings.

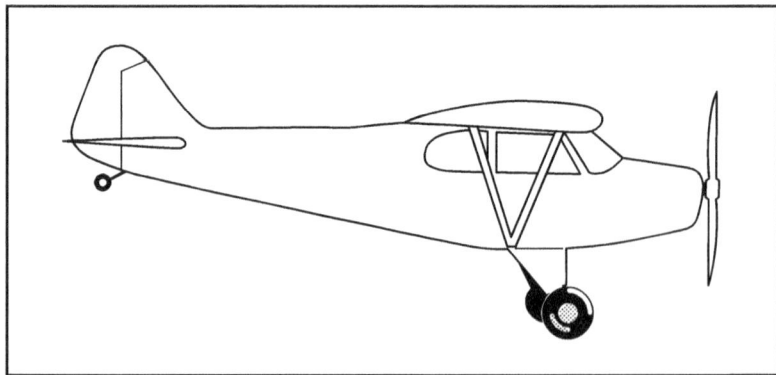

Figure 2-12: A Basic Airplane

Important Ratios

Comparing various ratios of forces acting on the airplane yields important insight into airplane performance. For example, the Lift-to-Drag ratio (L/D) provides a measure of the efficiency of the wing at a given angle of attack. Plotting these ratios graphically reveals a curve similar in shape to a typical coefficient of Lift curve: as angle of attack increases, L/D increases, then peaks, then decreases.

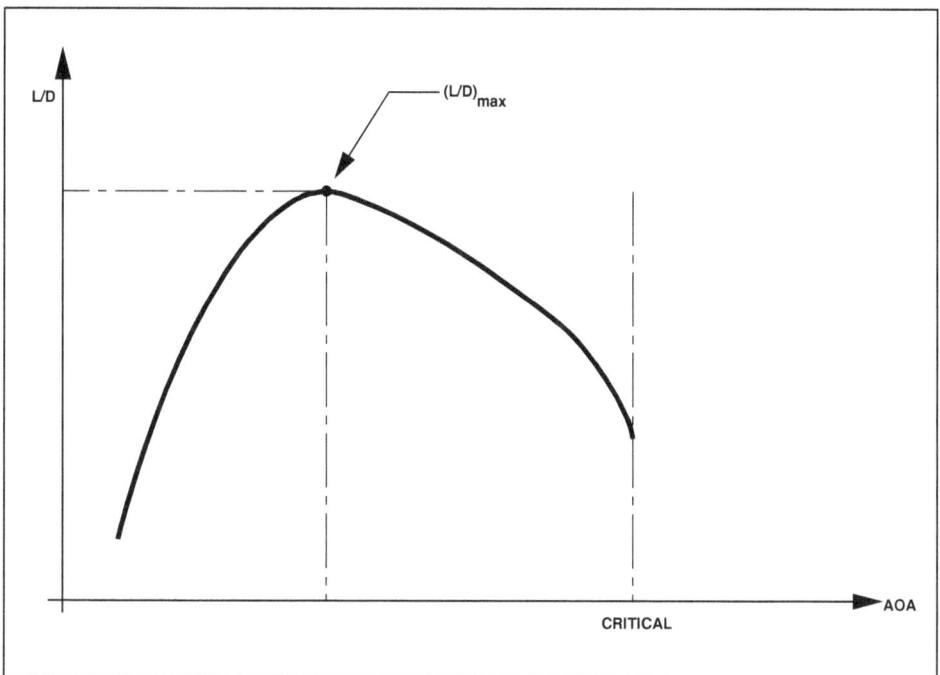

Figure 2-13: Lift-to-Drag Ratio vs. Angle of Attack

The peak is called (L/D)max. Flight at (L/D)max results in maximum glide range (zero wind conditions). Our wing operates at peak efficiency at the angle of attack corresponding to (L/D)max. If our engine quits, gliding at (L/D)max will maximise our range from a given altitude. (L/D)max also represents our glide ratio, which generally ranges from 6:1 to 10:1 in many light airplanes. We'll discuss (L/D) in more detail in Chapter 10—Glides.

The Lift-to-Weight ratio (L/W) is a measure of the g-load on the pilot and airplane. It's significant from structural and physiological standpoints, especially when manoeuvring. Airplanes designed for Normal category operation, for instance, must be able to sustain design limit loads up to +3.8 g's and -1.52 g's without structural damage. A 60 degree turn imposes a load of +2.0 g's; a loop, a load of +4.0 g's. We'll discuss g-load in more detail in Chapter 5—Curved Flight.

Power loading—an indirect measure of Weight-to-Thrust—is the ratio of Weight-to-Power (W/P). It hints at the overall performance one might expect from an airplane. For instance, the Power loading of a popular light trainer is around 15 pounds per horsepower, but a high performance aerobatic biplane can have a Power loading as low as 6 pounds per horsepower. Consequently, the corresponding rates of climb are strikingly different—700 feet per minute in the trainer, 2,700 feet per minute in the biplane.

The theory of flight is based on a simple premise: create enough Lift to offset Weight. Unfortunately, an inseparable entourage of other forces and side effects accompanies Lift: Lift begets Drag and instability; Negative Lift provides stability, but increases our total lifting requirement; Drag requires Thrust for altitude control; Thrust generates P-factor, slipstream, and gyroscopic precession, which require corrective actions by the pilot; and so on. Juggling these forces and their side effects is an integral part of piloting an airplane.

We've designed a basic flying machine using fundamental aerodynamic principles. In fact, our airplane incorporates a number of streamlined, winged shapes bolted together for stability and control: main wing, horizontal and vertical stabilisers, propeller blades, movable control surfaces. Even the fuselage resembles a blunt wing. We could enhance the design by adding secondary control surfaces like trim tabs, or by adding high lift devices like flaps designed to increase coefficients of Lift while decreasing flying speeds, or by adding dihedral for increased roll stability, but this airplane will do for now.

We could devise other designs using Bernoulli's and Newton's principles, too. We could incorporate multiple engines, low or multiple wings, multiple tail sections or no tail at all, or even secondary wings—canards—located in front of the main wing. The possibilities are almost endless, but we'd be spending our time dreaming about flight like Bernoulli and Newton once did. We have a flyable airplane right now. Let's learn how to control it so we can begin to master the art of flight!

3
Roll, Yaw, and Pitch

Flying requires us to transition from the two-dimensional world of everyday experience to the three-dimensional realm of flight. This transition can be difficult, but it must be complete to pilot an airplane safely. From birth, we learn to live on a seemingly flat Earth bound by the horizon. We instinctively respond to the horizon, relating our experiences with descriptive words such as "left", "right", "up", and "down". Various cues—trees, mountains, walls, our sense of balance—reinforce our two-dimensionality, defining what's "normal".

Flying, on the other hand, breaks our bond with the Earth. It challenges our normal view of the world and provides the thrill of three-dimensional freedom of movement. Airplanes cannot know what's normal, nor can they discern left from right, up from down. Airplanes are unaware that a horizon even exists. Instead, they react to the relative wind, which can come from **ANY DIRECTION**.

To communicate with the airplane, we must speak its language and adapt ourselves to a three-dimensional environment. Imposing two-dimensional thinking on an all-attitude machine increases the risk of misunderstanding between pilot and airplane. Proficiency means thinking as an airplane might think. Only then will the airplane become an extension of ourselves, rather than a machine with an apparent will of its own.

The first concept we must understand is that all airplanes are governed by the same aerodynamic principles. It doesn't matter whether it's an aerobatic airplane, a basic trainer, a complex aircraft, or a twin. Each is capable of entering an unusual attitude. The relative performance and operating limitations certainly vary between aircraft types, but the concepts of roll, yaw, pitch, angle of attack, Lift, and Drag remain constant.

We describe the airplane's position relative to the horizon as its **ATTITUDE**. We deflect ailerons, rudder, and elevator into the relative wind to control our motion around three separate axes: the roll axis, the yaw axis, and the pitch axis. Consequently, all flight manoeuvres consist only of roll, yaw, and pitch components.

Of course, the flight axes intersect at the airplane's center of gravity. The center of gravity (c.g.), therefore, signifies the origin of roll, yaw, and pitch. Since the c.g. is an integral part of the airplane, roll, yaw, and pitch movements are independent of the airplane's attitude. Control inputs obviously influence our attitude, but how the airplane moves around its flight axes has nothing to do with where the horizon is.

16 — Emergency Manouvre Training

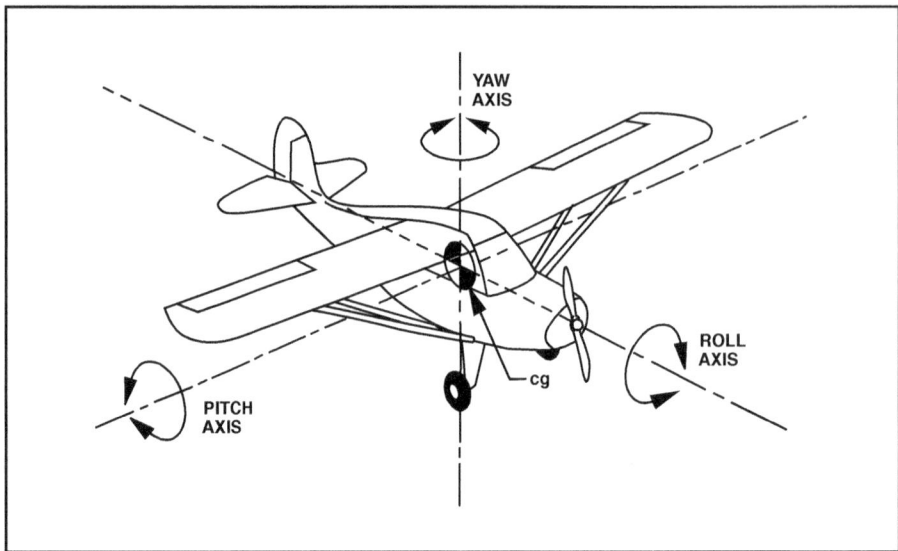

Figure 3-1: The Three Flight Axes

Because our mental attitude directly affects the airplane's attitude, we must interpret roll, yaw, and pitch movements correctly. Learning to perceive movements relative to the pilot—rather than to the horizon—improves our ability to control the airplane in any attitude. Let's now define roll, yaw, and pitch from the pilot's point of view:

Roll

Ailerons control movement around the roll axis. Deflecting them from side to side rotates the nose of the airplane from our head to our hip. The wingtip travels from head to hip as well. Although the airplane can be placed **IN ANY ATTITUDE**, roll will always appear as a head-to-hip movement relative to the pilot.

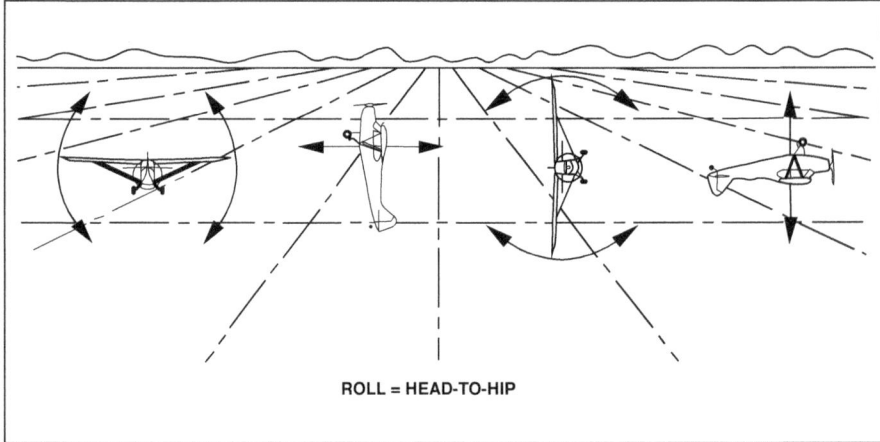

Figure 3-2: Roll Relative to the Pilot

Yaw

The rudder controls movement around the yaw axis. Deflecting the rudder from left to right slides the nose of the airplane from ear to ear. The wingtip moves ear-to-ear as well. Although the airplane can be placed **IN ANY ATTITUDE**, yaw will always appear as an ear-to-ear movement relative to the pilot.

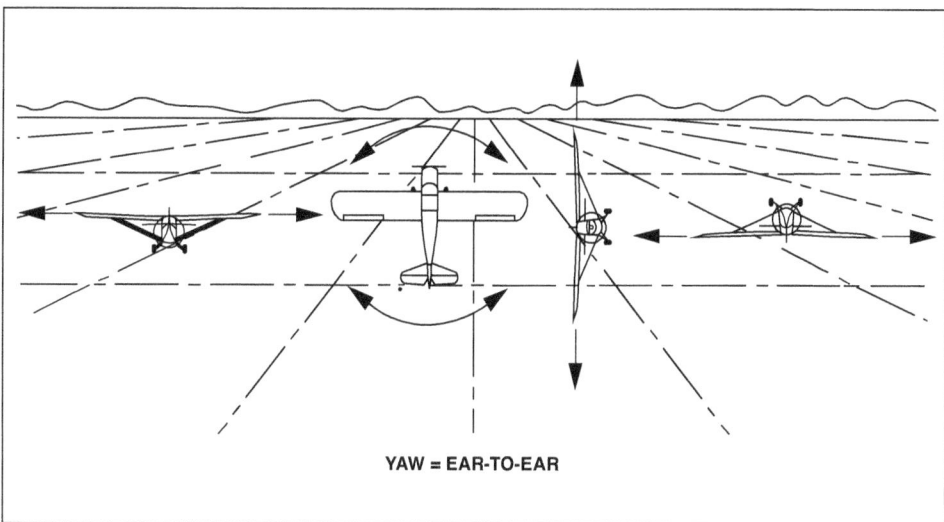

Figure 3-3: Yaw Relative to the Pilot

Pitch

The elevator controls movement around the pitch axis. Elevator inputs do not necessarily move an airplane "up" or "down". Fundamentally, the elevator rotates the nose from our head to our feet. The wingtip rotates head-to-feet in pitch as well. Back elevator pressure pulls the nose and wing toward your head; forward pressure pushes them toward your feet. Although the airplane can be placed **IN ANY ATTITUDE**, pitch will always appear as a head-to-feet movement relative to the pilot. As we'll see in upcoming chapters, pitch also controls a multitude of other parameters, including angle of attack, airspeed, g-load, and curved flight.

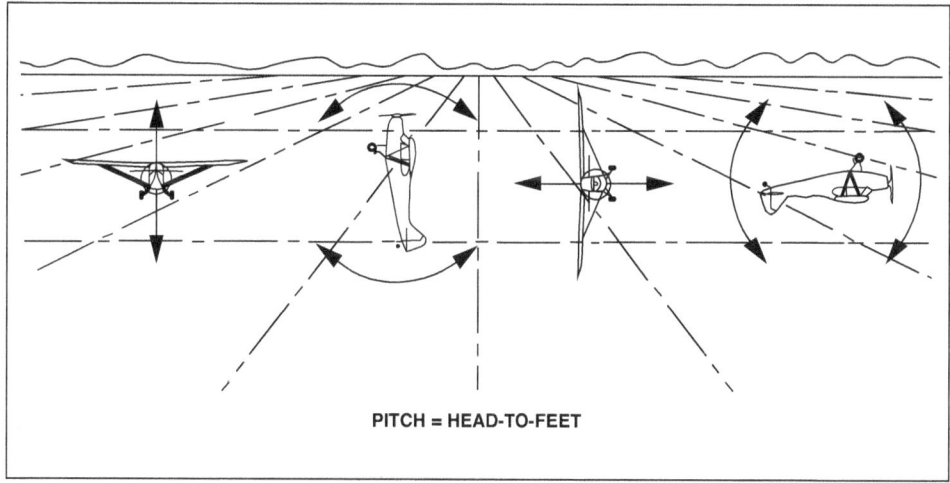

Figure 3-4: Pitch Relative to the Pilot

Interpreting roll, yaw, and pitch as described above reduces fixation on the horizon. It also reduces preoccupation with the airplane's attitude. We're then better able to control the airplane with the appropriate combination of inputs. In addition to the primary control movements, however, several secondary roll, yaw, and pitch effects routinely appear when flying. Let's review these secondary effects, bearing in mind that although different designs may exhibit them in varying degrees, the principles remain the same.

Secondary Roll Effects

RUDDER INPUTS: Yawing an airplane induces a roll in the same direction as the applied rudder. For example, left rudder swings the right wing into the relative wind while the left wing retreats from the relative wind. Altering the airflow changes the Lift generated: the right wing experiences an increase in Lift; the left wing, a decrease in Lift. The Lift differential causes a left roll toward the deflected rudder.

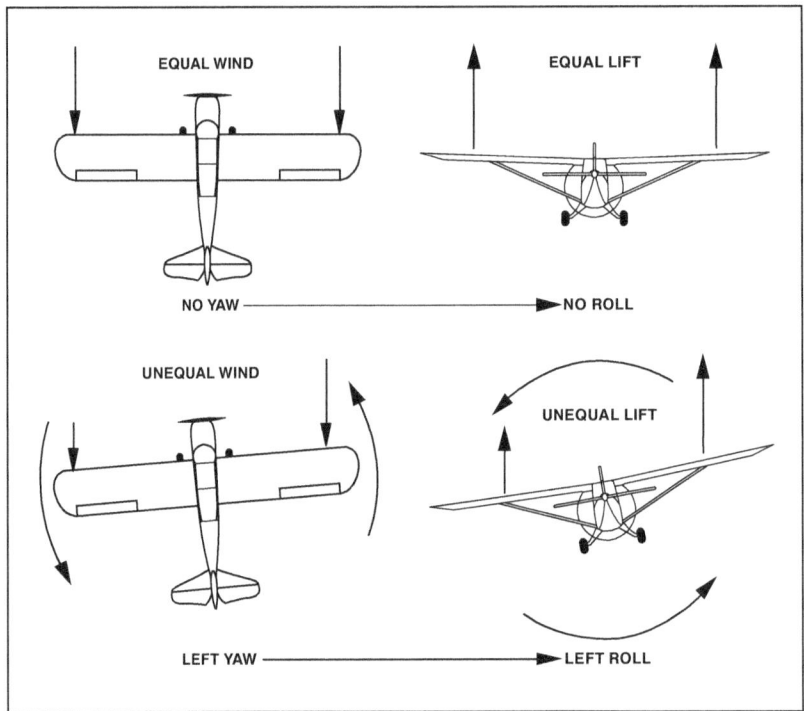

Figure 3-5: How Yaw Induces a Roll

ASYMMETRIC POWER: Asymmetric power settings in twin engine aircraft can cause a secondary roll as well. The engine developing more Thrust yaws the airplane, thereby inducing a roll toward the engine developing less Thrust.

TORQUE: The term "torque" is sometimes used as a generic label for all of the effects associated with a rotating propeller—torque, P-factor, slipstream, and gyroscopic precession. In this book, torque refers strictly to the equal-but-opposite reaction of the airplane to the rotating prop. The other effects will be treated separately.

As the prop turns clockwise (viewed from the cockpit in a single-engine airplane), the torque reaction tries to rotate the airplane counterclockwise. The magnitude of the reaction depends partly on the size of the propeller compared to the rest of the airplane, the prop's rotational speed, and the engine horsepower. In most light airplanes, torque-induced-roll generally cannot overpower the natural damping in roll provided by the wings; otherwise, right aileron would be needed to counter it.

Secondary Yaw Effects

Several secondary yaw effects are inherent in the design and operation of propeller aircraft. The rotating prop can be responsible for up to four secondary yaw effects. Torque, P-factor, and spiral slipstream are three effects that can generate left yaw. They usually become significant during low airspeed, high power flight. Gyroscopic precession is the fourth effect, occurring as a result of changes in pitch. Precession can generate left or right yaw, depending on the type of pitch input.

TORQUE: As mentioned earlier, torque is the equal but opposite reaction to the rotation of the prop. Normally a roll reaction, it may appear as a secondary yaw effect when on the ground. Rapidly advancing the throttle during takeoff, for example, may momentarily roll sufficient additional weight onto the left main gear to cause the airplane to veer (yaw) to the left. Right rudder counteracts this action.

P-FACTOR: P-factor stems from asymmetric propeller Thrust and appears during slow flight at high power settings. The blades of our propeller are actually small wings developing Lift as they rotate. Viewed from the cockpit during slow flight, the descending blade effectively experiences more relative wind than the ascending blade. This difference causes an imbalance in Lift, which ultimately yaws the airplane to the left.

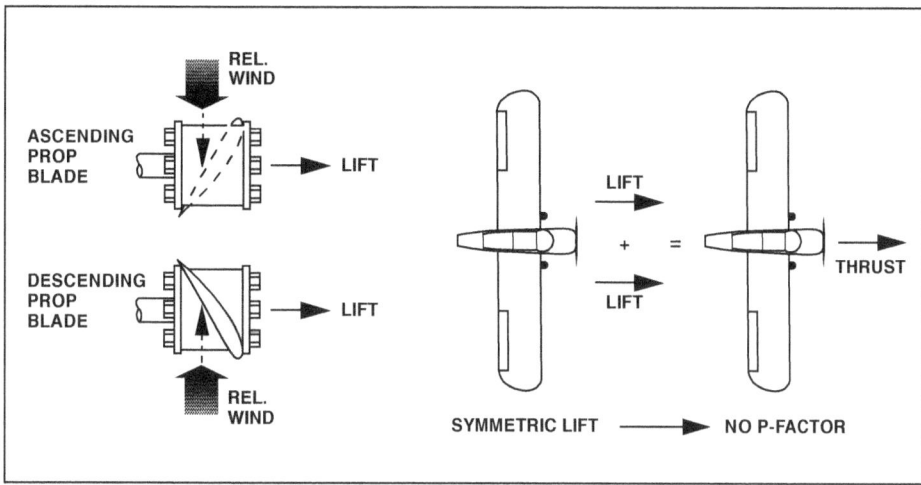

Figure 3-6: Developing Thrust without Forward Motion

To illustrate P-factor, let's apply the principles reviewed in the last chapter (Basic Aerodynamics). Imagine sitting stationary on the ground, on a no-wind day, with the engine idling at 1,000 rpm. Remember, prop blades are small wings moving through the air. The relative wind on each arises exclusively from, and points in the opposite direction to, the rotation of the propeller. A snapshot of the prop as it passes through horizontal shows each blade developing the same amount of Lift. These Lift forces are actually Thrust components, which might pull the airplane forward if we weren't holding the brakes.

Let's now take a snapshot during level cruise flight. The only difference between this picture and our first one is the addition of a relative wind component representing our forward motion through the air. The combined effect of propeller rotation and forward motion tilts the relative wind slightly on each blade, but they're still equal in magnitude. Consequently, both blades still produce the same amount of Lift, so P-factor is not yet present.

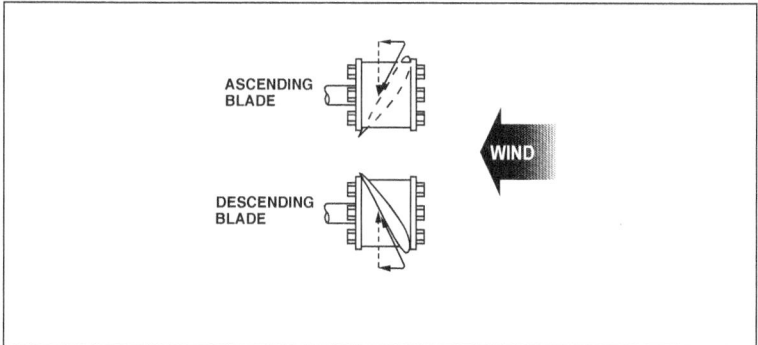

Figure 3-7: Adding Level Cruise Flight & Propeller Rotation Wind Components

Let's take three more snapshots corresponding to slower and slower flight at a constant altitude. Propeller rotation and our forward motion still contribute separate wind components to the equation. Notice, though, that the angles between these components are no longer equal on the two prop blades. The overall relative winds differ, too. As the airplane rotates to higher angles of attack, the effective wind on the descending blade grows while the wind on the ascending blade shrinks. (Note: at a ninety degree angle of attack, the airplane propeller is called a helicopter rotor! The "descending" blade is then called the "advancing" blade and the "ascending" blade is the "retreating" blade.)

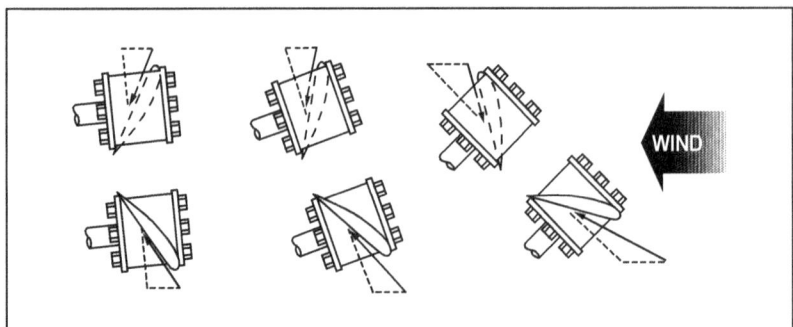

Figure 3-8: Increasing the Angle of Attack in Level Flight

The total Thrust developed acts at the center of the propeller when Lift is equal on each blade. During flight at high angles of attack, however, an imbalance in Lift occurs. The combined force now no longer acts at the center of the prop; it slides off-center, moving out along the descending blade. This off-center force produces a left yawing moment around the airplane's center of gravity. Right rudder pressure cancels this P-factor effect.

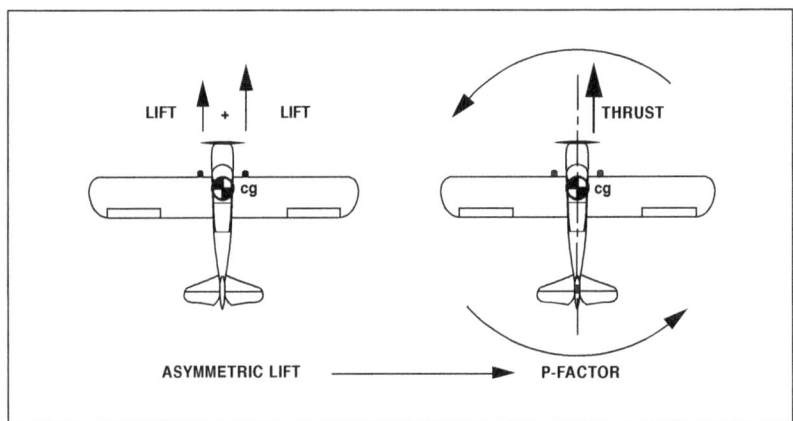

Figure 3-9: Developing Thrust at High Angles of Attack

SPIRAL SLIPSTREAM: A spiral slipstream of air rotates clockwise behind a turning prop. The slipstream curls around the fuselage and strikes the left side of the vertical stabilizer, tending to yaw the nose to the left. Once again, right rudder corrects this. Propeller slipstream can contribute significant left yaw, especially during slow flight at high power settings.

RIGGING: Aircraft design generally incorporates elements that reduce the impact of secondary yaw effects. These design features, though, can sometimes contribute their own yaw effects. For example, torque, P-factor, and slipstream are always present in varying degrees with a rotating prop. Airplane rigging, however, often eliminates the need for continuous right rudder pressure during level cruise flight (usually by offsetting the vertical stabilizer). Under high power/low airspeed conditions such as climbs, P-factor and slipstream overpower rigging effects, necessitating right rudder pressure. Under low power/high airspeed conditions such as descents, on the other hand, airplane rigging may dominate, creating the need for some left rudder pressure.

GYROSCOPIC PRECESSION: Pitch inputs may give rise to a secondary yaw effect from gyroscopic precession of the rotating propeller. The physics governing precession isn't important; just remember that the propeller resists changes to its geometric plane of rotation (if you try to move it, it will resist you). This resistance points in the same direction as the applied force, but its effect appears 90 degrees ahead in the direction of rotation (clockwise as viewed from the cockpit in most light airplanes).

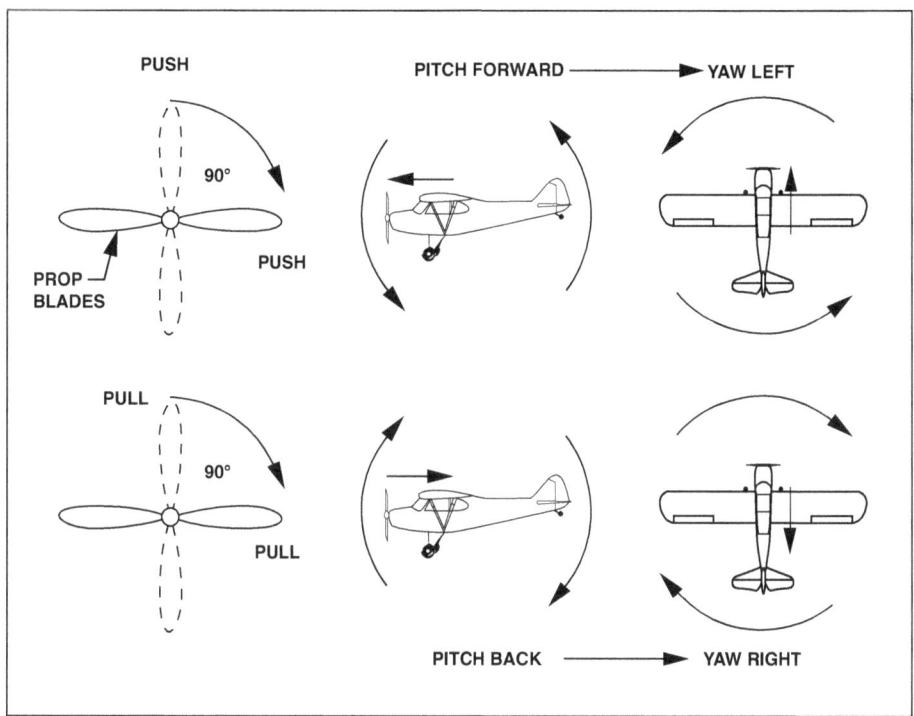

Figure 3-10: How Pitch Inputs Induce Changes in Yaw

To visualize pitch-induced precession more easily, imagine sitting in an airplane with the prop stopped vertically. Imagine being able to reach out and hold the top blade with your right hand as though it was the stick or yoke. Imagine pushing to simulate a forward elevator input. Rotate the prop 90 degrees clockwise (i.e.: precess it!). Pushing now yaws the nose to the left. Start over, but this time imagine pulling back on the prop blade. Rotate the prop 90 degrees and keep pulling. The nose now yaws right.

Because many light airplanes have relatively low horsepower-to-weight ratios and relatively small, lightweight propellers, the precession effect is often negligible. Also, pilots generally don't make large, rapid pitch changes, thus many pilots haven't experienced this effect. If precession was significant, pulling on the elevator control would require simultaneous left rudder pressure; pushing would require simultaneous right rudder pressure. Pilots flying high performance aerobatic airplanes often must compensate for gyroscopic precession. Also, conventional gear (taildragger) pilots must apply more right rudder to counter precession whenever they raise the tail during the takeoff roll.

ADVERSE YAW: Aileron (roll) inputs induce a secondary yaw effect called adverse yaw. Although Drag's contribution to adverse yaw is the easiest to identify, Lift is the primary driving force behind it. A complete description of this yaw effect, therefore, must include the significant role Lift plays.

A deflected aileron modifies the wing's local angle of attack and influences the local relative wind. Left aileron, for instance, increases the local angle of attack on the right wing, thus creating more Lift and Drag than on the left wing. The Lift differential generates a left roll while the extra drag induces some right yaw. As the wings move in roll, however, the relative wind changes.

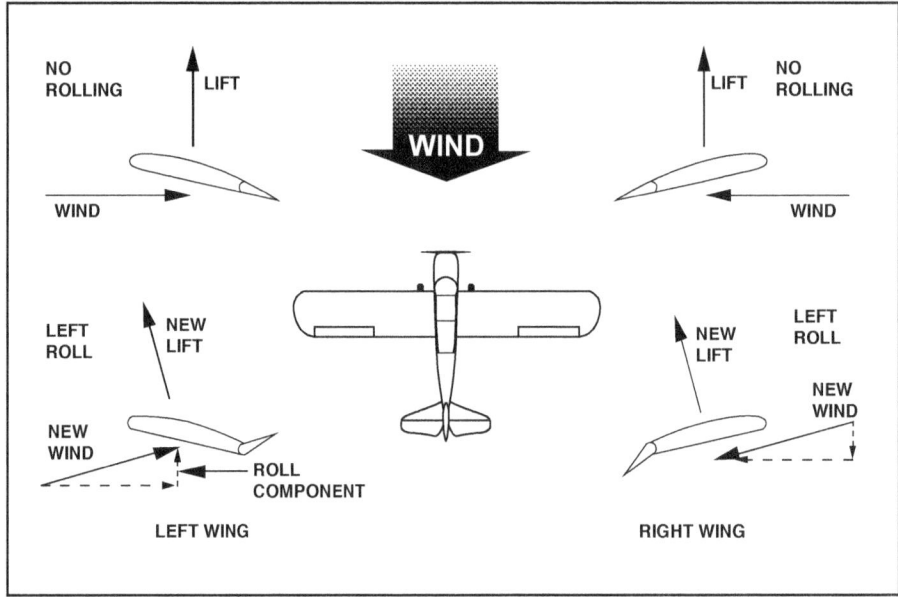

Figure 3-11: Aerodynamic Changes due to Left Roll

Prior to the left aileron input, the relative wind points directly opposite to the airplane's forward motion. As the left wing begins to drop in roll, it experiences a small wind component opposite to its downward travel. The right wing experiences a small wind component opposite to its upward travel. Adding these roll-induced wind components to the relative wind opposing our forward motion yields new, composite relative winds on each wing (Chapter 8—Overbanked discusses this in more detail).

Let's now draw new Lift vectors perpendicular to the new relative winds. Notice that the new Lift vector leans slightly forward on the left wing, but slightly rearward on the right. Resolving these vectors into horizontal and vertical components reveals horizontal Lift components pointing in opposite directions. These components simultaneously pull the left wing forward and the right wing aft—adverse yaw in action!

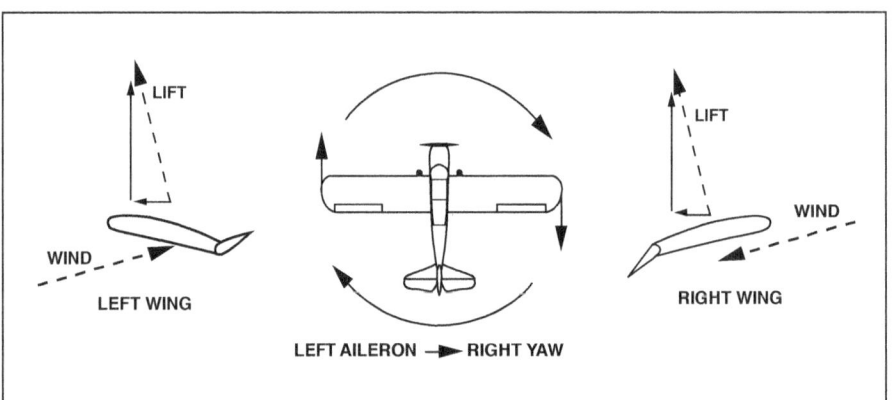

Figure 3-12: Lift's Contribution to the Adverse Yaw Phenomenon

Horizontal components of Lift are largely responsible for the adverse yaw phenomenon. Aileron movements may actually provide the strongest secondary yaw effect. To cancel the attendant right adverse yaw, left aileron inputs require left rudder pressure. Similarly, right aileron inputs require right rudder pressure to cancel the resulting left adverse yaw. Rudder should always be coordinated with your aileron inputs.

Secondary yaw effects can arise whenever we change the position of the ailerons (adverse yaw), the elevator (gyroscopic precession), or the throttle (torque, P-factor, slipstream, rigging). Consequently, we should expect to make a commensurate rudder adjustment whenever we change any of the other primary control positions. Although its application is often subtle, the rudder is a dynamic control surface nonetheless. Unfortunately, it tends to be the airplane's least exercised control.

As we'll see, proper yaw control becomes increasingly important when operating near critical angle of attack. The rudder's primary function is to **CANCEL YAW**, keeping the airplane in coordinated flight. Based on the above discussion, we can anticipate the following actions: Climbs require right rudder pressure; descents require left rudder pressure; left aileron inputs require left rudder inputs; right aileron inputs require right rudder inputs; changes in pitch require changes in rudder pressure; changes in throttle position require changes in rudder position. Our feet must be active during flight.

Secondary Pitch Effects

RUDDER INPUTS: Yawing an airplane with the rudder not only induces a roll, but it also induces a pitch change through gyroscopic precession of the rotating propeller. To visualize the precession effect, imagine sitting in an airplane with the prop stopped horizontally. Imagine being able to grasp the right propeller blade with your right hand. Pushing or pulling on this blade moves the airplane about the yaw axis.

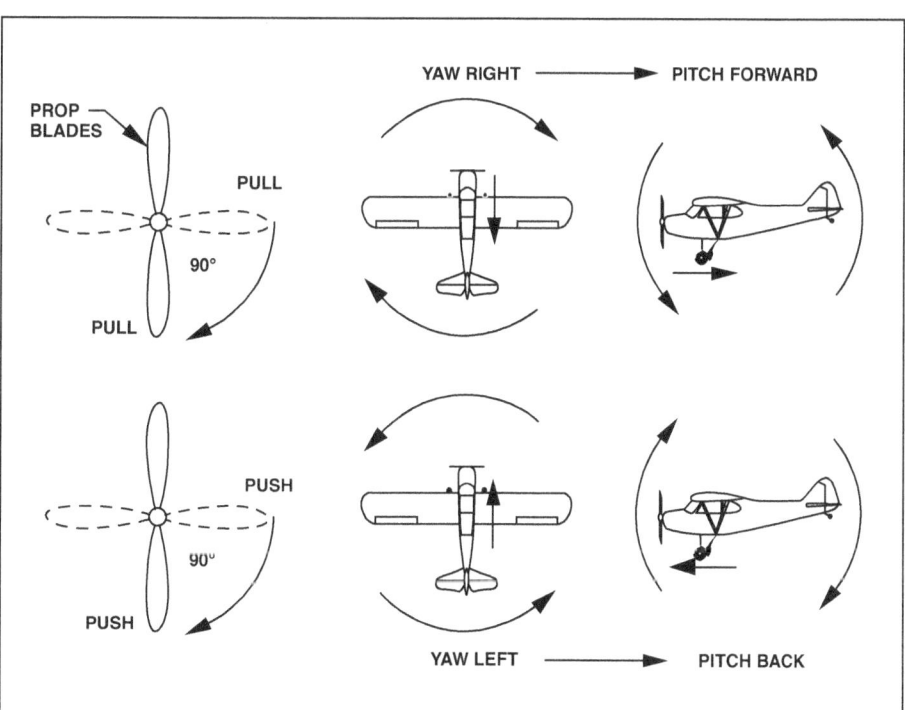

Figure 3-13: How Yaw Inputs Induce Changes in Pitch

To simulate right yaw, imagine pulling on the prop blade. Imagine rotating the prop 90 degrees clockwise to "precess" the yaw input. Continue pulling. The result is now a pitch change toward our feet. Maintaining a constant pitch attitude would require a pull on the elevator control when applying right rudder, if precession was a factor. Now repeat the process, only this time imagine pushing on the propeller blade to simulate some left yaw. Rotate the prop 90 degrees clockwise and keep pushing. The result is a pitch change toward our head. Thus, maintaining a constant pitch attitude when applying left rudder might require a simultaneous push on the elevator control.

Compensating for rudder-induced pitch changes becomes important when transitioning into and out of slips, especially when making large, rapid rudder inputs. Also, pilots flying high performance aerobatic airplanes must compensate for precession during the pivot at the top of the Hammerhead Turn manoeuvre.

POWER CHANGES: The effect power changes have on pitch becomes more pronounced during high power, low speed situations such as climbs, slow flight, and go-arounds. For example, a single engine airplane with the propeller up front (known as a tractor configuration) normally generates pitch-back moments as power is applied and pitch-forward moments as power is reduced, especially when the horizontal stabilizer is within the main wing's downwash. Adding power increases the downwash, producing a pitch-back moment; thus to maintain a constant pitch attitude, additional forward elevator pressure may be necessary. Similarly, reducing power produces a pitch-forward moment; thus, additional back pressure may be needed.

FLAPS: Flaps often influence pitch attitude as they move. Many low-wing airplanes, for example, tend to pitch forward as flaps deploy, back as they retract. Many high-wing airplanes, on the other hand, tend to pitch back as flaps deploy, forward as they retract. The amount of pitch change depends on airspeed and the degree of flap movement. For example, rapidly deploying full flaps at Vfe produces a stronger pitch change than lowering the flaps incrementally at speeds below Vfe.

Flying is a dynamic interaction between the pilot and the airplane. It demands that we become equally fluent in roll, yaw, and pitch. Even though back elevator inputs are the most natural, realize that we cannot fully control the airplane with aft elevator alone. A wide range of aileron, rudder, and forward elevator also exists to enhance the airplane's controllability. Although each control is capable of preventing an unusual attitude, misapplied each can also generate one. We must anticipate, therefore, the secondary effects of our inputs and react accordingly.

As we'll see in upcoming chapters, the key to dealing with overbanked configurations lies with aileron inputs; the key to spin prevention and recovery lies with rudder inputs; the key to stall recovery lies with elevator inputs. But before exploring our flight envelope further, let's discuss another fundamental concept of aircraft control: the relationship between pitch and power.

4
Pitch and Power

Pilots have debated the question, "What controls airspeed and what controls altitude?" for years. Unfortunately, the true identity of pitch and power controls often is obscured during flight training. Instead of enlightening student pilots about this fundamental piloting technique, several popular training manuals tend to mask it in confusion. Comparing excerpts from the FAA's own *Pilot's Handbook* and *Flight Training Handbook* demonstrates how befuddled this issue can become:

> *"it is a fallacy to think that an airplane climbs because of 'excess lift'. It does not; the airplane climbs because of power available over power required." Pilot's Handbook, FAA AC 61-23B, p. 29.*

It sounds like power controls altitude, but let's check the other publication:

> *"Power control is the control of power or thrust by use of the throttle to establish or maintain desired airspeeds in coordination with the attitude changes." Flight Training Handbook, FAA AC 61-21A, p. 60.*

Wait! Does power control airspeed? Let's read some more:

> *"if changes have been coordinated, the airplane will still remain in level flight but at a higher speed when the proper relationship between thrust and angle of attack is established. If the angle of attack were not coordinated (decreased) with this increase of thrust the airplane would climb." Flight Training Handbook, FAA AC 61-21A, p. 267.*

OK, it seems that maybe power controls altitude after all. Let's find one more passage to be sure:

> *"Significant changes in airspeed will, of course, require considerable changes in pitch attitude and pitch trim to maintain altitude." Flight Training Handbook, FAA AC 61-21A, p. 62.*

Whoa! So pitch controls altitude now?

Confused? Sadly, misunderstanding the function of pitch and power can lead to inappropriate and often dangerous reactions by pilots during critical flight operations. Let's wipe the slate clean and take a closer look at what's really going on: When we talk about altitude and airspeed, we're talking about two forms of the same thing—**ENERGY**. One form of energy is Potential Energy, which has been **STORED** for future use. The second form is Kinetic Energy, which is the energy of **MOTION**.

For instance, drawing a bow and pointing an arrow toward the sky stores potential energy in the tension created by pulling back on the bowstring. Releasing the bowstring rapidly turns potential energy into kinetic energy as the arrow whistles skyward. But as the arrow gains height, it slows down. In other words, kinetic energy is transformed back into potential energy. When the arrow reaches its peak, kinetic energy is zero, but it now has lots of potential energy in the form of altitude. As the arrow begins to fall earthward, potential energy is converted back into kinetic energy. The more altitude the arrow uses up, the more speed it gains.

Clearly, altitude is stored energy; airspeed is kinetic energy. It should also be clear that flying is a continual process of trading back and forth between altitude and airspeed energies. Like the arrow example, we always gain one at the expense of the other. We cannot have airspeed without expending some form of altitude, and vice versa. Remember these important points. Also consider the four possible energy combinations and their ramifications on safe, controlled flight:

1. High/Fast—This energy combination offers an abundance of both potential and kinetic energies. With lots of energy at our disposal, it's the safest configuration.

2. High/Slow—This combination offers an abundance of potential energy, but it's deficient in kinetic energy. Since altitude can be sacrificed for airspeed if necessary, it's a relatively safe configuration.

3. Low/Fast—This is the combination preferred by the skilled airshow performer (lots of speed close to the ground). It offers an abundance of kinetic energy at the expense of potential energy. Airspeed must be traded for altitude. Since the margin for error here is small, flying like this is better left to paid professionals.

4. Low/Slow—This energy combination is deficient in both potential and kinetic energies. No safe exchange of energy is possible. Unless the airplane is a foot or two above the runway, the pilot could be in serious trouble. Avoid this highly dangerous combination.

Energy Management

To understand how we manage airspeed and altitude energies, let's simulate flight in a glider. After all, what's true aerodynamically for gliders must be true for powered airplanes. For ease of illustration, let's assume no wind or thermal activity. First, we must somehow elevate the glider above the ground. Let's push it up a nearby hill, expending some of our own kinetic energy to add potential energy to the glider.

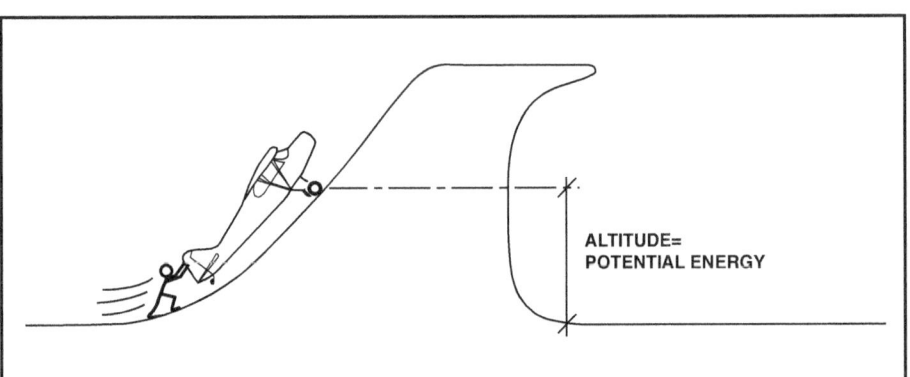

Figure 4-1: Increasing Altitude Increases Potential Energy

At the top, let's launch ourselves and trade the altitude we worked so hard to get into the kinetic energy of flight. Regardless of our elevator position, we travel in only one direction—down. Our descent profile clearly is affected by our choice of airspeed, but only indirectly. In fact, with the exception of the descent profile corresponding to best glide speed, we can glide along other flight paths at two different airspeeds: one faster and one slower than best glide.

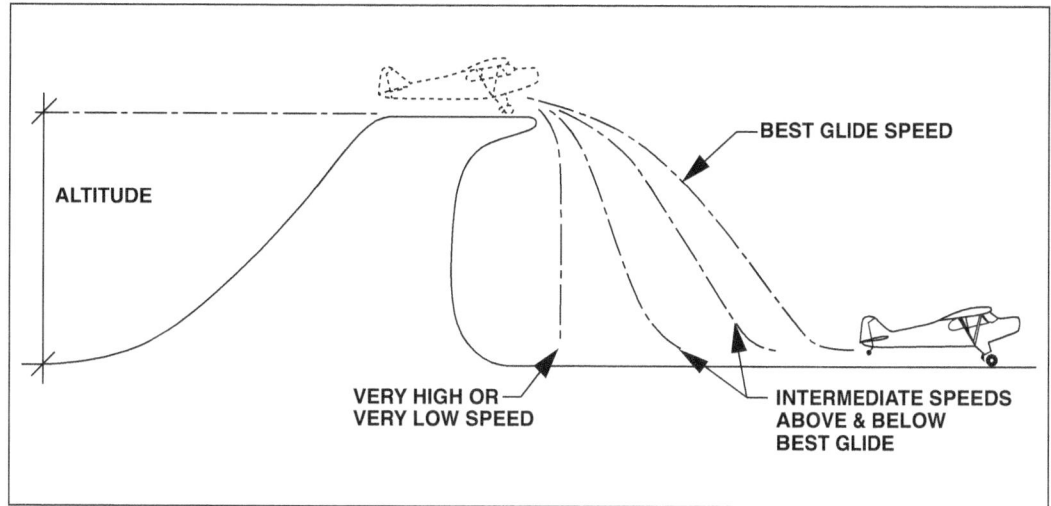

Figure 4-2: Converting Altitude into Airspeed

Steady flight requires balancing the aerodynamic forces. Since we don't have a powerplant developing Thrust, the force of gravity is all that's available to offset Drag. Using some of the airplane's own Weight, gravity pulls the airplane earthward, trading altitude for airspeed along the way.

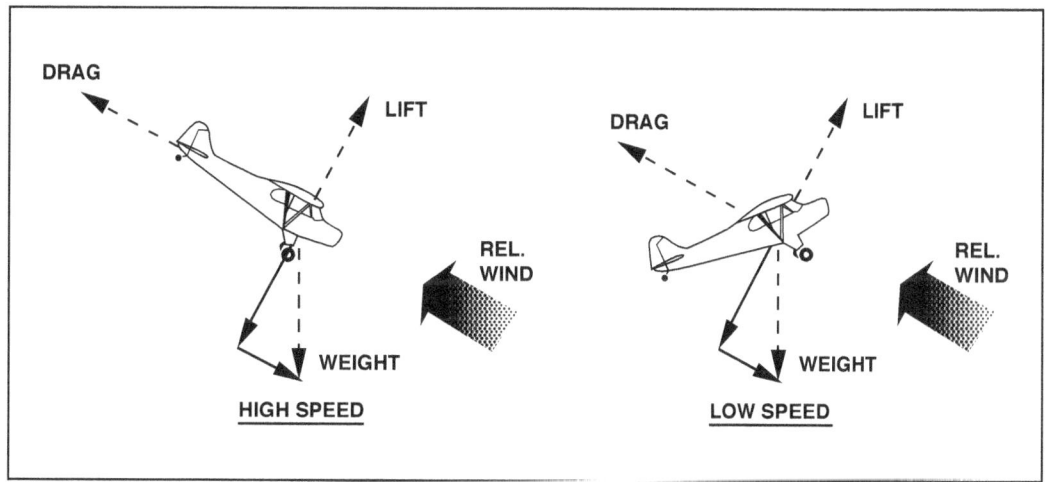

Figure 4-3: Force Balance in a Glide

Varying our elevator position during the glides, we observe transient changes in airspeed and altitude as we trade back and forth between kinetic and potential energy. The net result, however, is always the same—we go downhill. Potential energy is continually expended overcoming Drag, thus we're prevented from ever returning to our starting altitude.

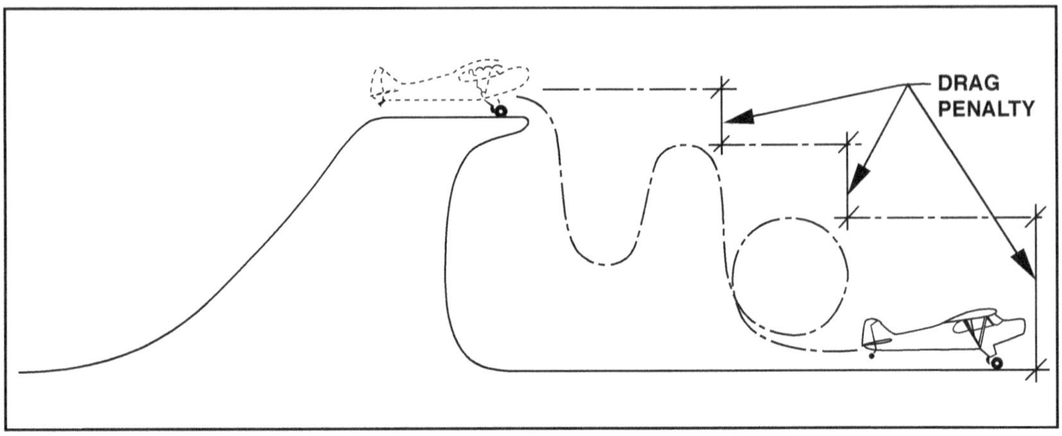

Figure 4-4: The Cumulative Effect of Drag on Altitude

Recall from Chapter 2—Basic Aerodynamics that angle of attack and airspeed are the ingredients needed to generate Lift. Each and every angle of attack comes packaged with a unique airspeed to create the right amount of Lift to balance a given aircraft Weight. Aerodynamically, airspeed responds directly to changes in angle of attack, which is controlled by the elevator.

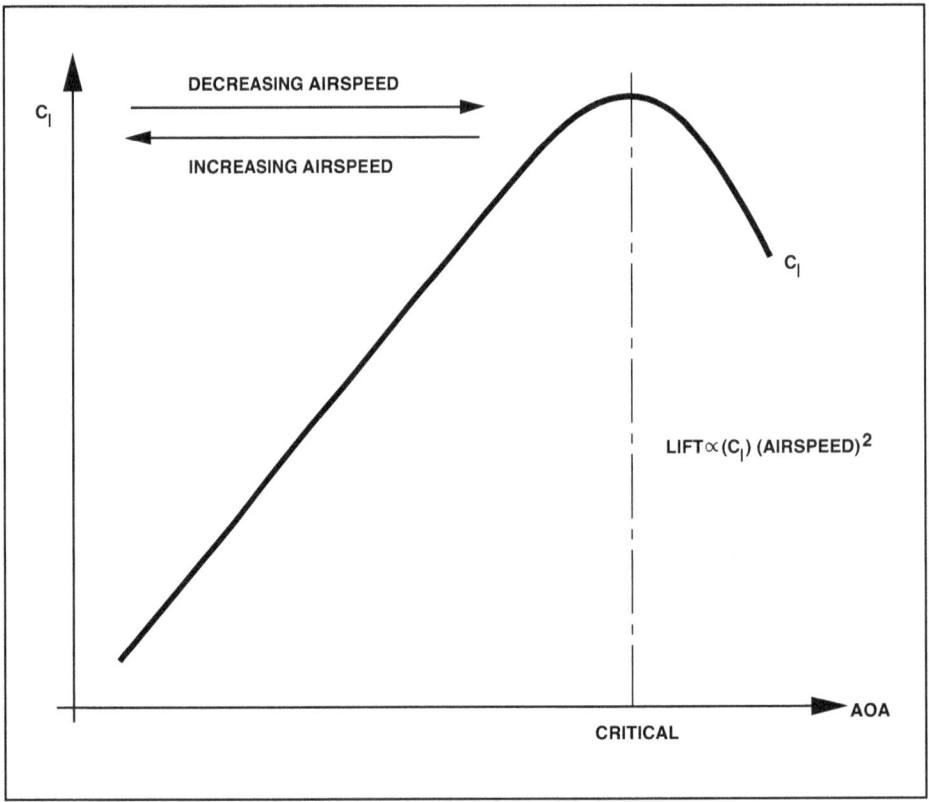

Figure 4-5: Linking Airspeed to Angle of Attack

Our quest to identify the airspeed control points to the elevator. Since elevator controls angle of attack, and changes in angle of attack are accompanied by changes in airspeed, the elevator **MUST** control airspeed. As the glider simulations confirmed, decreasing the angle of attack—pushing on the elevator—increased our airspeed; increasing the angle— pulling on the elevator—decreased our speed. Each elevator input, though, ultimately resulted in a net loss of altitude, but with varying airspeeds. Therefore, elevator **MUST** be controlling airspeed.

Power must be our primary altitude control, if the above observations are true. Rather than deducing this by elimination, let's prove it by "motorising" our glider. Rather than expending our own energy pushing the glider up the slope, we can now "drive" the motor-glider to the top of the hill using the engine. In other words, we can use power to increase the glider's potential energy—that is, altitude.

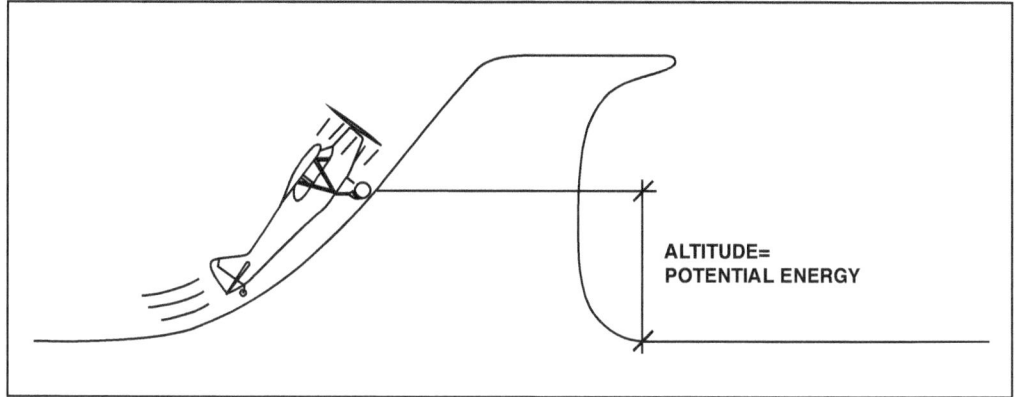

Figure 4-6: Using Power to Increase Potential Energy

Once we reach the top, we can cut the power and glide back down, controlling airspeed via elevator position. But we can do more now: Instead of confining ourselves to an airspeed and its corresponding descent profile, why not use power to alter the profile while maintaining the same airspeed? Power gives us control over our altitude profile. It provides a range of profiles not inherently available to the glider pilot, including climbs and level flight. Fundamentally, we use power to raise the airplane above the ground, thus increasing its potential energy.

The most significant difference between an airplane and a glider isn't necessarily what you can see—an engine and propeller, but rather, it's what you often don't see—the **FUEL**. Fuel is Potential Energy stored in the tanks, waiting to be converted into Kinetic Energy. Fuel is **LIQUID ALTITUDE**. We pour altitude into our tanks every time we fuel an airplane. Some of this latent altitude was converted into literal altitude before we launched our motor-glider from the hill. The advantage airplanes have over gliders is the ability to control altitude precisely, by burning fuel. Clearly, power is our primary altitude control.

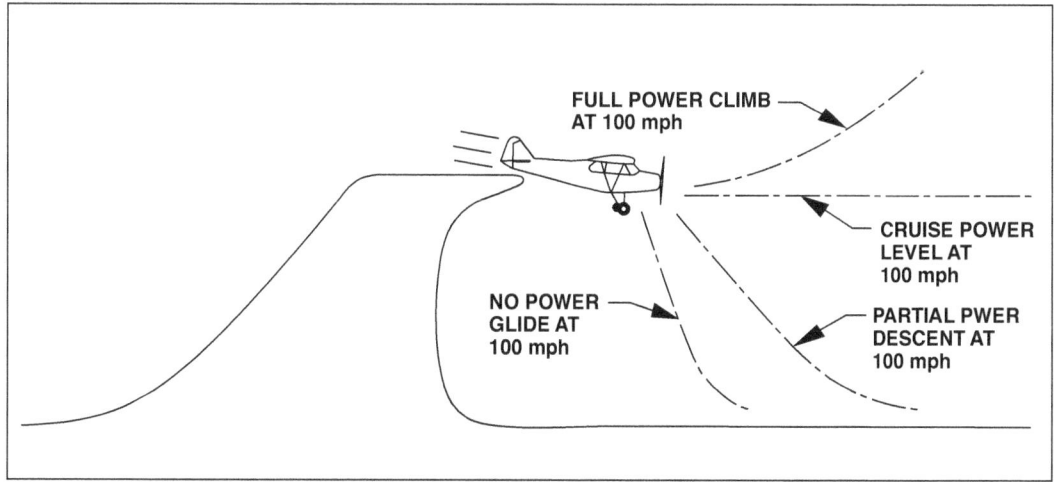

Figure 4-7: Controlling the Altitude Profile with Power

Of course, power pilots don't begin their flights by "driving" up a hill. Instead, aircraft engines convert fuel into airspeed rapidly during the takeoff roll along a level runway. Fuel is then traded for altitude during a constant-airspeed climb. Leveling off and flying at a particular speed requires burning more liquid altitude. If we deplete the fuel in the tanks, energy stored as altitude above the ground must then be exchanged for glide airspeed.

Here's a summary of the key points made so far:

1. Pitch (elevator) is our primary airspeed control.

2. Power (throttle) is our primary altitude control.

3. Fuel (potential energy) is liquid altitude.

4. Gaining or maintaining airspeed (Kinetic Energy) requires consuming some form of altitude (Potential Energy).

Transient phases of flight tend to complicate the pitch and power issue. But we can still demonstrate the validity of pitch-for-airspeed and power-for-altitude with a simple test: Starting from level flight at 60 mph, descend until the airspeed reaches 100 mph, then climb until the airspeed returns to 60 mph. Let's perform this exercise twice, first without power, then with power. Let's also follow the same descent and ascent profiles during each test run.

A specific amount of altitude is consumed to increase the airspeed from 60 to 100 mph without power. Drag then causes us to reach 60 mph prematurely during the ensuing climb, forcing us to level off below our starting altitude. Without power, the net result in this test is a loss of altitude.

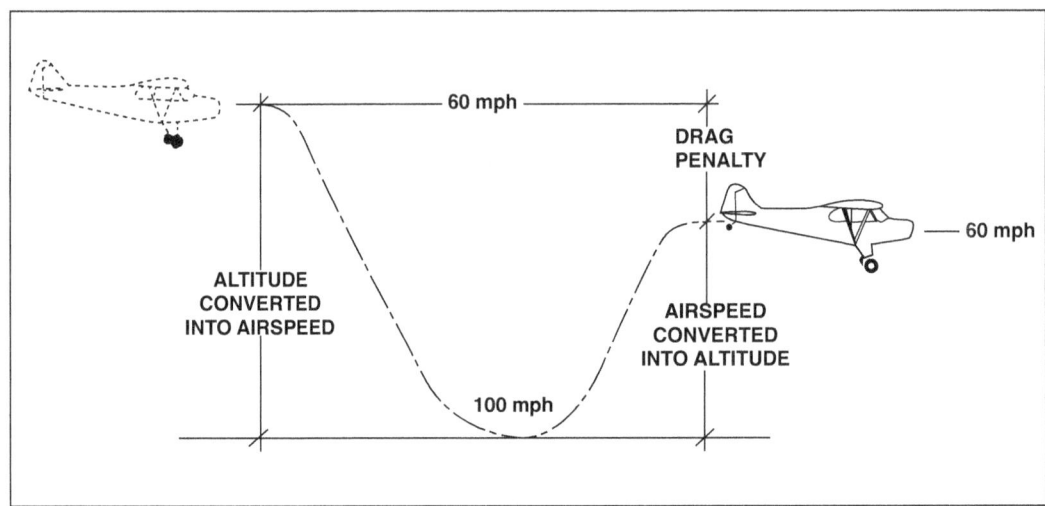

Figure 4-8: Dive/Climb Test Performed without Power

Given the same descent profile, the powered descent gains airspeed faster per foot of altitude lost. Fuel is expended in exchange for airspeed in this case. We reach the desired speed sooner, thereby conserving some altitude. With the aid of power, we then climb back to our original altitude and fly away at 60 mph. We could even continue to climb **ABOVE** our original starting altitude, holding a constant airspeed.

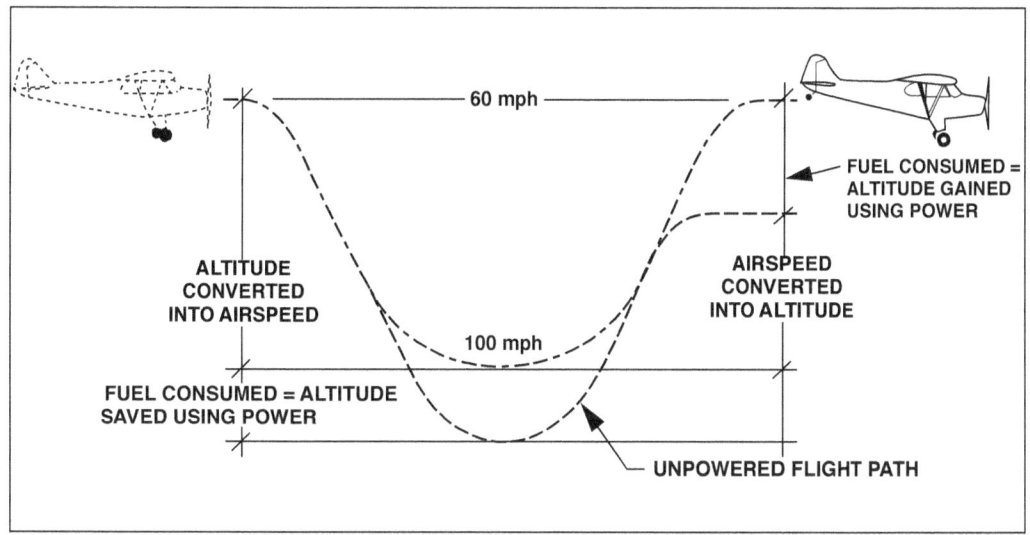

Figure 4-9: Dive/Climb Test Performed with Power

We can fly at many different airspeeds, with or without power. As illustrated above, however, power has more to do with altitude control. It's also evident that pitch and power are closely linked, and changes in one impact the other. The relationship between pitch and power is analogous to that between ailerons and rudder: they work in tandem.

We studied the forces acting on an airplane in steady, level flight in Chapter 2—Basic Aerodynamics. Let's expand our earlier force balance to include normal climbs and descents. For simplicity, let's consider only those Thrust, Drag, and Weight components acting parallel to our flight path. In level flight, Weight does not enter into the balance; therefore, Thrust must equal Drag exactly. When climbing or descending, though, some of the airplane's Weight is inclined along our flight path. Thrust can no longer just equal Drag; its magnitude is influenced by a portion of the airplane's own weight.

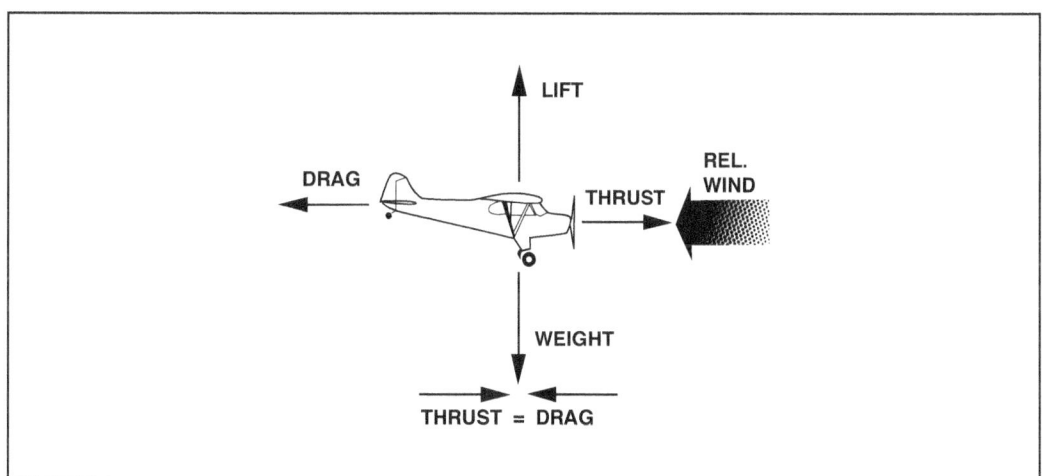

Figure 4-10: Force Balance in Level Flight

Notice what happens in a climb: Weight, which always points toward the center of the Earth, no longer directly opposes Lift. Part of the airplane's Weight now acts in the same direction as Drag. A forces-balanced climb is only possible if Thrust is increased enough to offset Drag **plus** part of the airplane's Weight. A climb at 80 mph, for example, demands more Thrust (and therefore, more Power) than level flight at 80 mph. Our **angle** of climb depends on the amount of excess Thrust available; our **rate** of climb depends on the amount of excess Power available.

Descending flight places the effect of gravity in our favor. Part of the airplane's Weight now acts forward, augmenting Thrust to counter Drag. A forces-balanced descent is only possible if Thrust is reduced sufficiently to compensate for the Weight component assisting against Drag. Descending at 80 mph, for instance, requires less Thrust (and therefore, less Power) than level flight at 80 mph. Thrust separates powered airplanes from gliders—without it, steady flight can only be achieved by using the downhill pull of gravity. It should be evident, then, that the ability to modulate Thrust gives us direct control over our altitude profile.

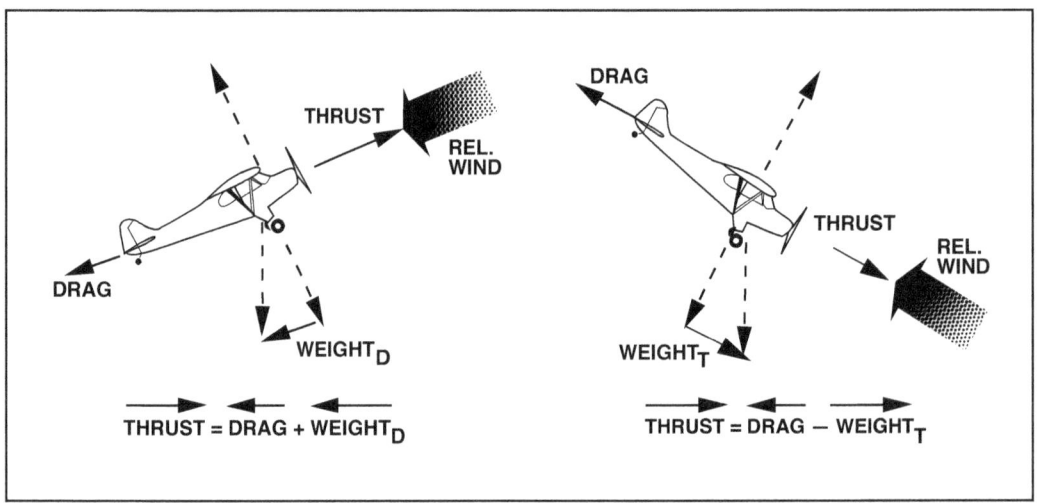

Figure 4-11: Force Balance in Climbing and Descending Flight

The Power Curve

Let's construct a performance diagram that displays the relationship between airspeed and power in steady, level flight. The diagram plots power as a function of airspeed for a given weight and configuration. We can superimpose power required and power available curves and identify some important airspeeds. On the high speed side, for example, the airplane achieves its maximum level cruising speed, Vh, when the power required equals the maximum power available. The available rate of climb is zero; therefore, we can only fly level with this airspeed/power combination. On the low speed end, the power required curve becomes vertical at the airplane's 1-g stall speed.

The amount of excess power available at a given airspeed defines our rate of climb. The speed corresponding to maximum rate of climb (maximum excess power available) is Vy. The lowest point on the power required curve is our maximum endurance speed. At this speed, we can remain in level, steady flight for the greatest amount of TIME. Maximum endurance speed also represents a cross-over point for the amount of power required; moving left or right away from this speed increases our power requirements.

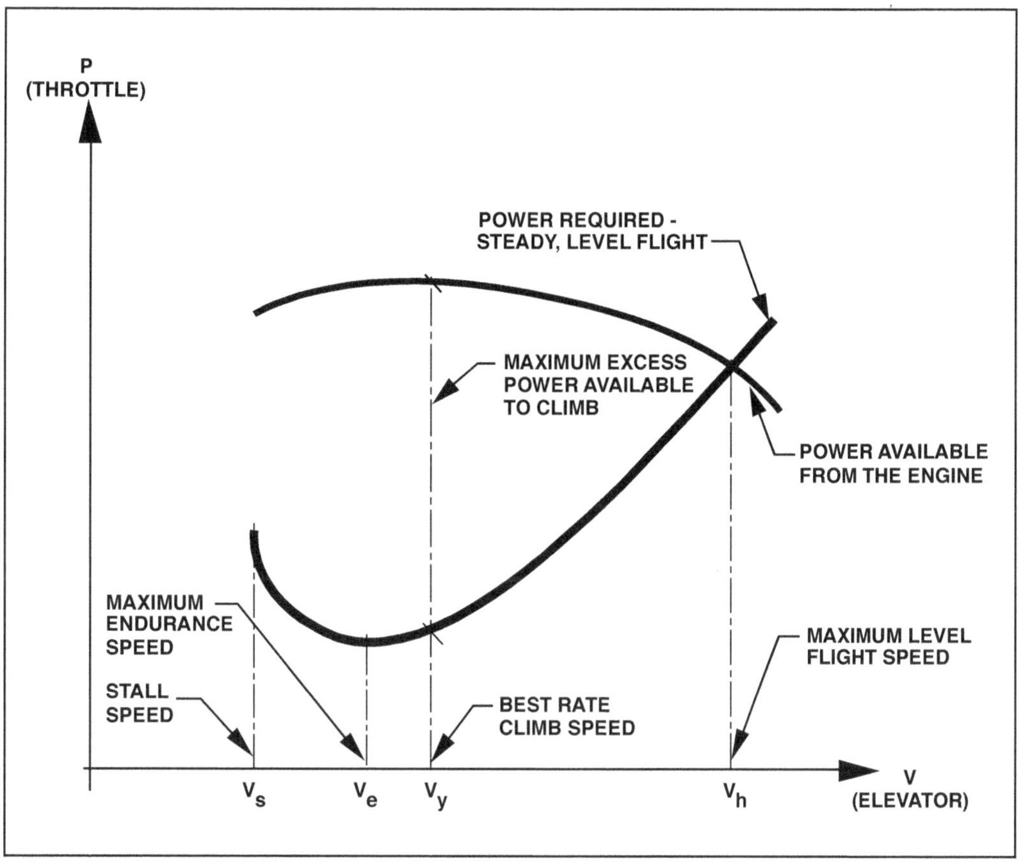

Figure 4-12: The Power Curve

The power required diagram is sub-divided into two regions, separated by the minimum power required/maximum endurance speed point on the curve. The area to the left is the "Region of Reversed Command", and is associated with the lower airspeeds encountered during takeoff, landing, and slow flight. The area to the right is the "Region of Normal Command", and is associated with the higher airspeeds encountered during cruise and non-slow flight manoeuvres. Let's pick an airspeed in each region and see what happens when we change the power setting or the airspeed. To make this more interesting, let's select the airspeeds so that **EACH ONE REQUIRES THE SAME POWER SETTING** in level flight. (So much for the power-controls-airspeed argument!)

If we hold the airspeed constant and change only our power setting, we'll effect a change in altitude. Varying the power slides us vertically above or below the power required for steady flight at a given airspeed. More power induces a climb; less power, a descent. To return to steady, level flight after a power change, airspeed must be increased or decreased by altering our angle of attack.

Coincidentally, in the Region of Normal Command, increases in power require increases in airspeed for steady, level flight. Decreases in power require decreases in airspeed. But look what happens in the Region of Reversed Command: Increases in power require **DECREASES** in airspeed, whereas decreases in power require **INCREASES** in airspeed for level flight. Hence the name, "Region of Reversed Command".

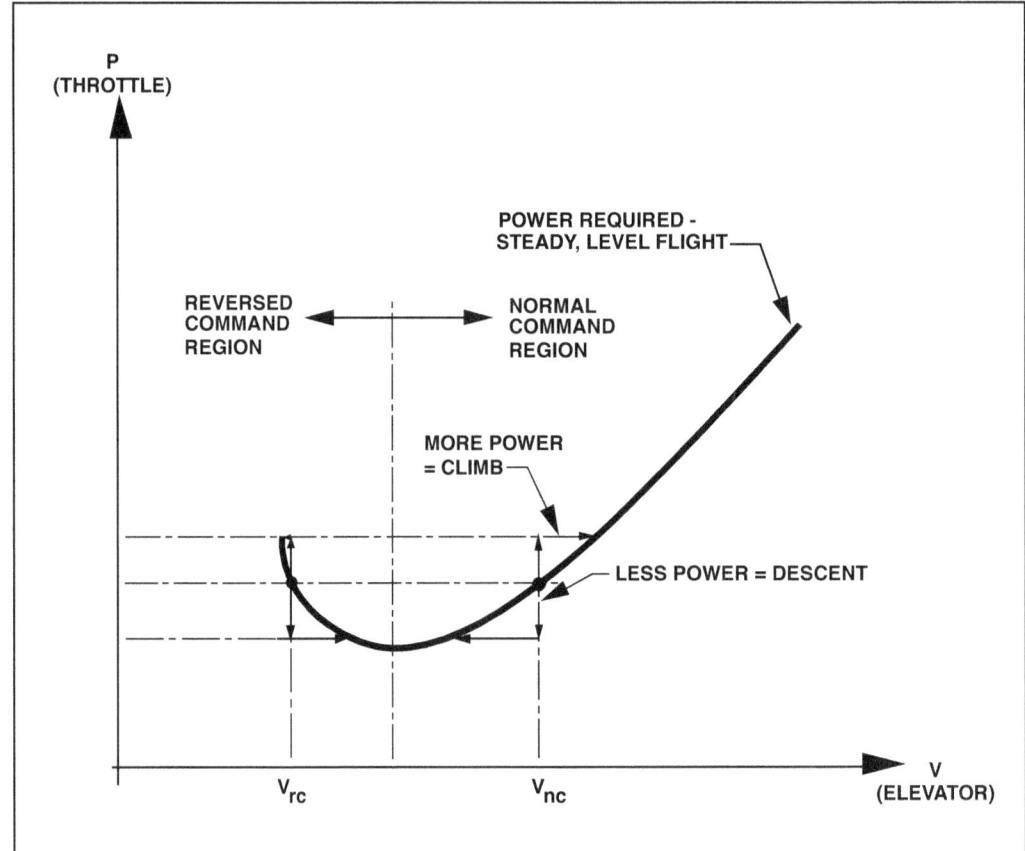

Figure 4-13: Effect of Power Changes on Level Flight

If we now keep the power setting constant and change only the airspeed, we'll effect a change in altitude as well. Varying the airspeed slides us horizontally away from the power required for level flight; thus, the airplane responds by climbing or descending. To return to steady, level flight after an airspeed change, we must adjust the power accordingly: reduce it if climbing, add it if descending.

In the Region of Normal Command, for instance, a higher airspeed requires more power to hold the same altitude; otherwise, the airplane descends. Similarly, a slower airspeed requires less power; otherwise, the airplane climbs. The opposite is true in the Region of Reversed Command: higher speeds require less power for level flight; lower speeds require more power. Otherwise, an increase in speed causes the airplane to climb; a decrease in speed causes it to descend.

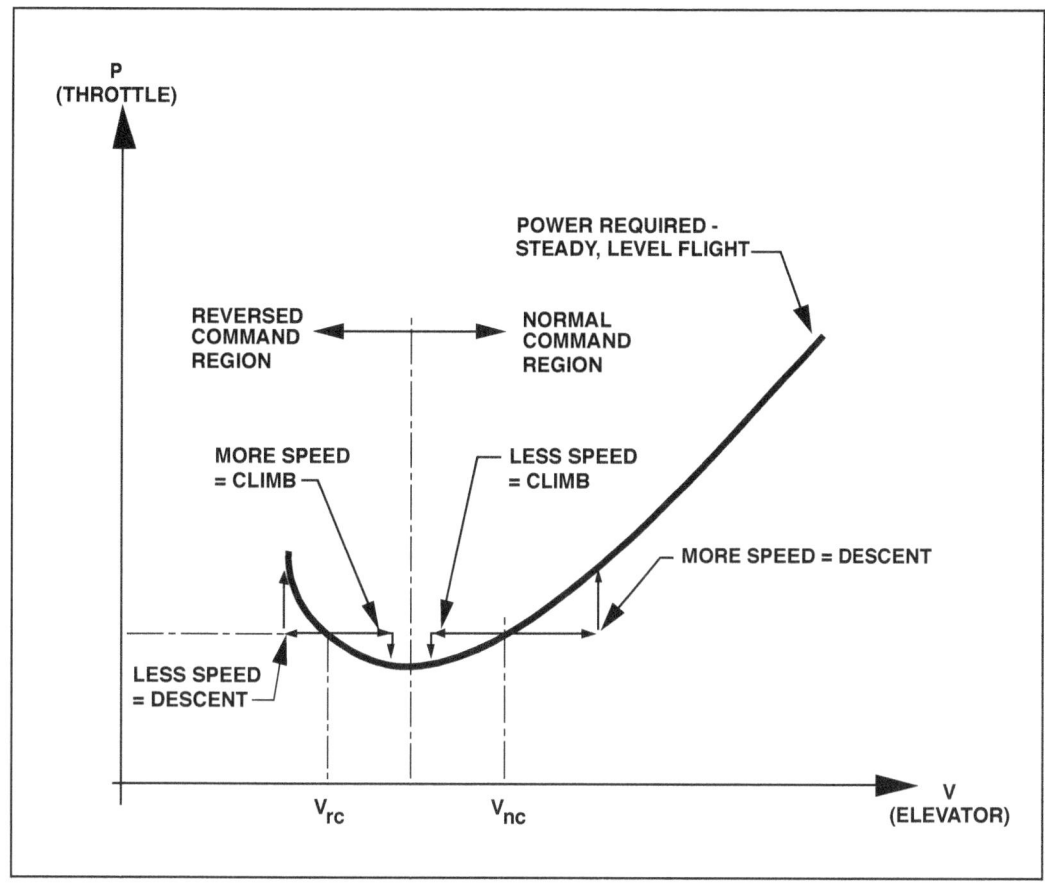

Figure 4-14: Effect of Airspeed Changes on Level Flight

Whether we're operating in the Region of Normal or of Reversed Command, steady flight requires coordinated changes in both pitch and power. Modifying one parameter affects the other. It's crucial, however, to understand the primary function of pitch and power controls and the effects of pitch and power inputs. To reiterate, elevator inputs control angle of attack and airspeed; throttle controls rate of climb and descent in all flight modes.

Since power and airspeed follow similar trends in the Region of Normal Command, it's often "convenient" to relate more power for more speed and less power for less speed—like "driving a car." This analogy is prevalent during commercial and instrument flight training, where the airplane is maintained in essentially level flight at all times, nestled comfortably within its operating limits. But flying is not at all like driving a car, especially during an emergency or whenever circumstances place the pilot near the edge of the airplane's capability.

Moreover, the airplane's natural tendency to maintain its trim speed is weakened considerably when changing power settings in the Region of Reversed Command. Controlling airspeed with elevator inputs is critical when on the back side of the power curve. Pulling on the elevator to gain altitude instead only elevates us to higher angles of attack and lower airspeeds. Pulling trying to stay "up", rather than pushing for airspeed, is a factor in many fatal airplane accidents.

Two classic examples where pulling back on the elevator control worsens the situation are the low, slow, dragged-in approach and the engine failure immediately after takeoff. Recall that low-and-slow is the worst energy combination possible. In the Region of

Reversed Command, pulling to stay "up" only amplifies the rate of descent. More power is then needed just to retard the increased rate of descent resulting from the pull.

If we're bleeding off airspeed at a faster rate than we're adding power, the airplane gets progressively lower and slower. Unchecked, the airplane eventually hits the ground, either in a stall/spin or while mushing at a high rate of descent. **BOTH** the throttle and the elevator must move forward to correct a low-and-slow approach. Applying power arrests the descent and allows us to reach the runway. Adjusting pitch gains airspeed, reduces our angle of attack, and improves our ability to climb in the Region of Reversed Command.

Pulling on the elevator control to stay "up" is also the typical reaction to an engine failure soon after takeoff. The correct response, however, must be a **PUSH** for airspeed. Even though pushing seems contrary to our normal instincts, it's one of the keys to controlled flight. Coping with critical flight conditions becomes difficult, if not impossible, unless we master this survival reflex. The significance of thinking in terms of pitch-for-airspeed and power-for-altitude will become apparent as emergency recovery strategies unfold in the chapters entitled Stalls, Powerplant Failures, Off-Airport Landings, and in the next chapter, Curved Flight.

5
Curved Flight

Airplanes carve just two shapes in the sky: straight lines and curves. The turn certainly is the most common form of curved flight. Although all pilots can perform this versatile manoeuvre, few can properly describe its mechanics. Unfortunately, an incomplete understanding of turning flight can lead to inappropriate control inputs during critical flight operations. Losing control of the airplane while turning is cited in many accident reports. Therefore, understanding turn dynamics is essential to control the airplane.

This chapter focuses primarily on the aerodynamics of turning flight. Different types of turns are discussed as well. Since improperly executed turns often precede fatal accidents, the need for proper coordination and proper turn technique cannot be overemphasised.

Current flight training typically focuses on only two elements pertaining to turns: First, the rudder doesn't turn the airplane. Second, the horizontal component of Lift is the force that turns the airplane. Many training handbooks and flight instructors, however, fail to continue beyond this to identify the true turn control. Consequently, many pilots know which control surface doesn't turn the airplane, but aren't sure which of the remaining two really does. When pressed to name it, many respond that ailerons turn the airplane. In actuality, the **ELEVATOR** is our primary turn control. Another look at our controls verifies this:

The rudder's primary function is to cancel the many yaw effects associated with flying: adverse yaw arising from aileron inputs; gyroscopic effects arising from elevator inputs; torque, P-factor, and slipstream arising from the use of power; yaw arising from airplane rigging. The rudder permits coordinated, ball-centered flight. Used correctly, it improves the quality and the efficiency of our flying. If all secondary yaw effects could be designed out entirely, airplanes wouldn't need this control surface (unless, of course, we wanted to perform slips and spins). The rudder was never intended to be a turn control.

Ailerons are our roll, or bank control. To illustrate their function, recall an airshow performance you may have seen. When the airshow pilot performs a full roll, does the airplane turn? No! When the airshow pilot performs an eight-point hesitation roll, stopping every 45 degrees, does the airplane turn? No! Even when the airshow pilot rolls to 90 degrees of bank and flies down the length of the runway in knife-edge flight, the airplane still doesn't turn.

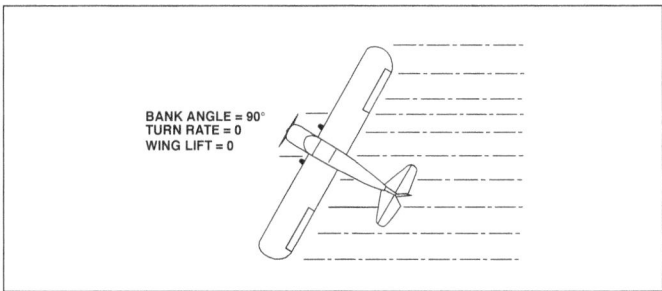

Figure 5-1: Knife-Edge Pass

Aileron inputs merely characterise our turns. They cannot, and do not curve our flight path. They do, however, permit a wide range of possible curves, facilitated by pointing Lift in different directions. With ailerons deflected, the airplane rolls; with ailerons neutralised, rolling ceases instantly and a bank is established. Unfortunately, banking tends to be the most dramatic and least natural part of a turn. It's this action, and not the often subtle, but necessary elevator input that erroneously leads pilots to perceive ailerons as the turn control. Later in this chapter, we'll see some turns that require aileron inputs **OPPOSITE** to the direction of flight.

Unconvinced, some pilots rationalise the apparent knife-edge flight anomaly by postulating that opposite rudder cancels the airplane's turning tendency. Opposite rudder doesn't have anything to do with preventing turns in knife-edge. Rudder deflection allows the fuselage to generate Lift like a wing, balancing the airplane's Weight. The airplane wouldn't stay airborne otherwise. Furthermore, since rudder controls the angle of attack of the **FUSELAGE**, and elevator controls the angle of attack of the **WING**, how can the rudder cancel the wing's Lift? It can't. Lift is a function of the wing's angle of attack. It's controlled with the elevator. The only way to neutralise Lift, which points straight at the horizon in knife-edge, is to reduce the angle of attack—with the elevator—until zero Lift is produced.

The elevator truly is our turn control. Roll, yaw, and power are the spices we mix with pitch to flavor our turns. Combining different proportions of these ingredients gives each turn a distinct character. Visualise the airplane moving from your head to your feet as you make pitch inputs. Regardless of your attitude, the flight path always curves. We alter our flight path by pushing and pulling on the elevator control. How we manipulate the elevator ultimately determines the turn's shape and quality.

Think about the curved flight we experience on a single trip around the traffic pattern: We rotate to a climb attitude on takeoff with back elevator pressure. We level off at pattern altitude using forward elevator pressure. We perform level crosswind and downwind turns, then descending base and final turns. These are done by banking with ailerons and pulling the nose around to a new heading with elevator. Lastly, back elevator pressure allows us to flare for landing.

We can demonstrate the validity of elevator as the turn control with more dramatic examples. How about a 360 degree turn starting with zero bank? The resulting manoeuvre is a vertical turn, also known as a Loop. Looping manoeuvres are better left to skilled aerobatic pilots flying aerobatic airplanes.

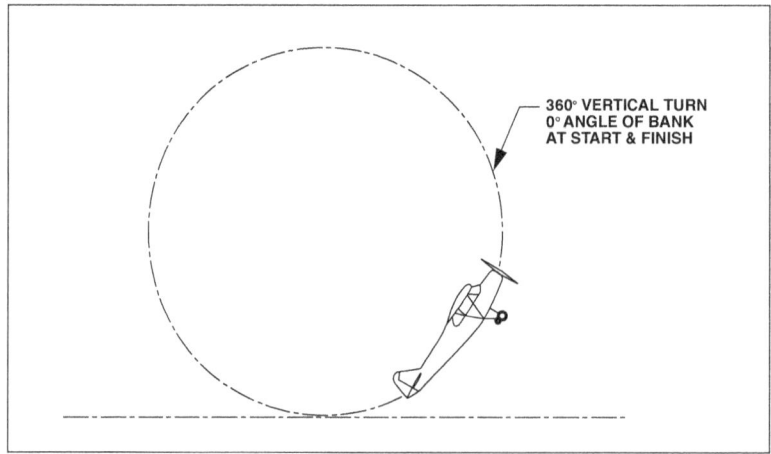

Figure 5-2: A Loop is a Vertical Turn

Thinking in terms of three dimensional space, many kinds of turns become possible. Each one is linked to movements relative to the pilot. Imagine some of the possibilities with just 30 degrees of bank to the left: We can fly a level turn by applying the correct amount of back elevator pressure. Too much back pressure initiates a climbing turn. Way too much pull starts a loop tilted 30 degrees from vertical. Insufficient back pressure yields a descending turn. A hefty amount of forward elevator carves an outside loop.

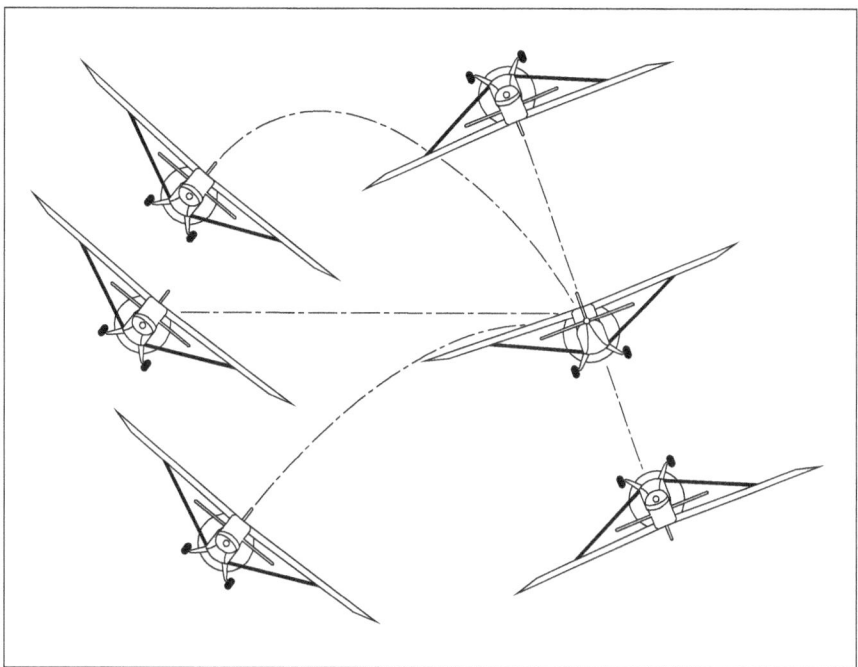

Figure 5-3: Various Turns Starting with 30 Degrees of Bank

None of these turns are freaks of nature. Each one is consistent with the laws of aerodynamics. We simply make use of the fact that elevator inputs curve our flight path. Some of these manoeuvres may be limited by one or any combination of aircraft design, energy, and pilot skill factors. What's available to us in a practical sense, however, should not obscure our understanding of what's theoretically possible in three dimensions: We can climb, descend, or even remain level; we can maintain a constant bank angle, or allow our bank to vary during climbs and descents—various forms of curved flight, all controlled through elevator inputs.

Forces in Turns

Forces develop any time mass is accelerated (see Chapter 2—Basic Aerodynamics). Acceleration occurs any time our airspeed **OR** our direction of flight changes. Since pushing and pulling on the elevator alters our flight path, and thus subjects us to acceleration (even though airspeed may be constant), it changes the forces acting on the airplane. We perceive these changes as g-load—total Lift divided by gross Weight—whenever the flight path curves.

For example, Weight must be balanced during a level, coordinated, right turn with 60 degrees of bank. Our Lift force, however, is now tilted 60 degrees from vertical. It no longer directly opposes Weight, which still points earthward. Let's resolve our Lift vector into two smaller components: a vertical Lift component, which must now become large enough to balance Weight; and a horizontal Lift component—called a **CENTRIPETAL FORCE**—which points in the direction of bank.

Equilibrium occurs vertically when the corresponding Lift component offsets the Weight of the airplane. But we can only change the magnitude of Lift two ways: by altering airspeed and angle of attack. Both of these are controlled with pitch. Back elevator pressure increases the total Lift when banked, thereby stretching the vertical and horizontal components. Doubling the g-load at 60 degrees of bank quickly balances the forces vertically, but they don't balance horizontally.

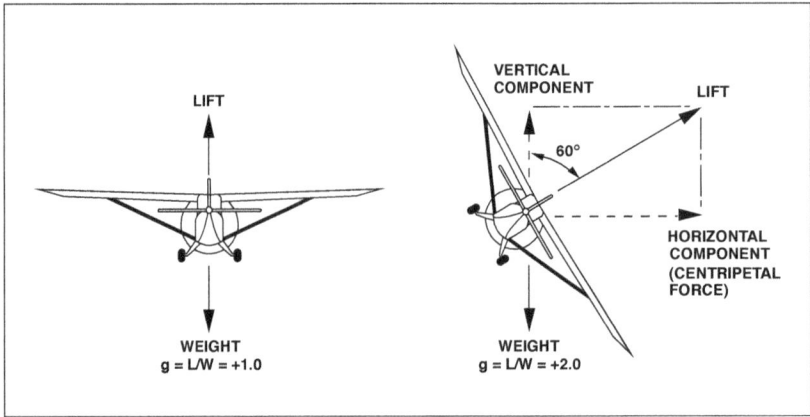

Figure 5-4: Forces in a Level Turn

It's the growing horizontal component of Lift that pulls the airplane away from a straight line. As the flight path bends under this unopposed force, the tail assembly continually weathercocks the nose into the changing relative wind. The result is a smooth, sweeping arc. Turning is actually a by-product of the Weight-balancing process. But as the loop demonstrates, an angle of bank isn't necessarily a prerequisite for curved flight.

G-Loads

We experience g-loads any time we apply ample elevator to alter our direction of flight. How rapidly we displace the elevator control, and in which direction, determine the magnitude and feel of the g-load imposed. Pulling the elevator control induces positive g's, which compress our bodies and pull us into our seat. Pushing on the elevator control induces negative g's, which stretch our bodies and push us out of our seats.

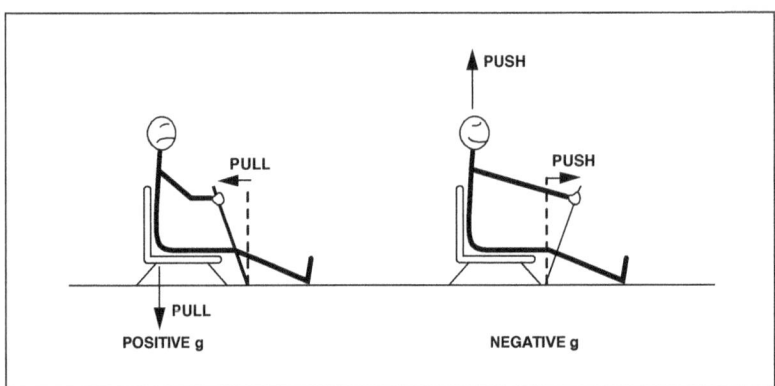

Figure 5-5: Correlating G-Load with Elevator Control Movement

G-load is important from physiological and structural standpoints. During straight and level flight at a constant airspeed, for instance, pilot and airplane experience +1.0 g (L = W). We feel normal and react to the effects of our normal body Weight. Under +2.0 g's (L = 2 x W), we experience twice our normal body Weight. Blood is pulled into the lower body, possibly causing some lightheadedness. Moving your arms now requires more effort. Structurally, Normal category operation is limited to +3.8 and -1.52 g's;

Utility category operation, +4.4 and -1.72 g's; and Acrobatic category operation, +6.0 and -3.0 g's.

G's are a measure of the effective Weight of an airplane in curved flight. The increased effective Weight affects aircraft performance as though it was an increase in the actual gross Weight. To fly along an arc, we must increase our angle of attack. This generates the extra Lift needed to support the Weight of the airplane. The g-load required varies with angle of attack. G-load remains constant when the correct mixture of airspeed and angle of attack are achieved.

The g's necessary to sustain a steady, coordinated turn also depend on our bank angle. As bank angle increases, g-load must increase. We must apply more and more back elevator pressure as the bank steepens in an upright turn, for example. But g-load doesn't increase appreciably until we approach 45 degrees of bank; consequently, the minimal elevator inputs required in shallow turns often go unnoticed. As bank angle and g-load increase, though, the elevator's role becomes more obvious.

BANK ANGLE (AILERONS)	0°	15°	30°	45°	60°	75°
+G-LOAD (ELEVATOR)	1.00	1.04	1.15	1.41	2.00	3.86

Table 5-1: G-Load during Turns vs. Bank Angle

We've been careful to avoid the elevator-equals-altitude and the elevator-equals-up pitfalls so far. Remember, the elevator controls pitch movements (head-to-feet), angle of attack, airspeed, g-load, and curved flight. Its relationship to up, down, or sideways is incidental. In the last chapter (Pitch and Power), we analysed the power requirements for steady, level flight as a function of airspeed. Increasing the g-load for a steady turn increases the power required. Hence, turning flight immediately results in a power deficiency, regardless of airspeed. Steady flight occurs when we move onto the power curve corresponding to the given bank angle. Unless we change power, airspeed, or a combination of the two, the power deficiency will cause the airplane to descend.

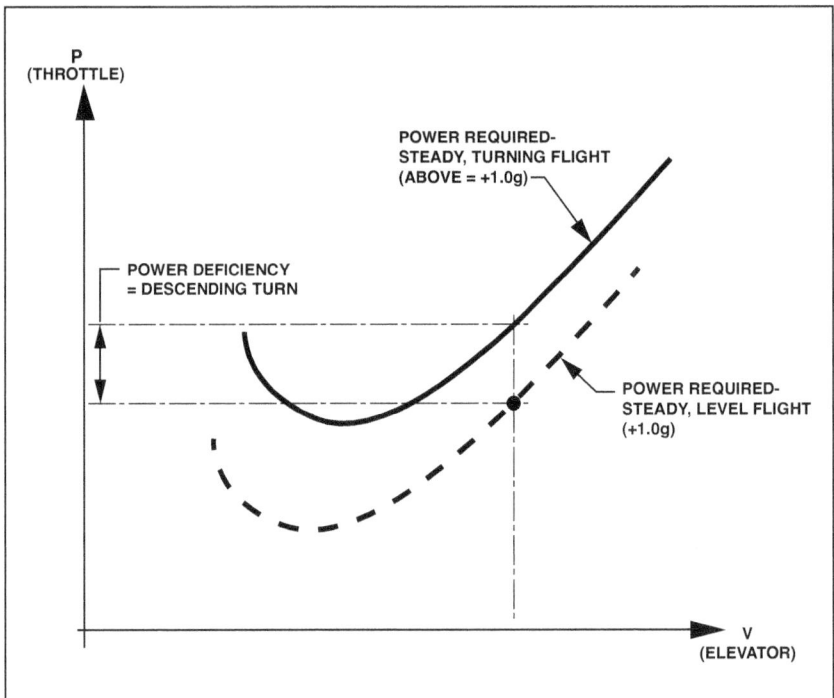

Figure 5-6: Turning Flight Increases the Power Required

A steady, level turn at 30 degrees of bank, for example, places us in a +1.15 g environment. To maintain a constant airspeed, we must add power to move from the +1.0 g power curve onto the +1.15 g power curve; otherwise, we'll descend. If we elect to keep the power constant, then we must decrease our airspeed sufficiently to move onto the +1.15 g power curve. Back elevator pressure in the turn takes care of this. Reducing speed too much results in a climb; not reducing it enough causes us to descend. Blending a slight increase in power while sacrificing some airspeed can also move us onto the +1.15 g power curve.

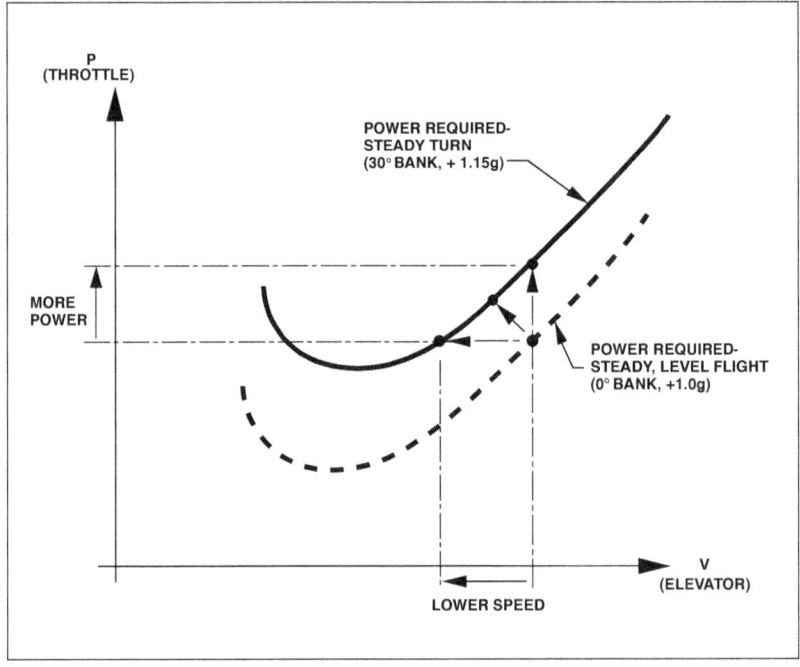

Figure 5-7: Balancing Pitch and Power during a 30 Degree Banked Turn

Although it's convenient to think back pressure holds our altitude when turning, it does not (at least, not directly). Back pressure decreases our airspeed, which decreases the power required for steady flight in the Region of Normal Command. In essence, we trade airspeed energy to hold altitude when pulling in a turn.

Increasing our Weight, whether it's by pulling in a turn, or by adding more passengers and baggage, shifts the power-required curve for steady flight upward and to the right. This trend highlights three significant operating characteristics when g-load and gross Weight increase:

1. Stall speed increases;
2. Excess power available for steady flight decreases;
3. The number of power and pitch combinations available for steady flight decreases.

Many of us know from practical experience that it's easier to lose control of an airplane in a steep turn than in a shallow turn. Steepening the bank shrinks your operating envelope. Hence, reducing the bank angle in any turn that has gone awry must expand the operating envelope. Reducing the bank immediately reduces the airplane's stall speed, increases the excess power available, and decreases the power required for steady flight. These properties give us better control over the airplane. This key point appears throughout this chapter and again in Chapter 8—Overbanked.

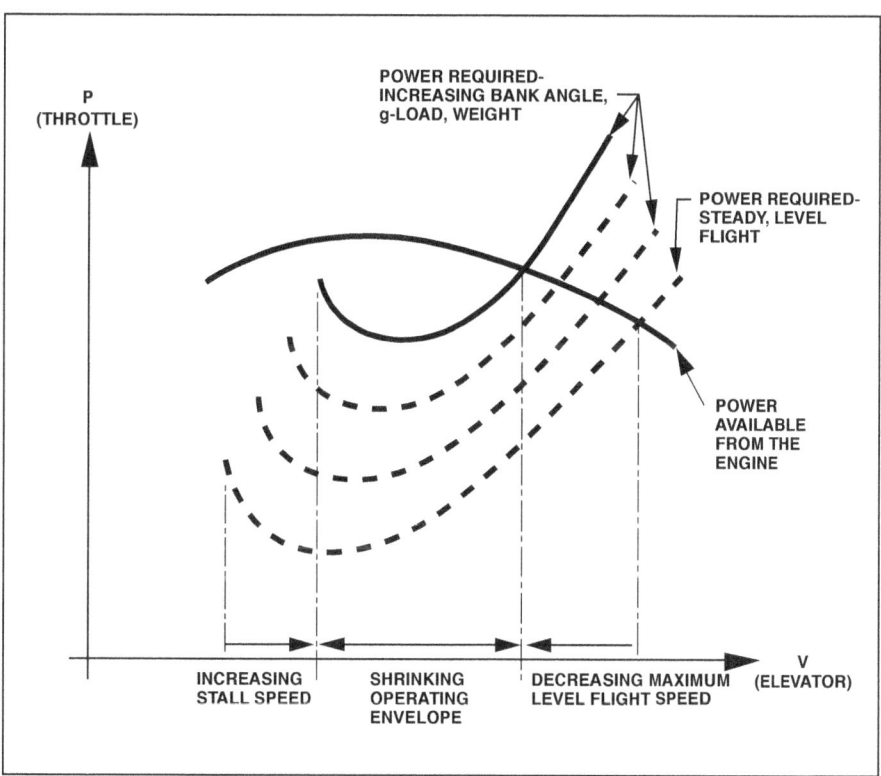

Figure 5-8: Increasing Bank Angle, G-Load, or Weight Increases the Power Required

The V-g Diagram

The V-g diagram offers a more useful representation of the relationship between g-load and airspeed. All of the parameters controlled by the elevator are presented here in one concise picture. For simplicity, let's consider positive g's only, and let's assume our airplane is certified in the Normal category. G-load is plotted vertically; airspeed, horizontally. Our operating envelope is bounded by two kinds of limitations: aerodynamic and structural. These limits appear as functions of airspeed and g-load. V-g diagrams are snapshots taken at a specific gross Weight, in a specific configuration, at a specific altitude, under a symmetrical g-loading (elevator inputs only—NO ROLLING).

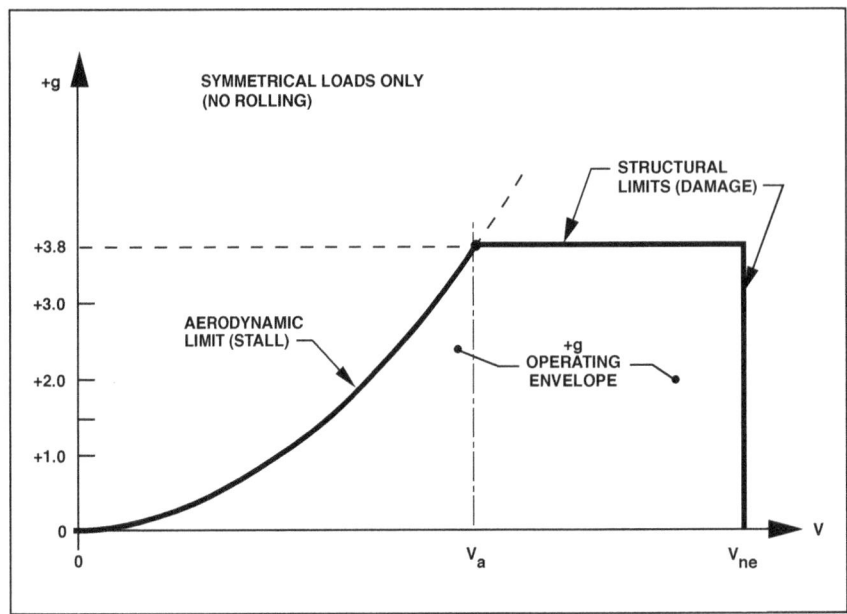

Figure 5-9: The V-g Diagram—Positive G Flight, Normal Category Limits

Stall speed always increases as g-load increases, as noted previously. The g-load and airspeed combinations resulting in a stall do have a practical limit, however. For example, Normal category operation is limited to no more than +3.8 g's. This represents a structural design limit and is the horizontal cap on the V-g diagram. Manoeuvring speed, Va, corresponds to the stall speed at the design structural limit. For a given gross Weight, manoeuvring speed is the pivotal point between aerodynamic and structural operating limitations. Its significance will become apparent in the next chapter (Stalls).

Our operating envelope has a maximum airspeed limit as well, called never exceed speed, Vne. Exceeding Vne, regardless of g-load, can cause structural damage or catastrophic structural failure. Each of the limiting factors on the V-g diagram—angle of attack, g-load, airspeed—is controlled primarily through pitch. Proper management of our elevator inputs, therefore, is paramount if we are to stay within the prescribed envelope, especially during an emergency.

Some interesting characteristics of coordinated turns can be illustrated on a V-g diagram. An airplane's turn radius, for example, is proportional to the square of its airspeed, but inversely proportional to the tangent of the bank angle (bank angle means g-load). Rate of turn, though, is proportional to the tangent of the bank angle, but inversely proportional to airspeed. Both of these parameters are independent of gross Weight and aircraft size. So, two different airplanes flying at the same airspeed and angle of bank will have identical turn radii and turn rates.

When bank angle is held constant, the turn radius will increase if airspeed is increased. Similarly, with constant airspeed, the turn radius will also increase if bank angle is decreased. The rate of turn, however, will decrease in both cases. More speed and/or less bank (lower g's) cause the airplane to cover more ground during a turn; thus, it takes more time to complete it. (The maximum turn radius and the minimum rate of turn occur at wings level: As bank angle decreases to zero, the rate of turn also becomes zero. G-load decreases to +1.0, but the turn radius becomes infinite. Straight-and-level flight, therefore, qualifies as a 1-g turn.)

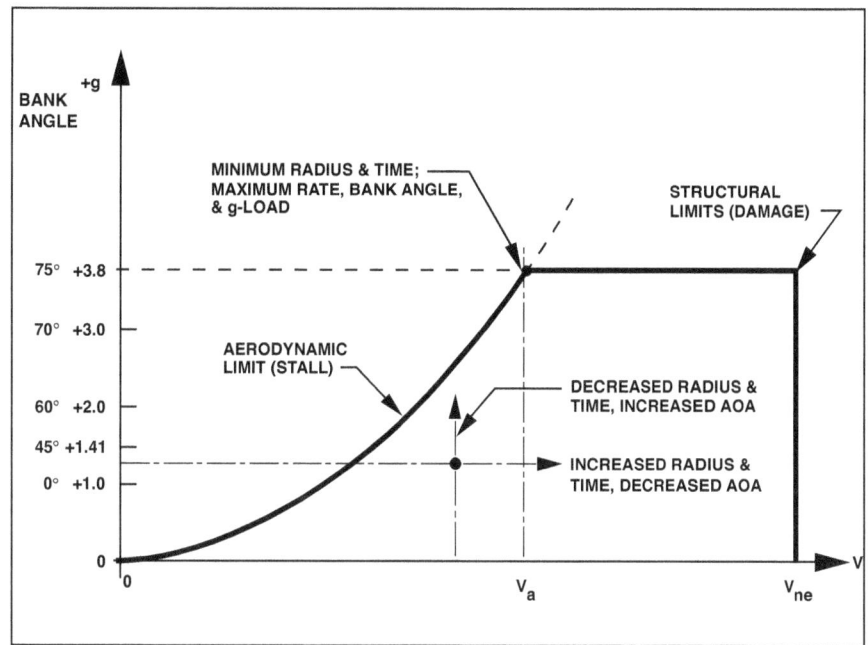

Figure 5-10: Illustrating Turn Performance on the V-g Diagram

When bank angle is held constant, turn radius will decrease as airspeed is decreased. Likewise, with constant airspeed, the turn radius will also decrease if bank angle is increased. The rate of turn in both cases increases. Less speed and/or more bank (higher g's) cause the airplane to cover less ground; thus it takes less time to complete a turn. (Theoretically, the minimum turn radius and the maximum rate of turn for a given speed would occur at 90 degrees of bank. Unfortunately, steady flight at this angle requires an infinite g-load—obviously impractical from a design standpoint.)

The V-g diagram reinforces several key relationships pertaining to curved flight. When turning, stall speed increases as bank angle increases. The g-load necessary to sustain steady, coordinated flight also increases as bank increases. Higher g's translate into higher angles of attack. Flight manuals usually provide tables listing stall speed versus bank angle for various configurations. Each listing is a point on the stall curve of a V-g diagram.

WEIGHT (LBS)	FLAP SETTING	ANGLE OF BANK (G-LOAD)			
		0° (+1.0 g)	30° (+1.15 g)	45° (+1.41 g)	60° (+2.0 g)
1600	UP	36	39	43	51
	10°	36	39	43	51
	30°	31	33	37	44

Table 5-2: Stall Speed during Turns vs. Bank Angle

The only way to modify your turn radius at a given airspeed is to alter the physical characteristics of the turn. Varying bank angle is usually the easiest way to accomplish this. Tighter turns require steeper angles of bank and higher g's. Looser turns require shallower angles of bank and lower g's.

We must be cognisant of the effects of airspeed and bank angle on turn performance when transitioning to higher performance airplanes. For instance, assume you're moving from a Champ into a light twin, from 60 mph to 120 mph in the pattern. Flying at twice the speed influences how we manage the traffic pattern. If we fly the twin at the same bank angle and distance from the runway as the Champ, our turn radius suddenly expands by a factor of four. We'll definitely overshoot the runway when turning final.

We must compensate for the effect higher airspeed has on turn performance: fly a wider pattern, for instance, if the bank angle is to remain the same; or, perform a tighter turn (more bank and higher g's) if the distance from the runway is to remain the same; or, blend a somewhat wider pattern with some additional bank. We also need to anticipate the effects higher approach speeds have during the round-out for landing. If we use our normal rate of pull in a faster airplane, the round-out must begin sooner. If we postpone the round-out, our pull suddenly needs to be tighter than normal. Otherwise, the runway might get in the way of the larger radius flight path, resulting in premature ground contact.

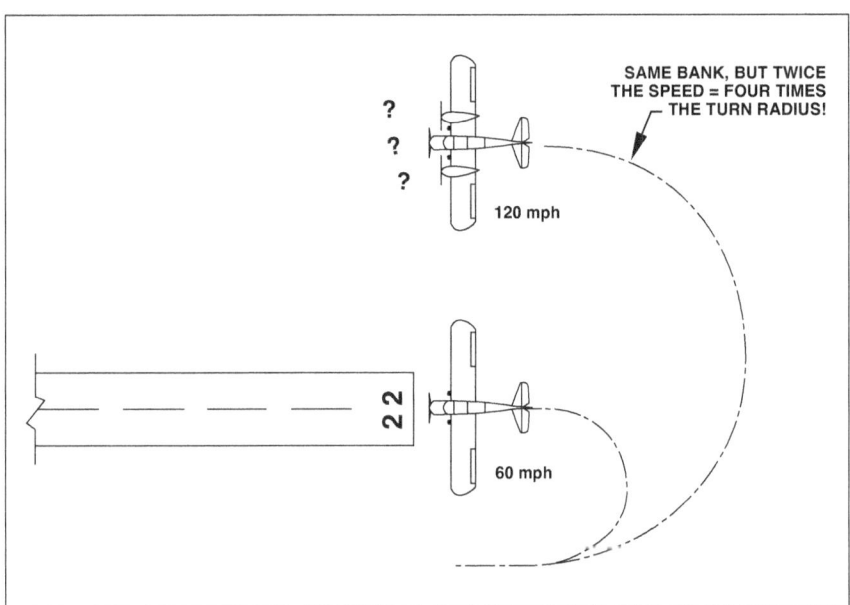

Figure 5-11: Effect of Airspeed on Turn Radius

Another parameter revealed on the V-g diagram is the minimum practical turn radius available. The tightest turn in a particular airplane at a given Weight occurs at manoeuvring speed, at the angle of bank that achieves the design g-load without stalling. In a Normal category design, for example, we would be banked almost 75 degrees, pulling close to +3.8 g's. In the Acrobatic category, we would be banked 80 degrees, pulling +6.0 g's. (Note how increasing the bank just five degrees—75 to 80—increases the g's 1.5 times!) These turns certainly qualify as maximum performance manoeuvres.

Regardless of the airplane's attitude, or the nomenclature used to describe its arcing motion, the control function of the elevator can be summed up in one simple formula:
AIRSPEED + G-LOAD = CURVED FLIGHT

Airspeed, g-load, angle of attack, and curving flight are all manifestations of the same control input: **ELEVATOR**. The fallacy of thinking and flying otherwise shows up all too frequently in aviation accident reports, many of which bear a striking resemblance to the one cited in the first chapter: *"The aircraft lost power on takeoff. Witnesses said the pilot apparently tried to turn back to the runway. The airplane entered a steep turn at low* *airspeed when it suddenly descended out of control."*

Why do pilots lose control of airplanes in these instances? Although distraction and panic understandably diminish a pilot's capacity to cope with in-flight emergencies, incorrectly believing that the ailerons turn an airplane while the elevator holds it "up" are equally significant. Moreover, when the pilot reacts with seemingly correct inputs, only to see the situation worsen, panic and distraction are compounded with confusion.

What we perceive to be a good approximation of reality near straight and level can have disastrous consequences when applied throughout the rest of the operating envelope. The scope of our flight environment is far broader than the 20 degrees of bank and the 15 degrees of pitch encountered on a routine cross country. Recognising that flight is a continuum of events in space, rather than accepting the shortcomings inherent in a single, two dimensional snapshot of this unique environment, ultimately improves our ability to control the airplane.

Based on the above, convince yourself of the following irrefutable facts and react appropriately:

1. To tighten your turn radius, you must increase the bank angle (ailerons) and the g-load (elevator).

2. As g's increase, airspeed may have to be increased as well to avoid an accelerated stall, regardless of your attitude.

3. Steep turns at low airspeeds—combining high g's with low kinetic energy— often will exceed the airplane's aerodynamic capability, especially close to the ground.

Helpful Hints

Turning flight commands striking a balance between angle of bank, airspeed, and g-load. These elements must complement one another to maintain controlled flight. We continually juggle roll, yaw, pitch, and power variables during turns. To manage these variables more efficiently, consider the following points: First, avoid physically leaning away from your turns just to keep your head perpendicular to the horizon. Keep your head aligned with your body instead. This gives you a better feel for the g-loads being imposed and a clearer picture of your elevator inputs. Head-to-foot pitch movements are easier to see when your head and feet form a line perpendicular to the airplane's lateral axis.

Rolling, whether it's to bank or to level the wings, requires aileron inputs. As the desired bank angle is established, aileron pressure must be relaxed; otherwise, you'll keep rolling. The rudder's primary function is to cancel yaw, except under special circumstances when excess yaw may be desirable (as in a slip to lose altitude). Coordinated flight requires blending rudder pressure with, and in the same direction as, your aileron inputs. Apply aileron **AND** rudder pressures whenever changing your bank angle. Also, assume all turns are coordinated—neither slipping nor skidding—unless stated otherwise.

Expect adverse yaw to be greater when rolling out of a turn than when rolling into it. We usually operate at higher angles of attack and lower airspeeds in turns compared to level flight, so more rudder pressure may be required when leveling the wings. Also, remember that slow flight requires right rudder pressure. It's not uncommon, therefore, to need some right rudder once the bank is established in a climbing turn, even in a left climbing turn. Let's now review the general recipes for some different turns, keeping in mind that the exact amounts of roll, yaw, pitch, and power needed will vary from airplane to airplane. Not all of the turns are possible in every airplane, either, nor do all of the recipes yield safe, healthy turns.

Shallow Turns

Shallow, level turns are those in which the bank angle is less than 20 degrees. They are characterised by almost imperceptible increases in g-load, and the natural stability of many airplanes tends to roll the wings back to level. Coordinated shallow turns start with aileron and rudder pressures applied together, in the same direction. Once the desired bank is attained, aileron inputs must be relaxed to stop the roll. A small amount of residual aileron pressure in the direction of the turn may be required, however, simply to keep the bank constant. The rudder must be readjusted as well to maintain coordinated flight. Slight (in some cases, imperceptible) back elevator pressure pulls us around to a new heading.

Pilots generally compensate for minor altitude deviations during shallow turns by adjusting their elevator pressure, rather than adjusting bank angle or power. Keep in mind, though, that elevator inputs directly affect our airspeed, which changes the power required for steady, level flight. Hence, we're trading off a surplus of one parameter (airspeed or altitude) for a deficiency in the other. Small elevator inputs during shallow turns have a minimal effect on the g-load experienced.

Medium Turns

Medium, level turns are those in which the bank angle is between 20 and 45 degrees. They are characterised by slightly higher, yet relatively small g-loads. The inherent stability of many airplanes tends to hold the bank constant. We start these turns just like shallow turns: aileron and rudder pressures together, back elevator pressure to curve the flight path.

In a properly rigged airplane, aileron inputs must be neutralised once a medium bank is established. The rudder is adjusted accordingly, since adverse yaw disappears when the aileron input is removed. Looking out at the wings should reveal no aileron deflection at all. If you can trim off the elevator pressure, you should be able to release the stick or control wheel while the airplane remains in a nice, medium-banked turn. This feature could come in handy if you ever get lost on a cross-country flight. By trimming such a turn over a specific point, you could momentarily free up both hands to locate your position on the sectional chart using a VOR cross-check. (Don't forget to remain vigilant for other traffic in the process.)

Steep Turns

Steep, level turns are those in which the bank angle exceeds 45 degrees. They are characterised by noticeable g-loads, which grow rapidly with increasingly steeper bank angles. Since the outside wing travels along an arc of significantly greater radius than the inside wing, it must travel faster to keep up. The outside wing generates more Lift as a result, causing the airplane to overbank into the turn. Once a steep bank is established, aileron pressure opposite to the direction of the turn may be required to keep the bank constant. Significant back pressure on the elevator is needed to sustain a level turn. Altitude excursions now are corrected more efficiently by reducing the bank angle.

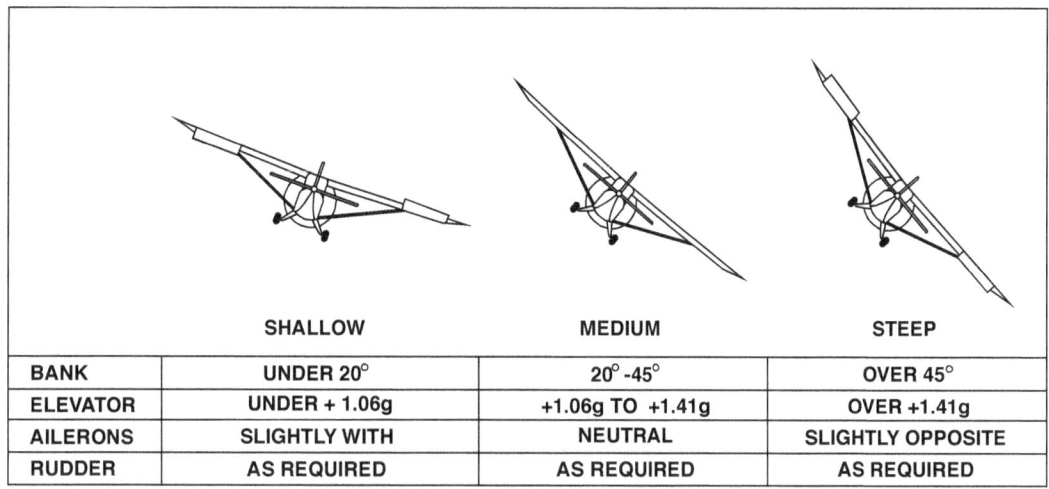

	SHALLOW	MEDIUM	STEEP
BANK	UNDER 20°	20°-45°	OVER 45°
ELEVATOR	UNDER + 1.06g	+1.06g TO +1.41g	OVER +1.41g
AILERONS	SLIGHTLY WITH	NEUTRAL	SLIGHTLY OPPOSITE
RUDDER	AS REQUIRED	AS REQUIRED	AS REQUIRED

Figure 5-12: Summary of Turn Characteristics

Steep turns provide vivid examples where a false belief that pitch controls altitude serves merely to aggravate turn characteristics. Where the elevator presents the illusion of altitude control in shallow turns (by trading off airspeed), it only tightens the steep turn. Pulling as the altimeter unwinds causes significant increases in g-load and angle of attack as airspeed builds. If you're having difficulty maintaining airspeed/altitude in a steep turn, release some of your back elevator pressure and shallow the bank with coordinated aileron and rudder pressures.

Climbing & Descending Turns

Climbing and descending turns inherently change our bank angle relative to the horizon. To illustrate this idiosyncrasy, picture an aerobatic airplane in wings-level flight (zero bank angle). Pulling into a half loop changes our bank relative to the horizon from zero to 180 degrees as the airplane executes a climbing turn. Rolling at the top of the half loop changes the bank back to level, upright flight. Similarly, pushing into a half outside loop results in an 180 degree change in bank, but along a descending curve. Rolling at the bottom returns the airplane to level, upright flight again.

Half loops place a greater demand on the pilot and the airplane and necessitate an aggressive exchange of airspeed and altitude (passengers may not appreciate such demonstrations, either). The less stressful normal climbing turn, on the other hand, requires a simultaneous roll input **OPPOSITE** to the direction of turn to prevent an increase in bank angle relative to the horizon. An 180 degree climbing right turn with 30 degrees of bank, for instance, requires some left aileron to hold a constant bank—pitching curves the flight path; rolling keeps us upright throughout. This combination of inputs is clearly evident during Chandelles.

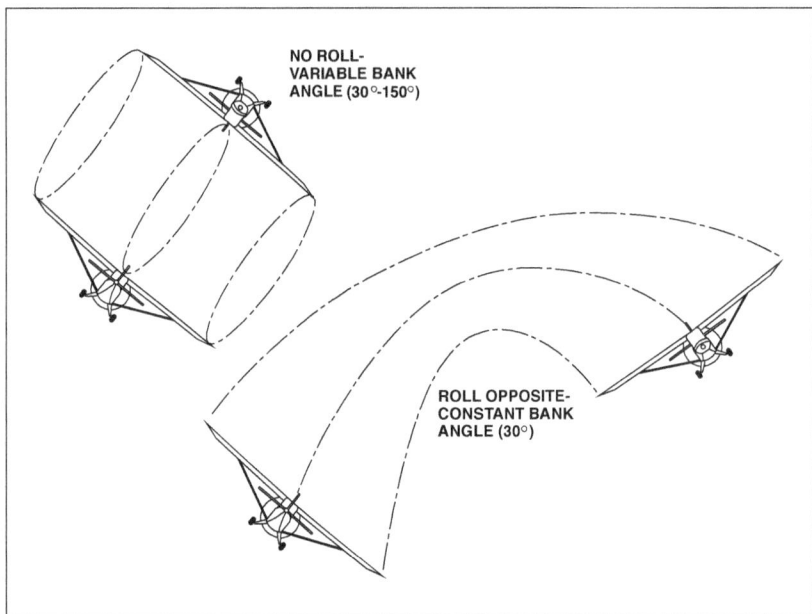

Figure 5-13: Effect of Climbing Turns on Bank Angle

Normal descending turns, on the other hand, require a small roll component in the **SAME** direction as the turn to hold a constant bank angle. Imagine descending along a huge, coiled spring. Continuously rolling into the turn allows us to follow the spring's curve. This effect appears during constant-speed, constant-bank spirals.

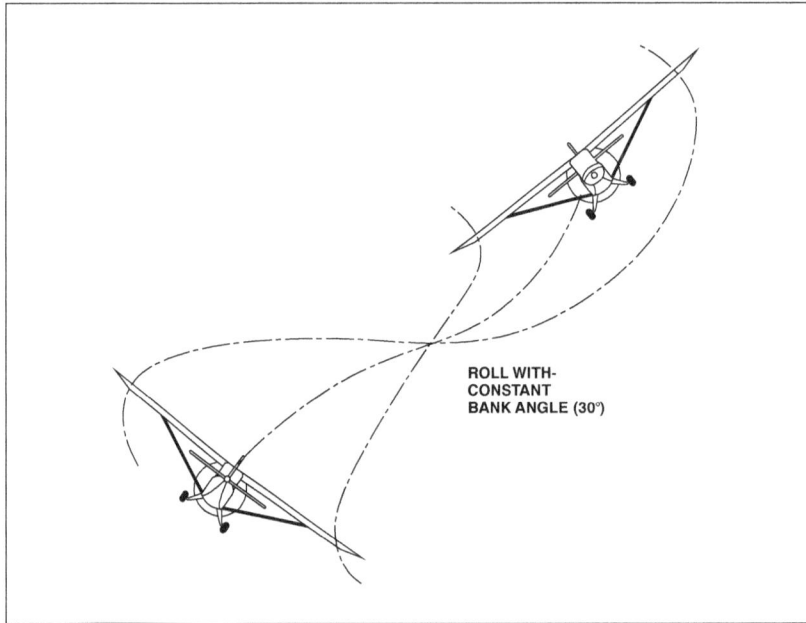

Figure 5-14: Descending Turn with a Constant Bank Angle

Skidding Turns

The underlying characteristic of all skidding turns is excess yaw in the direction of the turn. They are uncoordinated manoeuvres. Typically, the unnecessary yaw is pilot-induced, with too much rudder being applied in the direction of turn. Both the deflected rudder and the inside wing point toward the ground when skidding while the slip/skid ball moves to the outside of the turn.

Excess yaw also generates a secondary roll in the direction of the skidding turn, thereby increasing the angle of bank. Yaw slices the nose earthward through the horizon as well. These actions alter the character of the turn and can negatively influence the pilot's perception. Incorrectly reacting with opposite aileron to counter the increasing bank angle and additional back elevator pressure to hold the nose "up" pave the way for the classic accidental spin from a skidding turn.

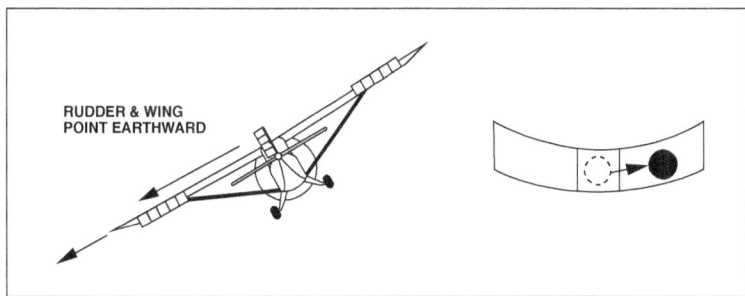

Figure 5-15: Characteristics of a Left Skidding Turn

Yaw coupled with roll near critical angle of attack excites autorotation (see Chapter 7—Spins). All of the ingredients for a spin are present in skidding turns. The strategy here is simple: **don't skid your turns!** Skidding turns serve no useful purpose. They are a sure recipe for disaster. They are killers. Rather than skidding, either add coordinated aileron and rudder pressure to increase the bank and to decrease the turn radius, or level the wings, go around, and try again.

Slipping Turns

The underlying characteristic of all slipping turns is excess yaw opposite to the direction of turn. Like skidding turns, slipping turns are uncoordinated. During a slipping turn, the inside wing points toward the ground. The deflected rudder, however, points skyward, opposite to the direction of turn. Slipping turns are useful for losing altitude quickly, particularly during a high landing approach. They're also instrumental when coping with in-flight control failures such as split flaps, jammed ailerons, or a stuck rudder.

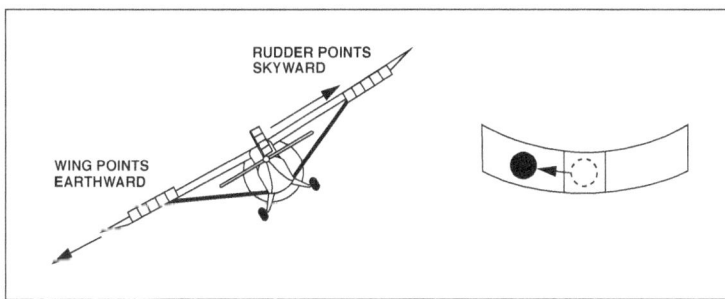

Figure 5-16: Characteristics of a Left Slipping Turn

Aileron pressure must be held in the direction of a slipping turn to maintain a constant bank angle. This pressure offsets the roll induced by the opposite rudder input. Yaw and roll, therefore, are not necessarily coupled as in the dangerous skidding turn. In fact, yaw and roll act in different directions, making a slipping turn somewhat spin resistant. Transitioning into and out of slipping turns requires precise control over your control inputs; otherwise, it's possible to transition into a spin-prone skid instead.

Slipping turns are performed by adding a little more bank, or reducing some rudder pressure, or a combination of the two, along with an increase in back elevator pressure. Looking down the inside wing reveals an upward deflected aileron. The slip/skid ball rests toward the inside of the turn. Since these turns are uncoordinated, turn rates will be slower than comparable coordinated turns.

Turn/Roll Combinations

The notion of elevator as the primary turn control and ailerons as the roll control is readily apparent to pilots trained in aerobatics. Among the most difficult manoeuvres to perform well, Rolling Turns provide the final litmus test of this concept. They clearly identify pitch as the turn control. After all, if elevator turns the airplane and ailerons roll the airplane, it should be possible to turn while rolling, right? Right! Rolling Turns demand concentration, timing, and control over your inputs (they also require higher performance aerobatic airplanes designed for the stresses imposed).

For example, a 90 degree Rolling Turn, with one roll in the direction of the turn (roll to the inside), requires that a slow roll be combined with a turn to a new heading 90 degrees from the original heading. The roll and the turn must begin and end at the same time, with constant roll and turn rates, with no altitude deviations. A right Rolling Turn requires a right roll; a left Rolling Turn, a left roll.

Inside Rolling Turns begin by rolling and pulling simultaneously. The airplane should be inverted half way through the turn—180 degrees of bank at 45 degrees of heading change. The pull then changes to a push, resulting in an outside turn for the second 45 degrees of heading change. The roll continues, blended with the push to arrive in upright flight 90 degrees from the original heading. Variable rudder inputs are used throughout to improve the shape and quality of this complex manoeuvre.

We can even perform Rolling Turns by rolling opposite to the direction of turn (roll to the outside). Roll left while turning right, or roll right while turning left. Many other turn/roll combinations are available as well. On the aerobatic side, Barrel Rolls are concocted by mixing a full loop (i.e.: vertical turn) with a full, albeit slow, roll. On the straight-and-level side, Commercial pilots blend pitch and roll inputs when performing precision Chandelles and Lazy Eights.

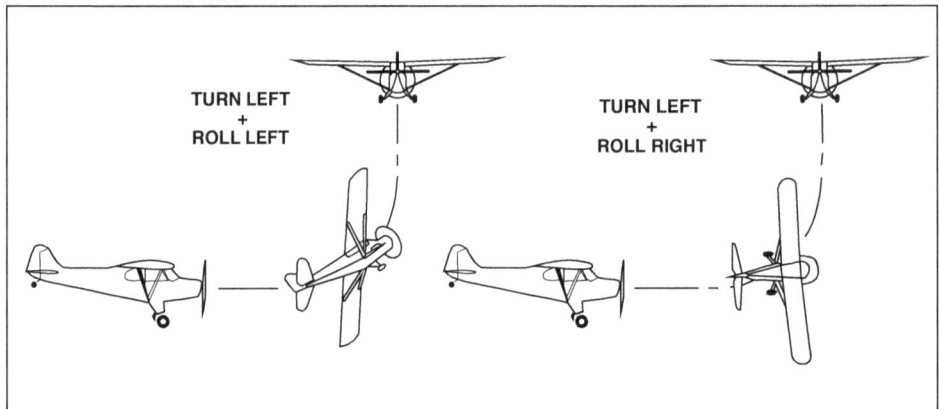

Figure 5-17: Rolling Turns

Spirals

Left to their own devices, most airplanes display a natural tendency to bank and turn by themselves. This tendency is called Spiral Instability. Spirals self-propagate and become tighter unless the pilot reacts appropriately to stop them. They can start from perfectly trimmed, straight and level flight, but spirals usually occur as a result of improperly executed turns, especially steep turns. They can also occur during stall recovery if the airplane is allowed to roll off heading as the angle of attack is reduced.

Spirals are steep, descending turns that become progressively tighter over time. They occur at relatively low angles of attack, and they display the same overbanking tendency common to all steep turns. Low angles of attack coupled with a healthy rate of altitude loss produce a rapid increase in airspeed. The low coefficients of Drag affiliated with low angles of attack also provide less resistance against the build up of high airspeed.

Attempting to arrest the descent and hold the nose "up" with more and more back elevator pressure aggravates a spiral. Since elevator is our turn control, and the spiral is a turn, additional elevator pressure further tightens the spiral. It also generates increased load factors on the airplane and the pilot. If airspeed exceeds manoeuvring speed, it's possible to achieve an airspeed/g-load combination that can cause structural damage.

The fundamental problem in any spiral is too much bank. Remember that as bank angle increases, the g-load for steady flight also increases. The operating envelope shrinks as well, with fewer power and airspeed combinations available for steady flight. As the bank continues to increase, pulling harder to generate the required g-load becomes futile. Either the wings will fall off or the ground will get in the way long before the elevator input can catch up with the steepening bank. Reducing the bank angle, on the other hand, immediately widens the turn radius, decreases the power required for steady flight, and makes it easier for the airplane to seek its level flight trim speed.

Spirals can descend quite rapidly. Reducing the power **FIRST** slows the rate of altitude loss and prevents engine overspeeding. Releasing back elevator pressure **NEXT** lowers the angle of attack, reduces the g-load on the airplane, and loosens up the turn. The **LAST** step is the primary recovery action: shallow the bank by rolling the wings level. Use coordinated aileron and rudder inputs, emphasising the aileron input. And don't pull on the elevator control. Once the wings are level, recover the pitch attitude with controlled elevator pressures, especially if the airspeed is high. This Power-Push-Roll hierarchy is developed more fully in Chapter 8—Overbanked.

Final Thoughts

In any emergency, it's important to isolate and then to address the primary problem. Rarely is our pitch attitude the **CAUSE** of an in-flight dilemma. More often than not, premature elevator inputs only aggravate the situation. Unfortunately, more back pressure tends to be an automatic response to adverse flight conditions. This reaction is nurtured by an incomplete understanding of the elevator's function. To review, these items are principally controlled by the elevator: pitch (head-to-feet), angle of attack, airspeed, g-load, curved flight, turns. These items are **NOT** controlled, reliably or principally, by the elevator: altitude, "up". Be sure this is crystal clear in your mind.

Once started, poorly executed turns and spirals do not continue because of your pitch attitude. They are driven by an intrinsic tendency to overbank; so, any time you botch a turn, don't pull harder. Instead, relax your back elevator pressure and roll toward wings level. These actions reduce angle of attack, g-load, stall speed, and the power required for steady flight. Conditioning yourself to avoid the pull reflex not only improves your control during turns, but it also forms a vital part of the recovery strategies discussed in upcoming chapters.

6
Stalls

Sustaining controlled flight hinges on the aerodynamics of air flowing around our wing. We reviewed the fundamentals of flight by designing a simple airplane in Chapter 2—Basic Aerodynamics. We identified and defined parameters common to all airfoils, including relative wind, chord line, angle of attack, and coefficients of Lift and Drag. We also constructed a typical graph plotting coefficients of Lift and Drag versus the wing's angle of attack. The information depicted on this graph reveals certain personality traits of our wing.

The coefficient of Drag, for instance, increases with increasing angle of attack. It's the penalty we pay to generate the Lift needed for flight. The coefficient of Lift, on the other hand, has a different fingerprint: as angle of attack increases up to the critical number, the coefficient of Lift increases. As angle of attack increases beyond the critical angle of attack, the coefficient of Lift decreases. Coefficients of Lift and Drag share a common trend below critical angle of attack—they both move in the same direction with changes in angle of attack. But above critical angle of attack, their trends diverge—they move in opposite directions as angle of attack varies.

Critical angle of attack signifies an important crossroad in a wing's operating efficiency. Beyond critical angle of attack, air flowing over the top of the wing no longer can follow its contour. It tears away from the surface, upsetting the once smooth airflow across the wing. Every time the wing exceeds its critical angle of attack, it experiences this turbulent separation of airflow, along with increasing coefficients of Drag and decreasing coefficients of Lift. This phenomenon occurs whether we fly aerobatic airplanes, basic trainers, twins, or jets, and can happen regardless of our attitude or our airspeed.

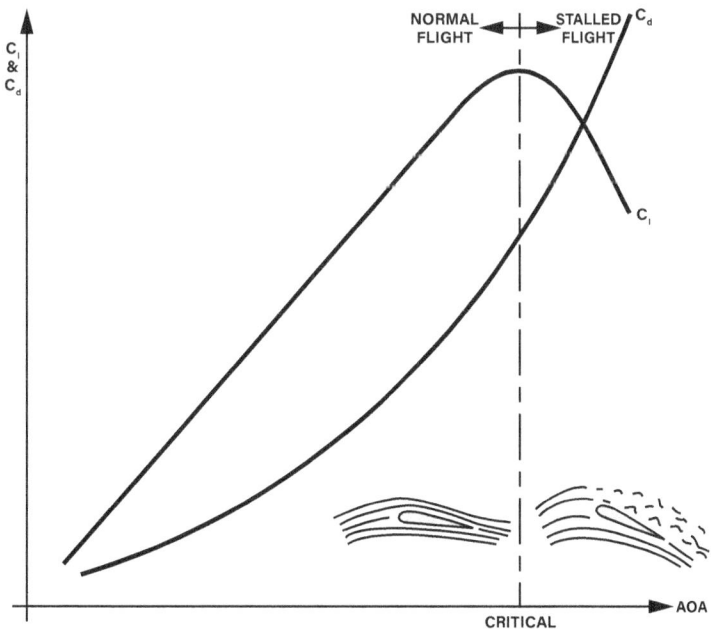

Figure 6-1: Coefficients of Lift and Drag vs. Angle of Attack

Flight beyond critical angle of attack certainly is less efficient than flight below critical angle of attack. Once airflow departs from the wing's surface, we enter the realm of stalled flight, which exists under a different set of rules from unstalled flight. Three aerodynamic flight modes may actually be available to a stalled airplane: Normal Flight, Autorotation, and Deep Stall. Normal Flight is unstalled flight; therefore, it occurs below critical angle of attack. Autorotation and Deep Stall both occur in stalled flight at angles of attack greater than the critical value.

Stalling a wing is analogous to trying to balance a golf ball on a pencil point. Like the golf ball, a stalled airplane immediately attempts to fall off the point, following the path of least resistance. Stalls are unstable and transitory by nature. A stalled airplane aggressively seeks a more stable configuration. Unfortunately, it isn't necessarily particular about which other mode it falls into, only that it happens as soon as possible.

Deep Stall has no practical value to the pilot. It's probably the least desirable of the three flight modes. Well designed airplanes, properly loaded within appropriate weight and balance limits, inherently resist the Deep Stall mode. We'll address Deep Stall in more detail later in this chapter.

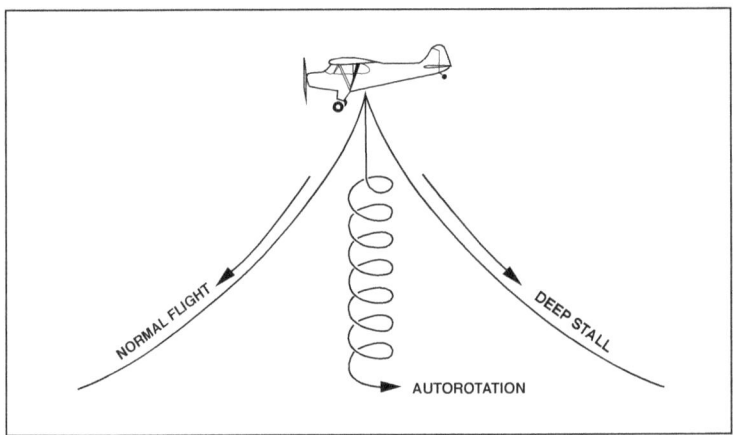

Figure 6-2: The Three Alternatives to Stalled Flight

Like Deep Stall, Autorotation occurs in the stalled region beyond critical angle of attack. Autorotation can be an interesting and challenging flight mode, given the right equipment, lots of altitude, and appropriate piloting skills. During critical manoeuvring close to the ground, though, Autorotation is often fatal. The spin is the most familiar type of Autorotation and is studied in the next chapter.

Of the three modes of flight, Normal Flight affords us the greatest manoeuvrability and the most control options. From the pilot's perspective, it's the safest, most desirable, and generally least stressful flight mode, too. Stall entry and recovery practice teaches us how to guide the airplane along the path back to Normal Flight, without getting lost in an Autorotation or a Deep Stall.

Stalls are purely a function of the angle of attack of the wing. In earlier chapters, we identified the elevator as our primary angle of attack control. The elevator, therefore, allows us to transition between stalled and unstalled flight. Additionally, we associate changes in coefficients of Lift and Drag, airspeed, g-load, curved flight, and pitch with elevator inputs. It appears as though the elevator serves a multi-faceted control function, based on all of the parameters attributed to it. Actually, all of these parameters are expressions of the same fundamental variable: **ANGLE OF ATTACK**.

Knowing precisely where the wing's aerodynamic operating limit is in any configuration is only possible through angle of attack measurements. Angle of attack indicators, though, are not standard equipment in most general aviation airplanes. Also, the graph depicting coefficients of Lift and Drag versus angle of attack paints an accurate picture of the elevator's control function, but unfortunately it doesn't relate well to our practical experience. We cannot perceive coefficients of Lift and Drag. Nor can we see our angle of attack in all flight attitudes.

The human body, on the other hand, can sense the effects of these parameters quite readily. Changes in airspeed, g-load, and flight path often can be heard, seen, and felt simultaneously. The sensations accompanying these changes usually indicate variations in our angle of attack. Correctly perceiving changes in the flight environment allows us then to infer our proximity to stalled flight.

We can transform the abstract information contained in the Cl and Cd versus AOA diagram into the same V-g diagram discussed in the previous chapter. Although we may lose something in the translation, we gain important operational knowledge about our airplane. The V-g diagram, simplified here for positive g flight in the Normal category, is a mosaic that truly reflects our actual flight experience. Remember, this single diagram depicts all of the elevator's control functions in one convenient place.

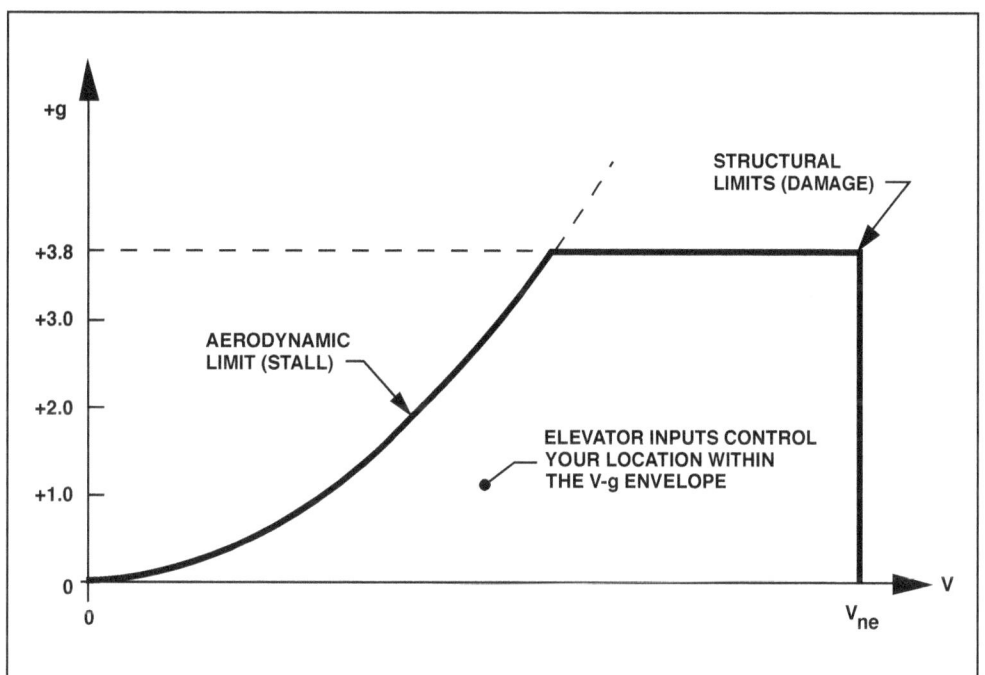

Figure 6-3: Practical Information Depicted on the V-g Diagram

Aerodynamically, an airplane is limited by the wing's critical angle of attack at and below manoeuvring speed, Va. A wide array of airspeed and g-load combinations can transition the airplane from unstalled to stalled flight. For steady, zero roll-rate flight (level turns, vertical loops) stall speed is proportional to the square root of the airplane's Weight. This can be an actual gross Weight, or an effective Weight (g-load) induced when manoeuvring. Since the coefficient of Lift at critical angle of attack is constant for a given airfoil, airspeed must vary in order for Lift to balance different weights in steady flight. For example, if our airplane stalls at 60 mph at a gross Weight of 1600 pounds, we can calculate stall speeds for other operating weights and plot the values on a V-g diagram.

ACTUAL WEIGHT (LBS)	EFFECTIVE WEIGHT AS G-LOAD (TYPICAL CORRESPONDING BANK ANGLE)				
	+0.5G (0°)	+1.0G (0°)	+1.15G (30°)	+1.41G (45°)	+2.0G (60°)
1400	40	56	60	66	79
<u>1600</u>	42	<u>60</u>	64	71	85
1800	45	64	68	76	90

Table 6-1: Stall Speed vs. Weight

The stall speed information tabulated here is similar to that presented in many flight manuals. As Weight, g-load, and bank angle increase, stall speed increases. As Weight, g-load, and bank angle decrease, stall speed decreases. Whether we move left, right, up, down, or diagonally through this table, the stall speed trend follows the general Weight trend. Different gross weights are represented by completely different stall curves on the V-g diagram, but different g-loads—changes in effective Weight—are represented by different points along the same curve.

The combination of airspeed **AND** Weight determines our angle of attack, and hence our proximity to stalled flight. The V-g diagram clearly illustrates this pivotal relationship. Pilots cannot know how close the wing is to stalling based on airspeed alone. We must be cognisant of the simultaneous effect of Weight. Unfortunately, most of our hands-on experience occurs in one attitude, at only one airspeed. Such limited exposure to stalled flight often obscures Weight's relevance and reinforces a dangerous affiliation with airspeed.

The bulk of our stall practice is performed upright in the landing configuration, with the wings level, at the reference speed Vso. Weight, the other half of the equation interacting with Vso, is often overshadowed by the events leading up to the stall. Only if we perform a +1.0 g deceleration, at the specified aircraft Weight, will the wing stall at the reference speed Vso. Banking the airplane and applying g-load in a turn increases the stall speed. Similarly, the +1.0 g stall speed is higher when fully loaded than when flying solo with the fuel tanks half full.

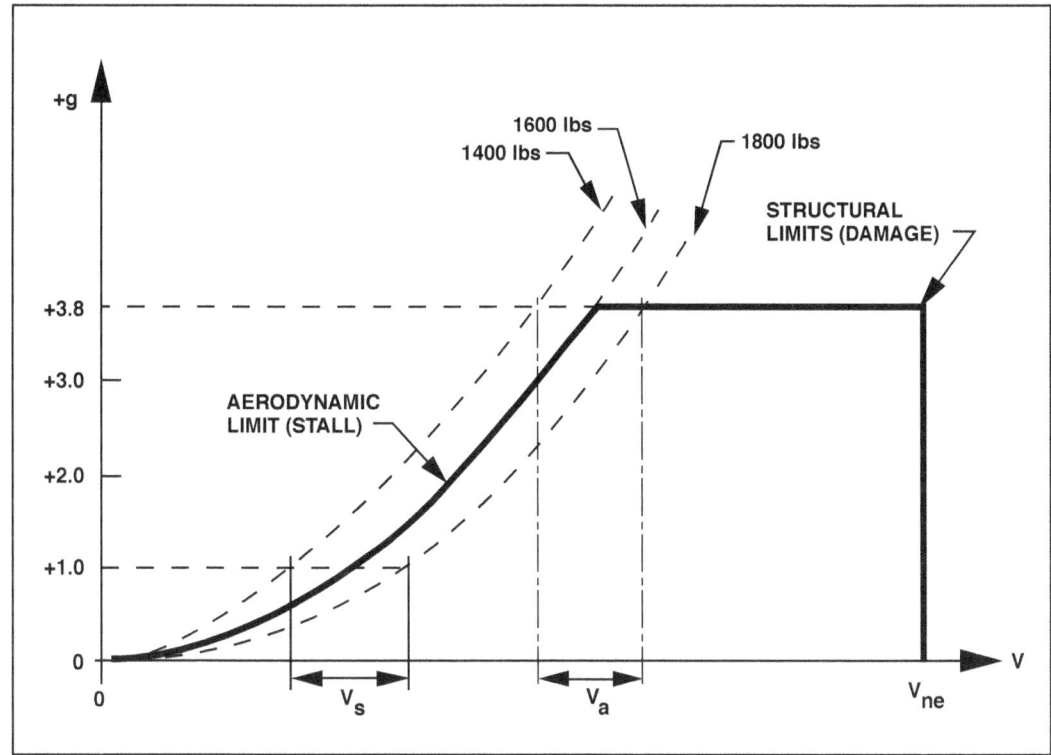

Figure 6-4: Effect of Weight Depicted on the V-g Diagram

Recognising and acknowledging the limitation in practicing stalls exclusively at Vso is extremely important. Such experience is useful only at a given Weight. Also, the pilot must maintain a normal, +1.0 g load on the airplane for Vso to be a valid stall speed. Since noticeable variations in pitch attitude and airspeed accompany Vso stalls, the pilot may perceive stalled flight occurring only as a result of a lack of airspeed. Vso certainly is a useful reference for normal takeoff and landing operations. However, the indispensable effect of Weight on all aspects of flight cannot be neglected. When loading the airplane with more Weight, as during a turn, emphasis must shift away from Vso to a higher stall speed.

Pilots who have had uncomfortable encounters with stalls during training, and who associate these encounters with airspeed, may erroneously believe they will be safe as long as they fly faster than Vso. Ironically, statistics reveal that few stall/spin accidents occur during +1.0 g flight at Vso—they occur, instead, while manoeuvring close to the ground, at higher g-loads, at airspeeds above Vso. So much for safety at higher airspeeds! The stall configuration usually practiced is only a single point in our operating envelope. We must appreciate the bigger picture represented by the V-g diagram, even though our practical experience may be limited to one very special case.

Flying the V-g Diagram

Since each parameter appearing on the V-g diagram is manipulated by elevator inputs, fore and aft control position can be used as a simple angle of attack indicator. Although stick and control wheel position cannot yield absolute angle of attack information, they do represent relative changes in angle of attack. We can select a point on the V-g diagram, alter airspeed and g-load variables via elevator inputs, and correlate these inputs with angle of attack trends during positive g flight.

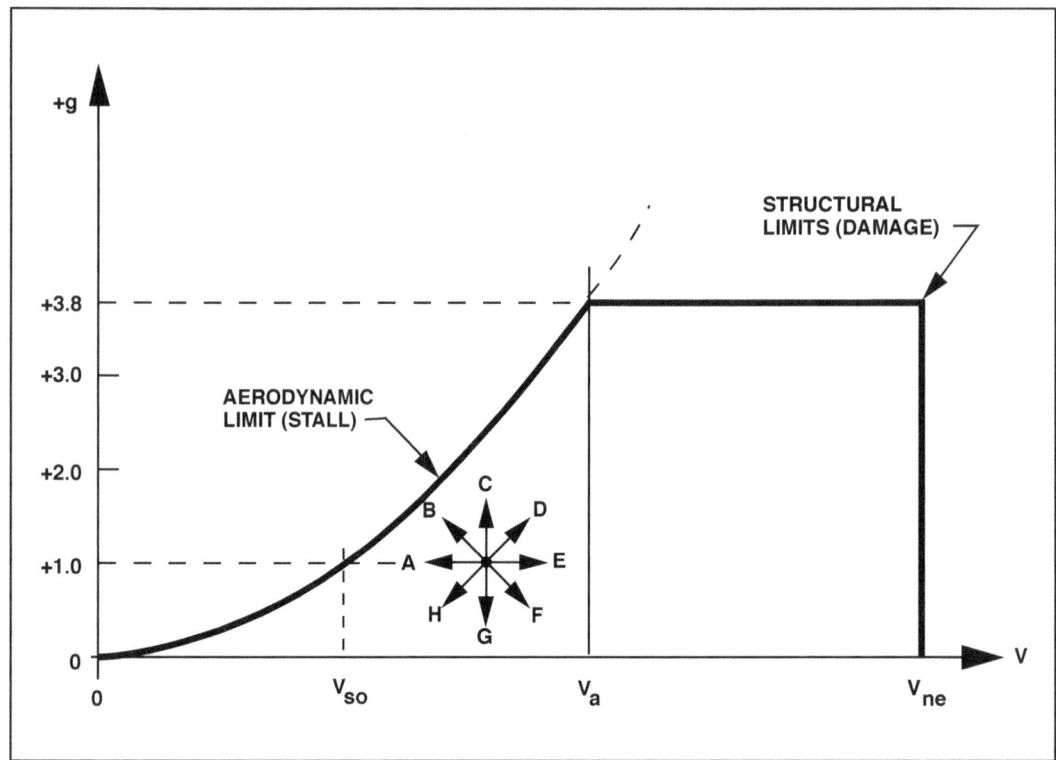

Figure 6-5: Flying within the V-g Envelope

Decreasing airspeed under a constant g-load requires aft movement of the elevator control. Decelerating along path A increases our angle of attack and moves us toward stalled flight. This is the exact path followed during routine stall practice. It happens to be the same undesirable path some pilots take trying to stretch a glide to reach a runway or an off-airport landing site. The constant elevator pressure held may have an assuring feel, but it does not maintain a constant angle of attack, nor does it improve glide performance. It moves us closer to critical angle of attack and reduces glide range.

An increase in g-load requires aft movement of the elevator control as well. This increases our angle of attack regardless of our airspeed trend. Pulling along paths B, C, or D elevates us to higher angles of attack. Path B represents an all-too-often route followed by pilots after an engine failure on takeoff: the tight, high g turn back to the runway. With low and decreasing airspeed, this is a direct route to an accelerated stall/spin accident.

We can move along path C simply by rolling into a turn at a constant airspeed. If the angle of bank selected requires more g-load than the airspeed can sustain, an accelerated stall results (provided we're below manoeuvring speed). Steepening the bank during a base-to-final turn at low airspeed, for example, places us at higher angles of attack and greater risk of an inadvertent stall.

Path D illustrates a simultaneous increase in g-load and airspeed trends. Pulling out of a dive or pulling on the backside of a loop are examples of flight along this path. Spirals also clearly display this same trend. As altitude is consumed in a spiral, airspeed is increased. Responding incorrectly with more pull on the elevator control increases g-load as well, ultimately tightening the spiral.

Under a constant g-load, increasing your airspeed requires forward movement of the elevator control. Path E takes us away from stalled flight. We fly along this path when accelerating from slow flight to cruise speed at a constant altitude. Adding power holds the altitude, forward elevator lowers the angle of attack and increases the airspeed. The initial phase of a properly executed go-around and an established dive angle to gain airspeed are other examples of flight along path E.

Regardless of our airspeed trend, a decrease in g-load requires forward movement of the elevator control, which decreases our angle of attack. Pushing along paths F, G, or H moves us to lower angles of attack. Path F might represent a push over from level flight to a descending attitude. The diminished g-load during the push lowers the angle of attack as altitude is converted into airspeed. An outside loop starting from the top begins down this path. We also follow a similar route during upright stall recovery.

We can reduce the angle of attack along path G by transitioning from a constant speed climb to a level attitude while holding the same airspeed. The angle of attack momentarily moves away from the critical value as the attitude changes. The process of leveling off in the traffic pattern after climb-out offers a practical demonstration of this.

Path H illustrates a simultaneous decrease in g-load and airspeed trends. This points toward an interesting possibility: unstalled flight at speeds below Vso. Of course, the g-load must be less than +1.0 as well. An enlightening demonstration is possible in most light trainers by initiating a steep climb from level cruise flight. As airspeed bleeds off and approaches Vso, gently push the nose over. Transition from the climb to a shallow descent along a ballistic curve. During the push, observe the needle on the airspeed indicator move below Vso, possibly resting for an instant against the peg as you float weightless over the top. Stalled flight is encountered only if you move the elevator control aft prematurely.

Skilled aerobatic pilots, flying aerobatic airplanes, experience this same phenomenon during the exciting Hammerhead Turn. The pilot first pulls the airplane to a vertical climb. As airspeed dissipates, forward elevator is used to hold the attitude. G-load is reduced as well, which prevents stalled flight. The turnaround occurs when airspeed and g-load are almost zero. Applying full rudder into the spiral slipstream from the propeller, which is the only air flowing over the airplane at the top of the manoeuvre, pivots the airplane. Sometimes mislabeled a "Hammerhead Stall" or "Stall Turn", a properly flown Hammerhead involves no stall at all.

Path H is a race to zero airspeed before the onset of stalled flight. If the rate of decrease in g-load is too slow, the airplane stalls. If g-load is decreased fast enough, we can slide under the stall curve and beat it to zero airspeed. After all, turbulent separation of airflow can only occur if we have airspeed and Weight. We need both to stall an airplane; stalled flight is impossible otherwise. Airplanes parked on the ramp on a calm day, for instance, **ARE NOT STALLED**. Granted, they're not generating any Lift either, but at least they're in a stable configuration!

Pulls on the elevator control ultimately increase our angle of attack. During critical phases of flight below manoeuvring speed, aft movements of the stick or yoke literally pull us into the critical edge of our operating envelope. Forward elevator movements push us away from the critical edge, lowering the angle of attack and providing a greater margin of safety from stalled flight. The exact position of the elevator control and the control pressure preceding stalled flight vary depending on power setting, trim position, and the type of manoeuvre. Even so, moving the elevator control aft from position A to position B positively pulls you closer to stalled flight. Displacing the elevator control forward from B back to A pushes you away from stalled flight. Pulling more when a manoeuvre starts to deteriorate generally makes matters worse. This theme appears time and again throughout this book.

(A similar analysis is possible for the negative g environment frequented by aerobatic pilots. The aerodynamic effect of pulls and pushes are reversed under negative g's: forward movements increase the negative angle of attack and move the airplane closer to inverted stalled flight. Aft movements decrease the negative angle of attack and move the airplane away from inverted stalled flight. Large aft movements not only move the airplane away from inverted stalled flight, but can transition the environment from negative g's to positive g's, whereby additional aft elevator control inputs will then move the airplane in the direction of upright stalled flight.)

Manoeuvring speed is a significant reference airspeed. At and below Va, our operating envelope is limited by the aerodynamic capability of our wing. Aft elevator inputs increase the wing's angle of attack and move us toward stalled flight. Above manoeuvring speed, our operating envelope is capped by the airplane's design structural limit. Aft elevator inputs still increase the wing's angle of attack; however, the airplane may bend or break under the g-load imposed before reaching stalled flight. To minimise exposure to structural damage, we must not allow the g-load to exceed design structural limits (+3.8 Normal, +4.4 Utility, +6.0 Acrobatic), nor should we allow the airspeed to exceed Vne.

Vertical gusts associated with turbulent air can subject our airplane to undesirable, structurally dangerous g-loads above Va. So, rather than risk bending or breaking the airplane in rough air, flight manuals generally recommend that we slow to manoeuvring speed. Since gust loads are beyond our control, reducing speed to Va ensures that turbulence can only increase the g-loading enough to stall the wing.

To illustrate how this works, assume you're performing a turn with 60 degrees of bank. This requires a +2.0 g pull on the elevator control. Encountering a +2.0 g jolt from turbulence now imposes +4.0 g's on the airplane (2.0 g's induced by the pilot plus a 2.0 g gust load induced by mother nature). Heaping the gust load onto the manoeuvring load bumps us into the structural damage/failure region of the V-g diagram above manoeuvring speed. Below Va, however, stalled flight intervenes before the full +4.0 g load is absorbed by the airframe. Stalled flight acts as an aerodynamic relief valve, limiting the g-load sensed by the airplane and preventing structural damage.

Manoeuvring speed, like any speed on the stall curve of a V-g diagram, is not cast in stone. It, too, varies with aircraft Weight. As we saw earlier, lower weights bend the stall curve up and to the left, resulting in a lower manoeuvring speed. Higher weights bend the stall curve down and to the right, ultimately increasing the manoeuvring speed. Lighter airplanes are more sensitive to turbulence than heavier ones, necessitating lower manoeuvring speeds. Should you encounter turbulence, especially severe turbulence, your first course of action is simple: **SLOW DOWN**. Position yourself on the V-g diagram to take advantage of stalled flight, should you need it. Flying precisely at manoeuvring speed for a given aircraft Weight offers the greatest margin of safety from aerodynamic and structural operating limits.

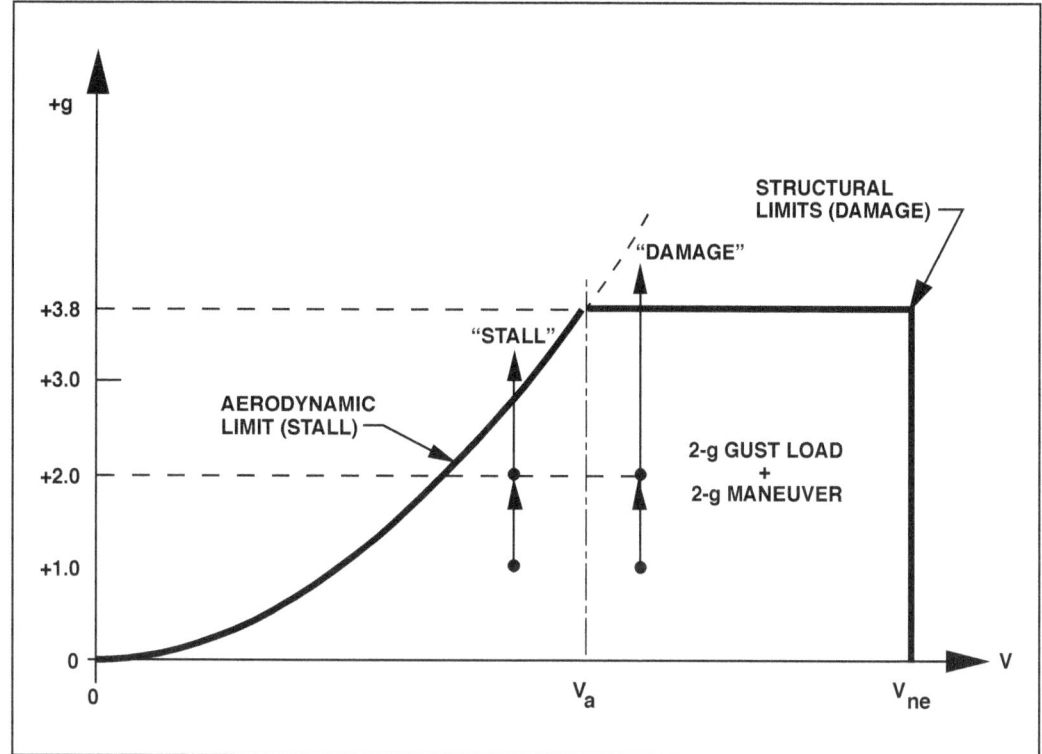

Figure 6-6: Taking Advantage of the Stall in Turbulent Conditions

Safe, controlled flight depends on recognising and recovering from stalls. Modern airplanes must meet specific criteria for certification in the Normal, Utility, and Acrobatic categories. This includes adequate and obvious stall warning during the course of normal operation. Since angle of attack indicators are not standard equipment in most light airplanes, we must learn to infer our proximity to the stall through indirect aerodynamic, mechanical, and physiological cues. None of these cues is fail-safe; integrated together, however, they can provide effective stall warning if the pilot pays attention to them.

Aerodynamic Cues

Several factors, including the wing's planform (its shape when viewed from the top), influence how a stall occurs. A progressive stall pattern, ideally beginning at the wing root and advancing outward to the wingtip, is the most favorable from the pilot's perspective. This characteristic combines early stall warning with good lateral control as airflow separates. Pronounced buffeting occurs as turbulent air spills from the wing root and strikes the empennage and tail section. Also, elevator authority and the stabilising effect of the horizontal stabiliser are weakened at the onset of the stall, pitching the airplane forward to a lower angle of attack.

A rectangular planform naturally displays such desirable stall characteristics. It's forgiving at high angles of attack when properly flown, offering plenty of aerodynamic stall warning with adequate roll control. For the light, low speed trainer, the rectangular planform is an ideal choice. However, the stability inherent in this planform does have disadvantages: rectangular wings typically create more Drag, are less manoeuvrable, and can be structurally cumbersome compared to other shapes.

Moderately tapering the wing planform satisfies the demand for higher speeds, lower Drag, and structural simplicity. The enhanced manoeuvrability afforded by this shape, however, results in less stability, particularly at high angles of attack. Airflow tends to separate throughout a moderately tapered wing all at once, resulting in poor lateral control and less aerodynamic warning.

A swept planform allows high speed flight and extreme agility (as demonstrated by fighters like the F-16), but such performance comes with a large instability penalty. In fact, several fighter designs require the use of on-board computers to keep them stable in flight. Swept wings inherently display undesirable stall behavior. Airflow tends to separate at the wingtips first, compromising aileron control with virtually no aerodynamic warning. Also, the center of pressure tends to slide ahead of the center of gravity as airflow separates, causing a rapid pitch **UP** into a deeper, more aggravated stall.

Several aerodynamic "tricks" are used to mimic the docile stall pattern of a rectangular planform while taking advantage of the improved performance of other shapes. Some wings have a slight twist built into them to vary the local angle of attack along their spans. Called "wash-out", the wing root is preset at a greater angle of attack than the wingtip, ensuring that the stall begins near the root. Attaching stall strips (or wedges) on the leading edge can trigger the stall at a specific location, usually near the wing root. Additional ways to tailor stall characteristics include changing the shape of the airfoil along the wingspan, adding stall fences or vortex generators, or cutting slots into the wing.

Unfortunately, aerodynamic stall warning can be thwarted by the effects of power, of turbulence, and of snow, ice, or frost accumulation on the wing. It can be defeated altogether by loading the airplane beyond its weight and balance limits. Skidding turns and other examples of poor coordination can transform otherwise docile stall behavior into more aggressive stalls.

Adding power in propeller-driven airplanes, for example, alters the stall pattern by delaying the separation of airflow from portions of the wing affected by the spiral slipstream. In single engine airplanes, airflow may not separate at the wing root first. It may separate farther outboard instead, resulting in more aggravated characteristics with little advanced warning. Slipstream effects in twin engine airplanes may also lead to similarly aggravated, deeper stalls with power on.

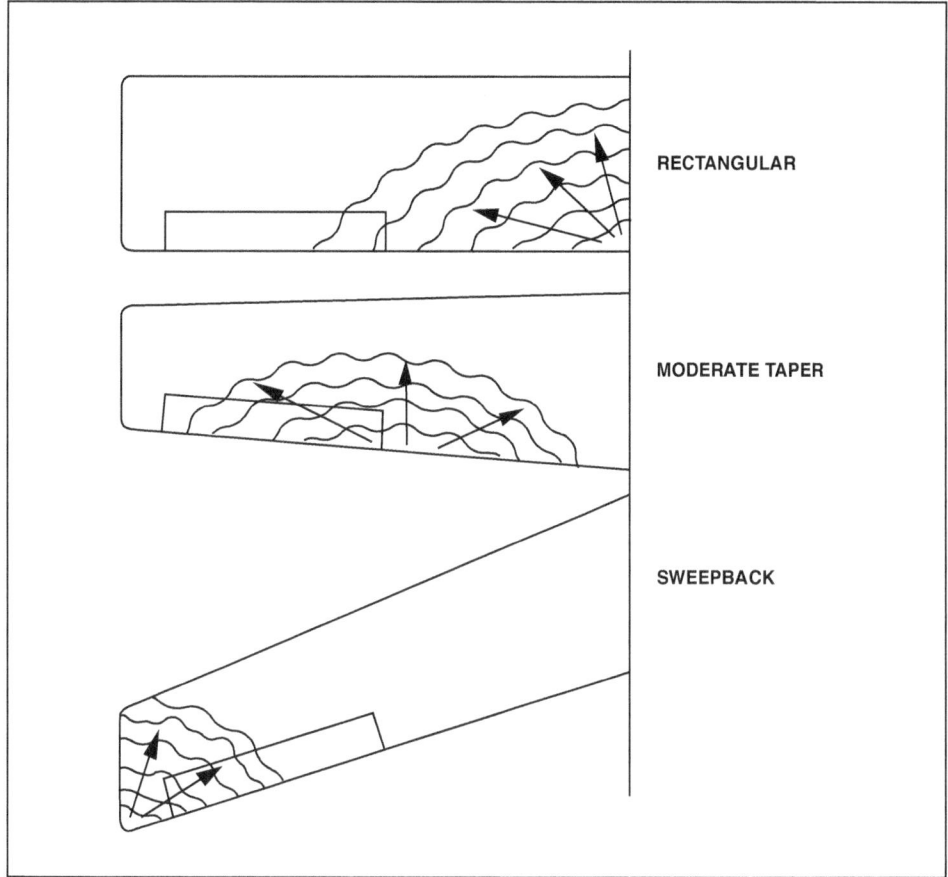

Figure 6-7: Typical Wing Stall Patterns

Uncoordinated flight can negatively impact stall progression, too. Yawing near critical angle of attack may defeat favorable stall characteristics built into the airplane. In fact, excessive yawing can result in airflow separation similar to that of a swept planform; airflow may depart near the wingtips, causing loss of aileron control and a sudden roll in the direction of yaw. Attention to yaw control near critical angle of attack assures more benign stall dynamics.

Altering the shape or the surface characteristics of a wing can also have a dramatic effect on stall behavior. Ice, frost, snow, surface damage (e.g.: dents along the leading edge), and possibly heavy rain can affect the performance of the wing. Surface irregularities tend to decrease Lift, increase Drag, reduce the critical angle of attack, and increase the stall speed. Modifications to the wing's surface, whether induced by mother nature or man-made, should be treated with caution. Remove accumulations of ice or frost completely before taking to the air, and avoid flight into known icing conditions.

Mechanical Cues

Continuous horns and warning lights are the most common means of providing mechanical stall warning. These devices are set to activate at least five knots prior to stalled flight, but they do have limitations. For example, one study found stall warning lights to be practically useless during day, VFR conditions, where pilot attention is primarily outside of the cockpit. Also, bright daylight makes it difficult to see if a warning light is on or off. Although continuous aural devices are usually better able to warn pilots of an impending stall, the same study found that pilots essentially "tuned them out" one third of the time when overloaded with other distractions.

Inlet air blockages, frozen or stuck stall sensing vanes, or electrical problems can render a mechanical stall warning system inoperative. A stall sensor located on one wing only—usually the left wing—is a potential weak link in the system as well. If both wings stall simultaneously, or if the left wing stalls first, as it might during a left descending turn, the stall sensor should detect the onset of stalled flight. But if the right wing stalls first, as it could during a steep, climbing turn to the left, the warning system may not activate until significant portions of both wings have exceeded critical angle of attack.

As noted earlier, the stick or yoke can be an effective mechanical stall warning tool. Since the elevator controls angle of attack, the direction in which it's moving determines our trend toward or away from stalled flight. The exact control position and control pressure preceding a stall depend on power setting, trim position, and the type of manoeuvre. Even so, realise that for every inch the stick or yoke is pulled aft during upright flight, the angle of attack will positively increase and the airplane will move closer to stalled flight. Forward control movements will lower the angle of attack and push the airplane away from stalled flight.

Correlating elevator movements with changes in angle of attack requires a light touch on the controls. When distracted or under duress, pilots subconsciously respond by tensing up and pulling the stick or yoke farther aft. As the earlier discussion of the V-g diagram revealed, an inadvertent pull coupled with a decreasing airspeed trend ultimately terminates in stalled flight. Our innate behavior must be modified so that we'll react instead with forward elevator. We need to respond to the airflow needs of the wing, not necessarily to an undesirable picture seen over the nose.

Physiological Cues

Aerodynamic and mechanical stall warning are useless if we become oblivious to our senses of sight, sound, and touch. Most stall/spin accidents occur during day, VFR conditions, so responding to physiological cues plays an important role in stall awareness. Continued stall practice fine tunes your senses to the changes in airspeed, g-load, and flight path preceding stalled flight. Witnessing telltale signs demands focusing attention on the airplane itself while ignoring its attitude relative to the horizon.

The ability to respond to physiological stall cues can be hindered by a high work load. Uncoordinated flight can confound the situation by causing sensory conflicts and interfering with stall warning signals. Concentrating on the wrong thing can prevent appropriate reactions, too. During stall practice, for instance, many pilots initially fight against stall cues in a futile attempt to keep the nose pointed "up", away from the ground looming in the wind-screen. Our top priority must be to give the airplane what it needs for controlled flight—a lower angle of attack. This can only be accomplished by moving the stick or yoke away from your body.

Regardless of the airplane's attitude, efficient stall recovery is a matter of responding correctly to airplane movements relative to the pilot. The basic stall recovery strategy boils down to two key actions:

1. Move the elevator control in the same direction that the nose of the airplane is moving;
2. Use the rudder to maintain coordinated flight. Everything else is secondary to these two stall recovery responses.

The only reason a wing stalls is excessive angle of attack; therefore, the only way to reduce the angle in an upright stall is with forward elevator. Pulling the elevator control farther aft as the nose drops only aggravates the situation. Instead, displace the elevator control forward smoothly until it feels like you're actually pushing the nose yourself, then freeze your input momentarily. Avoid immediately backlashing the stick or yoke into a secondary stall. Use rudder inputs to keep the airplane on a straight line to Normal Flight; otherwise, the airplane might stray into a spin.

Applying power during stall recovery conserves altitude. Unfortunately, it can also delay the recovery if its secondary effects are not anticipated. A burst of power at high angle of attack and low speed increases torque, P-factor, slipstream, and downwash effects. All of these can have a destabilising effect, especially in the typical single-engine airplane trimmed for slow flight. Adding power prematurely may also increase our angle of attack and could generate pro-spin yaw, both of which are counterproductive to stall recovery.

Illustrating the supporting role power must play is easily done: Picture performing a power off, wings level stall at a safe altitude, with the airplane properly rigged, trimmed for slow flight, and loaded within weight and balance limits. If we let go of the elevator control the moment the nose pitches toward our feet at the stall, the stick/yoke immediately follows the nose straight forward, unstalling the wing. What happens next if we just sit there? The airplane obviously will gain speed in a dive. Once it reaches the trim speed, it'll level off of its own accord, without power.

Airplanes are designed to fly, but oftentimes they're hindered from doing the right things by the pilot. Power does not unstall the wing—the elevator does. Power controls our altitude profile (Chapter 4—Pitch and Power). During stall recovery, subtle changes in the timing of elevator and throttle actions can have a significant impact on recovery characteristics. The recovery process will be more efficient if we move the elevator slightly ahead of our throttle input, mimicking what the airplane would do hands-off. Accept some altitude loss initially, in exchange for a lower angle of attack, increased airspeed, and better control. Blend power in smoothly only as needed to conserve altitude, staying coordinated throughout.

As with the application of power, the timing of aileron inputs is important as well. Using ailerons at high angles of attack requires finesse and discipline, especially since they're an integral part of the surface from which airflow is tearing away. Many airplanes lose significant aileron authority at the onset of stalled flight. This is typically followed by the loss of elevator authority, and finally rudder effectiveness as the stall progresses.

Flailing the ailerons around when at high angles of attack generates large amounts of adverse yaw and can aggravate stall characteristics. For example, examine what happens when adding left aileron to level the wings in a stall: The downward deflected aileron near the right wingtip increases the local angle of attack. In stalled flight, this results in **LESS** Lift—just the opposite of what happens in Normal Flight. Instead of rolling to wings level, the airplane may roll into a steeper right bank even though left aileron is applied. Increased Drag also yaws the airplane to the right as the airplane slides into a spin. During stall recovery, focus on moving the elevator forward first, without deflecting the ailerons errantly.

Let's now look at some of the general tendencies we might expect when stalling single-engine airplanes. Regardless of the airplane's configuration, react with forward elevator to unstall the wing. Use the rudder to maintain coordinated flight before, during, and after the stall. Introduce aileron inputs—coordinated with rudder—only **AFTER** the application of forward elevator.

Approach-To-Landing Stall

An approach-to-landing stall usually begins with the wings level and the power idle. A 1-g deceleration is initiated. Coordinated flight is maintained throughout, and aileron inputs are avoided at the stall. The nose and the wingtips rotate toward our heads, moving in the same direction as our aft elevator input. At the stall, the nose and wingtips pitch forward, toward our feet. Stall characteristics are typically relatively docile as airflow departs evenly from both wings. Recovery is initiated with forward elevator. Rudder inputs hold the heading and keep the wings level until airflow is reattached.

Departure Stall

The basic configuration in a departure stall is a wings-level climb with takeoff power. Maintain coordinated flight throughout, without haphazard aileron inputs at the stall. The nose and the wingtips initially rotate toward our heads, moving in the same direction as our aft elevator input. As speed decays, more and more right rudder is needed to offset power effects and to maintain coordinated flight. Also, expect power to cause a slightly more aggravated stall than the approach-to-landing stall.

The nose and wingtips still pitch forward at the stall. The right rudder loses effectiveness simultaneously as well, so expect power effects to roll and yaw the airplane to the left unless we compensate with additional right rudder. (If right aileron is used instead, the airplane may snap hard to the left at the stall.) Recovery is initiated with forward elevator and enough right rudder to maintain a heading and to keep the wings level. If the amount of right rudder is inadequate, the airplane recovers banked and off heading to the left. Too much right rudder causes us to be banked and off heading to the right.

Under-The-Bottom Stall

Under-the-bottom stalls are accelerated stalls. The basic configuration involves turning flight in which the inside wing stalls first. The airplane might then yaw and roll sharply into a steeper bank (possibly even inverted) as the nose pitches forward. This stall behavior is often encountered in descending turns, in skidding turns, and in steep, level turns. Uncorrected, these stalls can quickly transition into a spin whose direction is the same as the initial turn direction (called an under-the-bottom spin).

Coordinated, descending turns have a roll component in the same direction as the turn in order to maintain a constant bank angle (Chapter 5—Curved Flight). This roll component causes the inside wing to operate at a slightly greater angle of attack; thus, it tends to reach critical angle of attack ahead of the outside wing. The asymmetric loss of Lift and rise in Drag on the inside wing can suddenly roll the airplane to even higher bank angles.

Skidding with rudder also induces yaw and roll components in the direction of the turn. The inside wing operates at a higher angle of attack as a result; hence, it tends to stall first. Applying opposite aileron to counter the yaw-induced roll could instigate aggressive tip stall behavior even sooner by further increasing the local angle of attack on the inside wing.

In a steep turn, maintaining a slight amount of opposite aileron cancels the inherent over banking tendency. Stabilised steep turns experience no net rolling component as a result. The downward deflected aileron and the corresponding increase in local angle of attack, though, could trigger an asymmetric stall on the inside wing.

Over-The-Top Stall

Like under-the-bottom stalls, over-the-top stalls are accelerated stalls. The basic configuration involves turning flight in which the outside wing stalls first. The airplane tends to yaw and roll from one side, through wings level, over to the other side in the process. This stall behavior is often encountered in climbing turns, in slipping turns, and in shallow, level turns. Uncorrected, these stalls can also transition into a spin, but the direction of rotation is opposite to that of the original turn (called an over-the-top spin).

As we saw in Chapter 5—Curved Flight, coordinated, climbing turns need a roll component opposite to the direction of turn to hold a constant bank angle. This roll component causes the outside wing to operate at a higher angle of attack; thus, it may stall first. The asymmetric loss of Lift and rise in Drag on the outside wing could roll the airplane over the top as the nose pitches forward.

A slipping turn induces yaw and roll components opposite to the turn direction as well. The outside wing tends to operate at a higher angle of attack, and so could stall first. Furthermore, holding ailerons in the direction of the turn to keep the bank constant increases the local angle of attack on the outside wing. As in the climbing turn, this configuration could cause the airplane to yaw and roll over the top upon exceeding the critical angle of attack.

Countering the underbanking tendency in shallow turns normally requires holding a slight amount of aileron deflection in the direction of the turn. The downward deflected aileron on the outside wing, with its attendant increase in local angle of attack, could trigger an asymmetric stall, possibly rolling the airplane over the top.

Prolonged Stall

Holding the elevator control aft once the nose pitches forward prolongs stall characteristics. Earlier, stalls were likened to trying to balance a golf ball on a pencil point. As the airplane is forced to remain in a stall, it begins to oscillate about all three flight axes, wobbling on the pencil point. Buffeting is generally quite pronounced, too. Moving the elevator forward as soon as the nose slips away from you averts such aggravated behavior and lessens the likelihood of advancing into a spin.

Demonstrating a prolonged stall stresses the importance of good coordination above critical angle of attack. Known by such names as the rudder stall exercise, oscillation stall, or falling leaf, the basic configuration usually involves a wings-level stall entered with partial power. Rather than recovering as soon as the nose pitches forward, the airplane is forced to remain stalled with aft elevator. The ailerons are kept neutral throughout. Only rudder inputs are used to keep the airplane on a heading and the wings level. The effect is like learning how to walk in stalled flight. Releasing the aft elevator recovers the stall and stops any stall-related gyrations.

Deep Stall

Light airplane wings stall at angles of attack ranging from 15 to 25 degrees. When operated within approved weight and balance limits, the airplane naturally pitches forward to lower angles of attack. A Deep Stall occurs when the airplane instead pitches to even higher angles of attack. The airplane may suddenly become unresponsive to elevator inputs in the process. The angle of attack in a Deep Stall can become quite large (even approaching 90 degrees), resulting in a steep descent with little forward speed. The rate of descent often depends on the airplane's wing loading: high when the wing loading is high, low when the wing loading is low.

Like Normal Flight, Deep Stall is a stable flight mode. Unfortunately, it's at the opposite end of the angle of attack scale, and it's usually non-recoverable. Deep Stall is a low speed/high Drag configuration, analogous to skydivers free-falling in the prone position, backs arched. Normal Flight, on the other hand, is a high speed/low Drag configuration, like skydivers free-falling head first, legs together and arms pinned at their sides. The airplane moves through the air essentially bellyfirst in Deep Stall, whereas it moves headfirst, like a dart, in Normal Flight.

Several conditions can cause a Deep Stall. Loading an airplane beyond its aft limit, for example, may slide the wing's center of pressure ahead of the airplane's center of gravity at critical angle of attack, resulting in pitch up (Chapter 2—Basic Aerodynamics). A low velocity wake also trails from the wing during a stall. If the horizontal stabiliser falls within this wake as the stall deepens, it could be rendered ineffective for recovery.

The aggressive tip stalls associated with swept wings and uncoordinated flight tend to shift wingtip vortices inboard along the wing. If these vortices impinge on the horizontal stabiliser, they could push the tail downward, pitching the airplane into a Deep Stall. The fuselage may start to behave like a thick, stubby wing at high angles of attack, too, generating its own Lift and shedding its own vortices. Lift from the fuselage could hold the airplane in a Deep Stall. In addition, vortices rolling off of the fuselage could curl around and push down on the horizontal tail, locking the airplane into the stall.

T-tail airplanes are more prone to Deep Stall effects than airplanes with a conventional tail configuration. Locating the horizontal stabiliser atop the vertical stabiliser removes it from the wake behind the wing and propeller, placing it in the free airstream during Normal Flight. Typically, this allows the use of a smaller horizontal surface/elevator, which reduces Drag and improves efficiency.

The drawback near stalled flight, though, is that a T-tail may not provide adequate aerodynamic stall warning. By design, T-tails tend to remain effective longer; hence, it could be possible to pull the airplane deep enough into a stall to engulf the tail in the wing's low velocity wake. Vortex trails from the wing might then push downward on the T-tail, stabilising the airplane in stalled flight. The T-tail itself may even stall as a result.

Light airplanes, including those with T-tails, are designed to avoid Deep Stall characteristics when operated within their prescribed limits. The general aviation pilot's best defense against the Deep Stall threat is simple: treat the aft center of gravity limit as a hard boundary. Never flirt with loadings beyond that limit—no matter what!

Tail Stall

This chapter has focused on stall behavior relative to airflow separation from our main wing. But the horizontal stabiliser is a wing, too. It has a critical angle of attack, so it can stall. It can also lose effectiveness at low speeds and forward centers of gravity. Chapter 2—Basic Aerodynamics illustrated how the horizontal stabiliser balances the pitching moment of our wing by generating a small amount of Negative Lift. Downwash from the main wing strikes conventional tail configurations at a negative angle of attack, which helps them generate this Lift. But turbulent airflow spilling from the main wing decreases the effectiveness of the horizontal stabiliser/elevator. The amount of Lift it generates is reduced, which in turn causes the airplane to pitch to a lower angle of attack.

Under normal circumstances, the main wing is designed to stall first; the tail itself remains unstalled. A legitimate tail stall threat does exist, however, in icing conditions. Ice accumulating on the leading edge of the horizontal stabiliser might act like a stall strip, triggering an inadvertent tail stall even though the main wing is below critical angle of attack. The airplane will suddenly pitch forward uncontrollably if this happens.

Deploying flaps in icing conditions also tends to increase the tail stall threat. Flaps amplify the downwash angle on a conventional tail, hence increasing its angle of attack. If a tail stall is encountered in icing conditions, raising the flaps first helps reduce the tail's angle of attack. Don't push the elevator forward until the flaps start retracting, though, as this could momentarily aggravate the tail stall.

To avert a tail stall, remove all ice (frost, too) before flying. Also, avoid flight into known icing conditions. If ice does accumulate, divert to a suitable runway where a no-flap landing can be made safely. Use a slightly higher landing approach speed (i.e.: lower angle of attack). If flaps must be deployed, use the minimum setting that will satisfy your needs.

Stall Speed vs. C.G.

Center of gravity certainly influences stall behavior, but it has nothing to do with the separation of airflow at critical angle of attack. Center of gravity does impact the effectiveness of our horizontal tail, though. Although not a stall in an aerodynamic sense, loss of elevator authority qualifies as a stall under a broader, more practical definition adopted by the FAA. FAR Part 1, for instance, defines stall speed (Vs) as *"the stalling speed or minimum steady flight speed at which the airplane is controllable."* FAR Part 23, which contains requirements for Normal, Utility, and Acrobatic category certification, defines Vso and Vs1 the same way. In other words, published stall speeds actually can signify one of two events: **EITHER** airflow separates (the main wing stalls), **OR** pitch control is lost (a tail stall of sorts).

Airplane design involves a constant trade-off between manoeuvrability and stability. The simple airplane designed in Chapter 2—Basic Aerodynamics strikes a balance between forces and moments, but only within a specified operating range. We illustrated the negative impact aft centers of gravity can have on stability earlier. On the other end of the scale, forward centers of gravity tend to affect airplane controllability, particularly while taking off, landing, and manoeuvring.

The stabilising effect of the horizontal tail ultimately depends on the speed of air flowing over it and the elevator's control power. Greater elevator deflection is needed to hold a constant airspeed as the center of gravity slides forward. We eventually run out of elevator authority at a certain combination of airspeed and forward center of gravity. The nose then pitches forward, reacting similar to a stall even though the wing technically may not be stalled.

Consequently, "stall speeds" listed at a forward center of gravity tend to be higher than those listed at the aft limit. They probably represent the control limit of the tail. "Stall speeds" listed at the aft limit are more likely to represent the aerodynamic limit of our main wing, complete with airflow separation and stall buffet. Remaining within the prescribed center of gravity limits becomes crucial: too far forward and control may be lost, too far aft and the airplane may become unstable. In upright flight, forward elevator is needed in both cases to lower the angle of attack and to gain airspeed.

Flaps

Deploying flaps increases coefficients of Lift and Drag and lowers stall speeds. Retracting the flaps always raises our stall speed. This realisation is critical to the safe execution of a go-around. Rushing to raise the flaps at a low airspeed could suddenly bump the airplane into stalled flight. The first course of action during a go-around is to apply takeoff power smoothly while pitching to an appropriate climb speed (usually Vy). Retract the flaps afterwards one notch at a time, maintaining control over the airplane during the process.

Final Thoughts

Next time you're practicing stalls at a safe altitude, pay particular attention to the downward trend displayed by the airspeed indicator. Listen for a simultaneous decrease in ambient noise levels. Look at and feel the direction in which you're moving the elevator control to initiate the stall. Feel the changes in control pressures as well. When practicing accelerated stalls, feel the g-load increase on your body as you pull back on the elevator.

Watch the nose of the airplane pitch toward you before the stall, then pitch away from you as airflow separates from the wing. Feel the stall buffet. Listen to the sound of turbulent air hitting the back of the airplane and acknowledge the stall warning horn. React to these signs with enough forward elevator to reattach airflow on the wing while working the rudder to maintain a heading. Once the angle of attack is below critical, introduce coordinated aileron and rudder inputs.

Take advantage of the stall recovery capability designed into your airplane. And don't exceed published weight and balance limits, not even a little bit. Within the limits, it must be possible to regain level flight from a stall without the airplane displaying an uncontrollable tendency to spin or to pitch into a Deep Stall. This **DOES NOT** imply nor does it guarantee that an airplane won't exhibit potentially dangerous post-stall gyrations if coaxed, only that it can be prevented from doing so through appropriate control inputs.

The next chapter delves into another aspect of stalled flight—Autorotation. It addresses spins and spin dynamics, and outlines the special rules that apply when operating within this fascinating realm.

7
Spins

Contrary to popular belief, spins are **NOT** caused by stalls. If they were, every stall we ever attempted would wind up rotating earthward. We highlighted the importance of developing good rudder skills near critical angle of attack in the last chapter. Proper coordination is essential for stall/spin awareness. It helps tailor more favorable stall characteristics and thwarts spinning tendencies. As we'll see, it's uncoordinated flight that can transform a routine stall into a spin.

Spins are extremely complex phenomena, and many variables influence their behavior. Although tremendous advances have been made in high angle of attack research, no one yet has all of the answers to the spin problem. Enough information is available, however, to be able to separate myth from reality and to offer practical advice on the subject. Let's start by defining some pertinent spin terminology:

SPIN aptly describes the manoeuvre, during which the airplane descends vertically along a tight, helical flight path while at stalled angles of attack. Smoke trailing behind a spinning airplane would etch a corkscrew in the sky. Although rotation occurs around all three flight axes simultaneously, it's the combined yawing and rolling motion that give the spin its classic look.

AUTOROTATION describes the self-propelling nature of a spin. As we'll see, the aerodynamics of Stalled Flight fuel Autorotation through a process called negative damping in roll. Normal Flight, on the other hand, favors positive damping in roll and adverse yaw, both of which oppose the rotary motion of a spin. These different characteristics explain why spins are associated with stalled angles of attack, even though the stall itself does not generate the spin.

COUPLE refers to a disturbance along one flight axis that induces changes along another axis. Couples can be either aerodynamic or inertial in nature. Yawing an airplane, for example, not only rotates it about the yaw axis, but it also generates a secondary roll about the roll axis (Chapter 3—Roll, Yaw, and Pitch). Ultimately, it's this yaw/roll couple that drives the spin.

INERTIA refers to the resistance of various components of an airplane to changes in their flight path. Think of the heavy parts of an airplane like the railroad cars of a freight train: Setting the cars in motion requires powerful locomotives to overcome their massive resting inertia. Slowly, the car closest to the front moves, followed by the second car, then the third, and so on down the line in a chain reaction. Once the train is rolling, it possesses tremendous moving inertia that tends to keep it rumbling down the tracks. We know intuitively that a train lumbering at five miles per hour would be considerably more difficult to stop than a bowling ball rolling at the same speed.

Like the cars of a train, masses concentrated along the wings tend to resist changes in roll. Wing-mounted engines, fuel tanks, tip tanks, and avionics pods possess roll inertia. Masses concentrated along the fuselage tend to resist changes in both pitch and yaw. Hence, fuselage-mounted engines and accessories, fuel tanks, passengers, and loaded baggage compartments possess pitch and yaw inertia.

PRO-SPIN refers to airplane design elements and control inputs that tend to contribute to Autorotation. **ANTI-SPIN** refers to design elements and inputs that tend to resist or counter Autorotation.

Spin Dynamics

Let's investigate spin dynamics by starting in Normal Flight with our wings level. Observe what happens if we induce yaw by applying some left rudder: As discussed in Chapter 3—Roll, Yaw, & Pitch, left rudder swings the nose to the left, increasing airflow over the right wing and decreasing it on the left. The difference in airflow causes a discrepancy in the Lift generated. A left roll ensues, indelibly coupled to our yaw input.

The yaw-induced left roll now influences the relative wind sensed by each wing. The relative wind associated with roll must be added to the relative wind associated with our forward motion. Picture long pieces of yarn attached to each wingtip. If the airplane only moves forward, yarn on each wingtip points aft toward the tail. If the airplane only rolls left, yarn on the left wingtip points upward and yarn on the right wingtip points downward. The combination of forward motion **AND** roll causes the wind to strike the left wing at a slightly higher angle of attack. The resulting wind on the right wing strikes it at a slightly lower angle of attack.

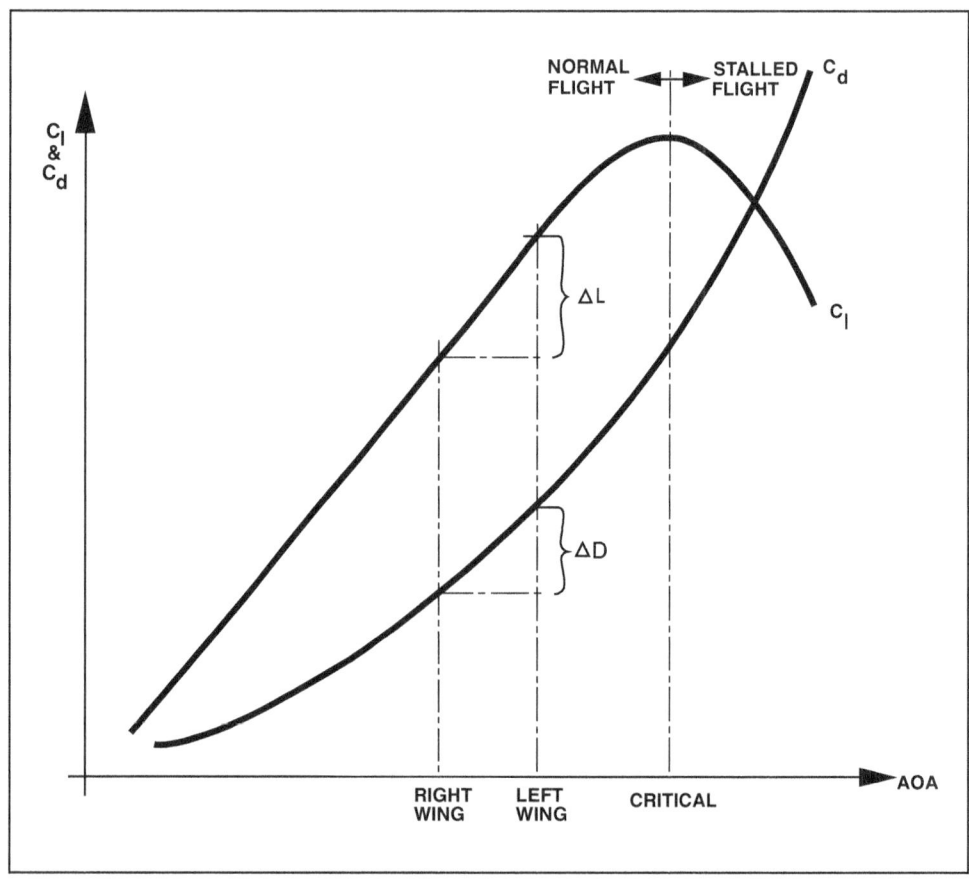

Figure 7-1: Effect of Yaw Input during Normal Flight

In Normal Flight, increasing the left wing's angle of attack produces a higher coefficient of Lift. Decreasing the right wing's angle of attack reduces its coefficient of Lift. Consequently, the airplane tends to roll back to level flight, disrupting the yaw/roll couple caused by our rudder input (i.e.: positive damping in roll). Also, the relatively small increase in Drag on the left wing is negated by the adverse yaw accompanying the secondary roll (review Chapter 3—Roll, Yaw, and Pitch). These elements have a stabilising effect against Autorotation; Normal Flight, therefore, is characteristically anti-spin.

Let's move over into Stalled Flight. Imagine performing a routine, wings-level, 1-g stall. Assume we reach critical angle of attack configured as follows: Power—idle, ailerons—neutral, flaps—up, slip/skid ball—centered, elevator control—held full back, center of gravity—within limits. At the stall, aerodynamic forces and moments try to pitch the nose forward, but no net yawing or rolling is present because we're perfectly coordinated. Using the rudder to remain coordinated throughout compels the left and right wings to remain at identical angles of attack. Each wing generates equal amounts of Lift and Drag as a result, even though they're both stalled. Stabilising forces are at work to return the airplane to Normal Flight, and no pro-spin couple is present to excite Autorotation.

Now picture another stall similar to the one above, except that we enter it while in uncoordinated flight. In fact, let's exaggerate matters by intentionally yawing the airplane with full left rudder as the nose pitches forward. As we saw in the Normal Flight example, the nose yaws left, inducing a left roll. The relative winds are affected the same way as well, resulting in a greater angle of attack on the left wing and a lower angle of attack on the right. The outcome in Stalled Flight, however, is quite different from Normal Flight.

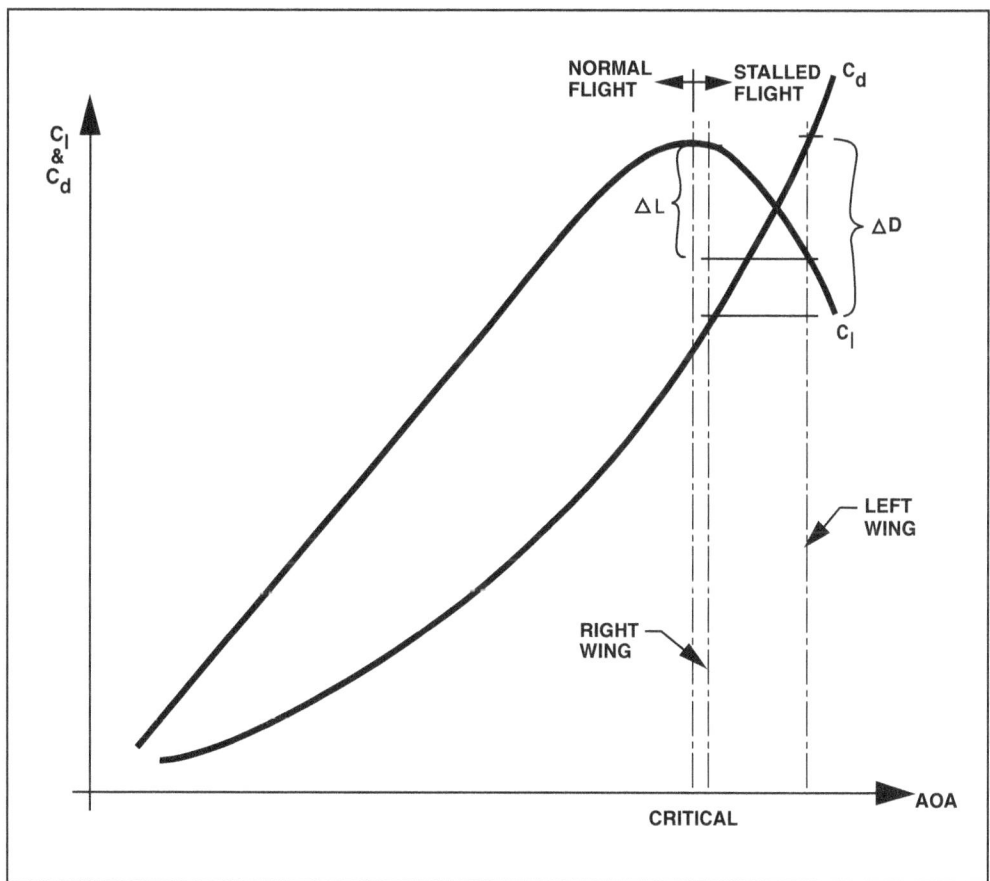

Figure 7-2: Effect of Yaw Input during Stalled Flight

The left wing now experiences a lower coefficient of Lift than the right wing; hence, the airplane rolls even farther to the left (i.e.: negative damping in roll). A significant differential in Drag to the left also exists, which overpowers adverse yaw from the roll and contributes to the left yaw. A pro-spin couple is formed, spawned by uncoordinated Stalled Flight. Although stalling is a necessary prerequisite to the development of a spin, it clearly is not the prime mover behind it. Excess yaw coupling with roll is the real culprit. Proper coordination, therefore, is paramount for spin prevention and is vital for stall/spin awareness.

Returning the wings to identical angles of attack unravels the yaw/roll couple and stops the spin. Naturally, opposite rudder provides the most direct and most powerful means to counter Autorotation in the light, single-engine airplane (especially when mass is nearly equally distributed between the wings and the fuselage). Applying full right rudder against a left spin, for instance, drives each wing's angle of attack together, breaking the yaw/roll couple. Rotation ceases, at which point the airplane returns to a coordinated, albeit stalled condition.

The airplane will remain in a coordinated stall if the rudder is then quickly neutralised and used to cancel other yaw effects; otherwise, the opposite rudder could induce another spin as the process begins anew. Returning to Normal Flight from here is a simple matter of reducing the angle of attack with the elevator. Coping with an actual spin, though, demands adhering to a specific set of rules. Reacting haphazardly with inputs reinforced during Normal Flight can adversely impact spin recovery characteristics. The critical sequencing of the rudder input to break the yaw/roll couple, **FOLLOWED BY** the elevator input to break the stall, will become apparent as this chapter unfolds.

How an airplane behaves during a spin—what it does, how it looks—characterises its spin mode. The spin mode encountered and its rate of rotation depend primarily on the yaw- and pitch-moment attributes of the airplane. However, spin entry conditions, airplane design features, and control inputs also influence spin behavior. Aerodynamic forces and moments trying to lower the nose, inertial effects trying to raise the nose, and gyroscopic effects arising from mass whirling around the three flight axes all shape the personality of the spin.

Spin modes are classified as either steep or flat, depending on the wing's angle of attack and the nose attitude relative to the horizon. "Steeper" refers to a lower nose position and relatively low, but still stalled, angles of attack. "Flatter" refers to a higher nose position and higher angles of attack. NASA has divided spin modes into four classifications: Steep, Moderately Steep, Moderately Flat, and Flat. The angle of attack ranges for each mode, which NASA defined somewhat arbitrarily, are listed in Table 7-1.

SPIN MODE CLASSIFICATION	STEEP	MODERATELY STEEP	MODERATELY FLAT	FLAT
ANGLE OF ATTACK RANGE	20° TO 30°	30° TO 45°	45° TO 65°	65° TO 90°

Table 7-1: NASA Guidelines for Classifying Spin Modes

Spin modes may also be steady, oscillatory, or cyclic in nature. A steady spin is one in which the nose attitude and rate of rotation remain constant throughout a given turn. In an oscillatory spin, the nose typically bobs up and down at various points during each revolution. The rate of rotation varies as the attitude changes, generally slowing as it flattens and increasing as it steepens. A cyclic spin usually displays periodic behavior spread over a number of turns. For example, the first few turns may be steep and fast, followed by a pitch up to a flatter, slower mode for a few turns, then returning to the steeper, faster mode, and so on.

A spinning airplane rotates around its spin axis, which has roll, yaw, and pitch motions superimposed upon it. The inclination of this axis and its location depend on the spin phase and on the type of spin encountered. For example, as a typical, light airplane falls into a normal spin from level, upright flight, the spin axis rotates from horizontal to vertical (or nearly so). It also moves aft from a point ahead of the nose toward the airplane's center of gravity. During steeper spins, the spin axis usually stabilises ahead of the center of gravity, on the inboard side of the spin. During flatter spins, the spin axis usually moves to the center of gravity, or close to it.

Like any good story, the complete Autorotation process has a beginning, a middle, and an end. The phases in the life of a spin are labelled incipient, developed, and recovery. Each has its own unique characteristics. The incipient and recovery phases are transient in nature, evolving with time. The developed phase is a steady-state condition. Let's take a closer look at these phases:

Incipient

The incipient phase is the action-packed first chapter in the spin story. Incipient spins are a transitional phase during which the airplane progresses from an aggravated stall to a pure Autorotation. This phase may last only two turns, during which time the rate of rotation tends to accelerate en route to the developed phase. Incipient spins are typically pilot-driven, especially in the early stages. The forces of Autorotation alone usually cannot sustain the spin, so pro-spin inputs must be held for it to continue. Merely relaxing your grip on the controls at the onset of rotation may stop an incipient spin in its tracks in many light airplanes.

All single-engine airplanes certified in the Normal category—as well as those certified in the Utility category that are placarded against intentional spins—have demonstrated recovery from one-turn incipient spins **ONLY**. Recovery capability from developed spins is not a design consideration for operation in these categories. Incipient spin demonstrations are merely checks of an airplane's controllability during aggravated stalls. No guarantees can be made about the prospects for recovery if rotation continues beyond the first turn. Simply put, you have a one-turn margin of safety in which to terminate the process.

Developed

The developed phase is the meat of the spin story. Fully developed spins represent a state of equilibrium between aerodynamic and inertia forces and moments acting on the airplane. Airspeed typically remains low and constant, either hovering 5 to 10 miles per hour above the 1-g stall speed (Vso), or flickering on the low end of the airspeed scale. The rate of descent can range from 8,000 feet per minute (91 mph) during nose-low spins to 5,000 feet per minute (57 mph) during flat spins.

Unlike incipient spins, developed spins are aerodynamically-driven. Sufficient differences in Lift and Drag on each wing exist to self-propel the spin. Should you release the controls in the developed phase, they'll tend to float more or less in the direction of rotation. For example, upon removing your hands and feet from the controls during a developed, upright spin to the left, the controls will tend to position themselves as follows: left aileron, aft elevator, left rudder.

The lack of mandatory, inherent spin recovery capability for Normal (and some Utility) category certification reduces the likelihood of recovery from a developed spin in many airplanes. The rates of rotation, spin attitudes, and gyroscopic effects, coupled with the diminished control authority associated with Autorotation, can make recovery from developed spins particularly difficult. Those airplanes placarded against intentional spins, as well as any airplane loaded outside of its approved weight and balance limits, may become inertially locked into a spin—like a runaway train—if it fully develops. Recovery then becomes impossible, even with the application of full anti-spin controls.

Unfortunately, specific cues may not be present to warn us that a non-recoverable spin is imminent. This is precisely why acute stall/spin awareness, good rudder coordination, and the ability to recognise and recover from the early stages of an incipient spin should be given due consideration during training. We must learn reactions that will skirt us around the developed spin phase before spin dynamics override our ability to control the airplane.

Recovery

Recovery certainly would be the happy ending to the spin story. Less desirable endings are also possible, unfortunately, unless several critical factors align in our favor. Spinning only ceases if and when forces and moments opposing Autorotation overcome pro-spin aerodynamics. Since yaw coupled with roll powers the spin, we must forcibly uncouple them to effect recovery. Full opposite rudder is the primary means through which this is accomplished.

During the recovery phase, the nose attitude typically steepens. The rate of rotation may accelerate momentarily as well, but it ultimately decreases to zero. Airspeed, relatively low and constant during the spin, quickly builds as the airplane returns to Normal Flight in a dive. When recovery is possible, it can occur in as little as a quarter of a turn, or it can take several additional turns depending on the airplane and the dynamics of the particular spin.

Inherent design differences between airplanes influence the effectiveness of recovery actions. Acrobatic category operation, for example, demands greater control effectiveness than flight within Normal or Utility category limits. Designs certified in the Acrobatic category must comply with more stringent spin test requirements, too. As a result, aerobatic airplanes tend to display good-to-excellent spin recovery characteristics **BY DESIGN**. On the other hand, since recovery capability from developed spins is not a design criterion for Normal (and some Utility) category certification, it's reasonable to assume that such airplanes might display poor recovery characteristics **BY DESIGN**.

No single factor can be used to predict spin characteristics or recovery potential. The combined influence of several variables must be considered, including the following parameters: the airplane's relative density; its inertia characteristics and the symmetry of its mass distribution; the wing design; the fuselage shape; the tail configuration; the size, location, and interference effects of various parts of the airplane; the center of gravity location; and the position and authority of the flight controls. Spins are recoverable only when the cumulative effect of these interacting variables favor recovery, **AND** of course, only when sufficient altitude exists.

Inertia Effects

Relative density is the ratio of an airplane's mass to its wing area, its wing span, and the local air density. It provides an indication of an airplane's resistance to changes in its configuration. All else being equal, a higher relative density tends to be more spin resistant. Unfortunately, a higher relative density also tends to resist recovery actions once a spin is initiated. Conversely, a lower relative density typically enters spins more readily, but also tends to respond quicker to recovery actions. An anvil with one inch wing stubs falling from the sky (maximum relative density), for example, will take much longer to rotate up to speed in a spin compared to a balsa wood toy glider (minimal relative density). Likewise, an anvil stabilised in a spin will be much more difficult to stop than the toy glider.

How mass is distributed throughout the airplane affects spin characteristics as well. As in our earlier freight train analogy, the inertia associated with mass located far from the center of gravity tends to make spin entry more difficult. Once spinning begins, though, inertia then tends to resist recovery actions. Spinning with an unbalanced load can adversely impact recovery, too, particularly when more mass is located on the outboard side of rotation. Spin recovery may be delayed or thwarted altogether, for example, if wing fuel tanks on the inboard side of the spin are empty while the outboard wing tanks are full.

Mass distribution also influences the anti-spin contribution of our recovery inputs. Rudder applied opposite to the direction of yaw directly counters the pro-spin yaw/roll couple. Opposite rudder tends to be the most effective anti-spin control in airplanes with a nearly equal distribution of mass between the wing and the fuselage (e.g.: light, single-engine airplanes). As more mass is transferred into the wings (e.g.: multi-engine airplanes), elevator inputs may play a more significant role along with full opposite rudder. As more mass is concentrated in the fuselage (e.g.: business jets, fighters), aileron position may play a more significant role along with the opposite rudder.

Wing Design

Spin recovery capability was once thought to hinge primarily on tail design. Research has shown, though, that the main wing can significantly influence spin and recovery characteristics. The wing may contribute strong pro-spin effects that simply overpower anti-spin features designed into the tail section. A wing rotating in a spin behaves a lot like a turning propeller. As such, it contributes pro-spin effects based on the same gyroscopic properties discussed in Chapter 3—Roll, Yaw, and Pitch.

For instance, as the wings roll left in a left, upright spin, inertia tries to raise the nose simultaneously, subjecting the wings to an upward pitch force. The pitch force, however, precesses ninety degrees in the direction of the left roll. It appears instead as left yaw, which contributes to flattening the spin and increasing its rotational speed. The precession effect becomes stronger as more mass is added to the wings. A properly sequenced nose-down pitch force (forward elevator), on the other hand, generates an anti-spin gyroscopic effect that can aid spin recovery. This anti-spin effect may be important for recovery, especially in wing-heavy airplanes.

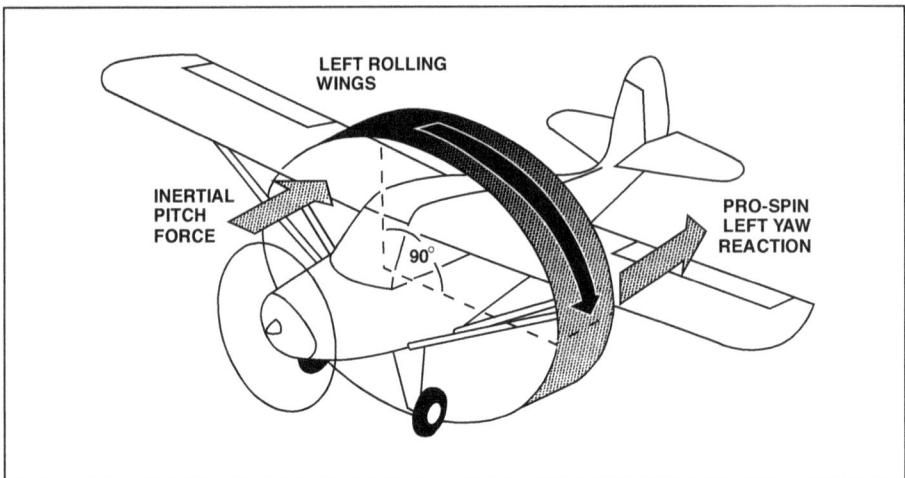

Figure 7-3: Pro-Spin Gyroscopic Effect due to Rolling Wings

Designers can improve airplane spin resistance and recovery capability by tinkering with the wing's shape and its location. Drooping selected outboard segments of the leading edge, for example, improves roll control during high angle of attack flight. Also, a high wing generally displays better recovery characteristics than a low wing on otherwise similar airplanes. Vortex generators can help to delay airflow separation longer before stalling, and can help to reattach airflow sooner during recovery.

Fuselage Design

The shape and mass distribution of the fuselage can either degrade or improve spin and recovery characteristics. A spinning fuselage acts like a skewed wing. As such, it could possibly generate a pro-spin Lift force that increases the rate of rotation and flattens the spin attitude. Research has found that a round top/flat bottom cross section contributes the strongest pro-spin effect compared to other fuselage shapes. But a rotating fuselage also projects a blunt, inefficient profile to the wind; therefore, it can offer significant anti-spin resistance to rotation as well. This resistance is referred to as "damping".

Airplanes with high damping (large side surface area) tend to spin slower. Airplanes with low damping (small side surface area) tend to spin faster and flatter. In cases where interference from the wing and tail section reduce damping by the aft part of the fuselage, pro-spin Lift generated by the nose could pull the airplane into a fast, flat spin. Adding nose strakes is one method of defeating pro-spin Lift on the front end. Adding ventral fins, protruding from the belly of the airplane, improves directional control and also tends to resist the development of flatter spin modes.

Rotating mass behaves like a gyroscope. In our upright, left spin example, the upward-pitching fuselage is simultaneously subjected to a left roll force. Precession rotates this force ninety degrees in the direction of pitch. The action of the left roll force appears as an anti-spin right yaw. The gyroscopic contribution of the fuselage, therefore, is naturally anti-spin. In some cases, the anti-spin contribution can be increased by applying ailerons in the direction of rotation, thus increasing the roll force to be precessed. In-spin ailerons can be a critical action required in fuselage-heavy aircraft with relatively small wings.

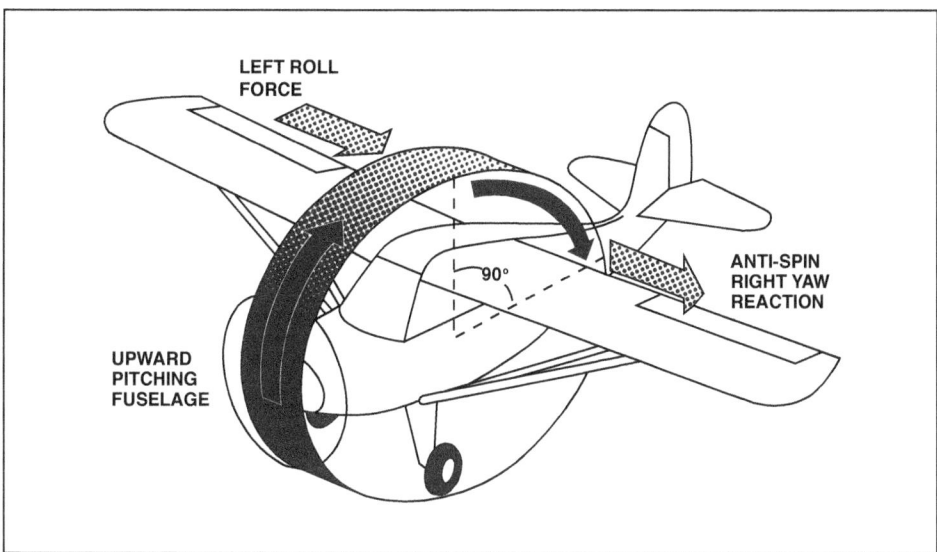

Figure 7-4: Anti-Spin Gyroscopic Effect due to Pitching Fuselage

Tail Design

The size and configuration of the tail section, while no longer viewed as the sole determinant of spin recovery capability, remains an extremely important part of the spin equation. Rudder applied fully against a spin directly opposes the yaw/roll couple. It's the most effective anti-spin input available in light, general aviation airplanes. Even though anti-spin gyroscopic effects from elevator and aileron inputs may take on more importance in wing- and fuselage-heavy designs, the effect of full opposite rudder against rotation remains crucial to successful spin recovery. A large rudder located as far aft of the center of gravity as possible generally offers better recovery potential than a small rudder close to the center of gravity.

The amount of rudder shielded during a spin is an important factor in tail design, too. The horizontal stabiliser on a conventional tail configuration, for instance, prevents airflow from reaching the upper part of the vertical stabiliser/rudder when in an upright spin. Hence, much of this area may be rendered useless for spin recovery. The blanketing effect of the horizontal stabiliser can be exacerbated by deflecting the elevator downward during an upright spin, which further reduces rudder power and decreases the damping effect of the tail.

A T-tail configuration minimises the shielding effect of the horizontal stabiliser/elevator in an upright spin, assuming it isn't prone to the adverse post-stall characteristics described in the last chapter (Stalls). Also, bear in mind that the primary advantage of a T-tail is the ability to incorporate smaller surfaces on the back end since they're located above the main wing's wake in Normal Flight. Smaller surfaces are more efficient in Normal Flight, but they may possess less control authority during Autorotation.

(Shielding effects from the horizontal stabiliser/elevator are relevant during an inverted spin, too. In general, more rudder surface is available to aid in recovery when inverted in a conventional tail airplane, less when inverted in a T-tail. Flipping the airplane upside down essentially places the conventional tail into a T-tail position, exposing more rudder to the wind. Conversely, the inverted T-tail is more akin to a conventional configuration, blocking more of the rudder.)

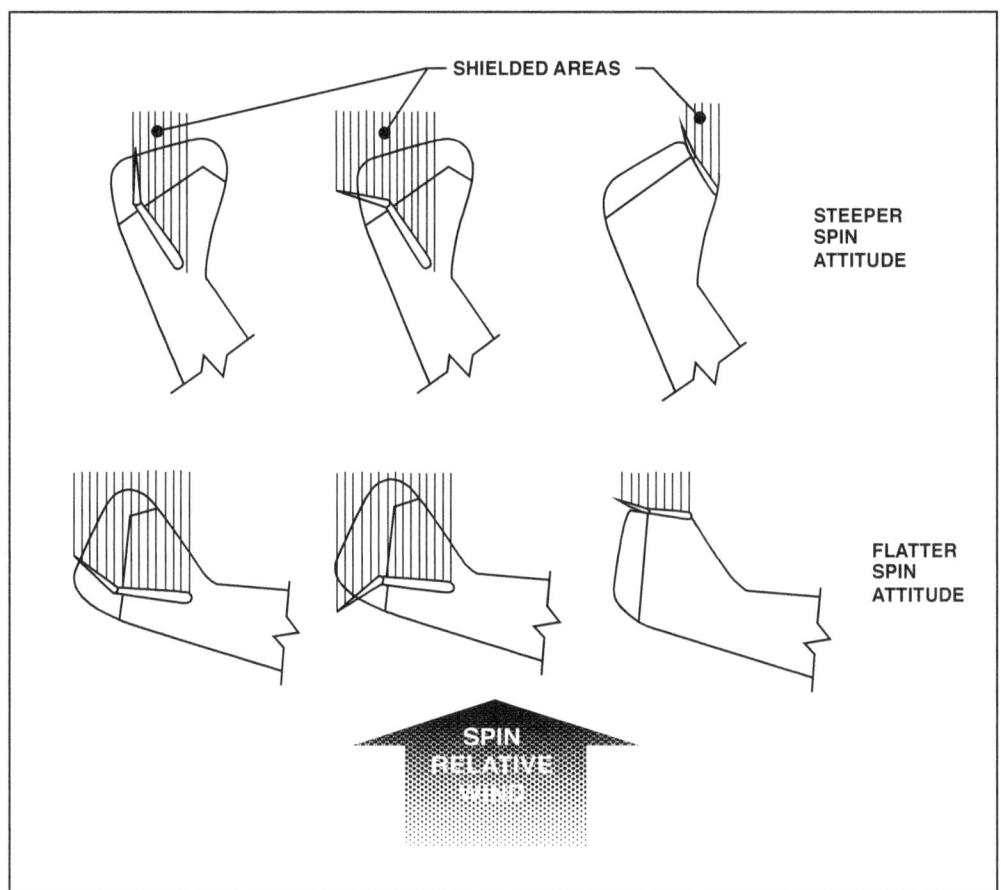

Figure 7-5: Possible Shielding Effects due to the Horizontal Stabiliser

Pilot-Controlled Variables

Spins possess certain inherent characteristics that are beyond our control, but we do have command over such elements as center of gravity and control positions. Spin recovery often depends upon how we choose to manipulate these elements. They can either be configured to contribute to a non-recoverable spin, or they can be used to tip the scales in favor of recovery. For example, we have direct control over weight and balance. Always load your airplane within its prescribed limits, without exception.

Center of gravity definitely influences stall and spin behavior. Attaining the high angles of attack necessary for Autorotation tends to be more difficult with a forward center of gravity. As a result, airplanes so loaded tend to be more spin resistant. All else being equal, a forward center of gravity provides a longer moment arm from the rudder and elevator; therefore, stronger anti-spin moments are possible when recovery inputs are applied.

Sliding the center of gravity aft, by comparison, shortens the moment arm and decreases the anti-spin potential of the rudder and elevator. It's also easier to achieve higher angles of attack and deeper stalls—and thereby generate stronger pro-spin forces and moments—at aft centers of gravity. Moreover, aft centers of gravity promote flatter spin attitudes. Although non-recoverable spins may be possible at any center of gravity position, they become increasingly more likely as it moves aft.

Power

Power translates us from one point to another while controlling our altitude profile in Normal Flight. During Autorotation, however, applying power tends to rotate us faster around the spin axis. Increasing the rpm of the propeller literally increases the rpm of the spin! The degree to which power influences spin dynamics depends on the size and weight of the prop compared to the rest of the airplane. It also depends on the spin's direction and speed, its angle of attack, and the ratio of roll to yaw.

Causing the propeller to turn at high rpm increases the gyroscopic forces acting on the airplane (especially when swinging a large, heavy prop). In a right spin with a clockwise-turning propeller (viewed from the cockpit), the right yaw component precesses clockwise ninety degrees. The gyroscopic effect appears now as a pitch force that tries to pull the nose to a steeper attitude. In a left spin, left yaw precesses into a pitch force that tries to pull the nose to a flatter attitude. Additionally, centrifugal (inertia) forces trying to raise the nose grow as the airplane rotates faster. This effect is analogous to twirling a rock on a string: speeding up the rotation causes the rock to rise.

Centrifugal and gyroscopic effects resulting from power tend to offset each other during right spins; hence, an appreciable change in pitch attitude may not accompany the increase in rotation. During left spins, centrifugal and gyroscopic effects are cumulative; hence, a noticeable flattening of the spin attitude could accompany the increase in rotation. Closing the throttle early during an inadvertent spin, therefore, minimises these detrimental effects.

Interestingly, it's not uncommon for an engine to run rough or even to quit during multiple-turn, power-on spins. Mounting centrifugal forces may unport fuel in the wing tanks, eventually leading to fuel starvation and prop stoppage. Unfortunately, by the time this occurs, gyroscopic and centrifugal effects contributed by the use of power may have already locked the airplane into a non-recoverable spin mode.

Ailerons

Spins are propelled by a yaw/roll couple. This couple results primarily from the aerodynamic properties of our wing in stalled flight. Moving the ailerons, therefore, directly influences these properties. Aileron inputs alter the proportion of roll-to-yaw in a spin. The airplane's response to such inputs is analogous to applying ailerons in Normal Flight. Let's compare aileron effects, assuming we're upright and banked to the left.

In Normal Flight, applying right aileron—opposite to the direction of bank—causes the airplane to roll to wings-level. Similarly, applying right aileron in a left spin—opposite to the direction of roll—also tends to level the wings. Autorotation continues, however, but now with a different mix of yaw and roll. Opposite aileron effectively reduces pro-spin roll and turns it into more pro-spin yaw. Recall that the roll force precesses in the spin, showing up as an anti-spin yaw effect. Diminishing this force, that is, impeding it with opposite aileron, decreases its anti-spin **YAW** contribution.

Deflecting the ailerons opposite to the direction of roll only serves to shallow the bank and intensifies the pro-spin yaw rate. Centrifugal effects, aggravated by the increase in yaw, may simultaneously swing the nose into a flatter spin attitude. Any roll or pitch oscillations tend to be dampened out in the process. The result could be a flatter, faster, steadier spin fortified with extra pro-spin yaw. Physically, you may feel as if you're being pushed toward the outside of the ensuing spin.

Applying left aileron in our example—in the same direction of bank—increases our bank angle in Normal Flight. Likewise in a left spin, left aileron tends to steepen the bank. Autorotation still continues, but now with more pro-spin roll at the expense of pro-spin yaw. Augmenting the roll force with in-spin ailerons tends to improve its anti-spin **YAW** contribution. Increasing the bank also tends to lower the nose into a steeper spin, amplifying any roll or pitch oscillations along the way. A steeper, faster, oscillatory spin may follow, possibly earmarked by a noticeable rolling motion. In addition, you may feel as if you're being pushed toward the inside of the spin.

In-spin ailerons may provide additional needed recovery power (more anti-spin yaw and steeper attitudes with lower spin angles of attack) to stop flat spins in some airplanes, and to stop spins in some fuselage-heavy, short-winged designs. We must consider, however, the potential downside effects associated with using in-spin ailerons during recovery. For instance, it's possible to confuse the roll generated by the ailerons as a prolonged spin, even though spin recovery has already taken place. The airplane could then transition abruptly from a spin into a high speed, high g, rolling spiral. Also, determining the direction of roll, then applying the correct input may be difficult in an unintentional spin, especially during an inverted spin. (During an inverted left spin, for example, the airplane yaws to the left from the pilot's perspective, but rolls to the right; therefore, **RIGHT** aileron becomes the "in-spin" aileron in an inverted, left spin.)

Based on the above discussion, we should anticipate the following responses: Applying out-spin ailerons (opposite to the direction of roll) tends to be a pro-spin input that's counterproductive to recovery. Applying in-spin ailerons (in the direction of roll) tends to favor recovery; however, using in-spin ailerons requires a good working knowledge of, and recency of experience with, the spin and recovery characteristics of a given airplane. The intent of emergency manoeuvre training is to take corrective actions early in the development of any unusual attitude. Minimising the potential for errors that may aggravate the situation is vital. Therefore, the most appropriate aileron position for recovery from an inadvertent spin in the standard, light airplane is neutral.

Flaps

Deployed flaps have a tendency to flatten the spin attitude and slow the rate of rotation. Flaps may shield airflow to the tail section as well, particularly in low wing airplanes. Anti-spin tail damping effects may be reduced as a result. If spin recovery is accomplished with the flaps deployed, it's possible to exceed the flap extension speed (Vfe) during the ensuing pull-out. Design structural limits, which can be as low as 2.0 g's with the flaps down, could also be exceeded. Raising the flaps during spin recovery, therefore, minimises their influence on spin dynamics and reduces the potential for structural damage during recovery.

Rudder

Spins are driven by a yaw/roll couple. The rudder can produce a direct anti-spin yawing moment to counter pro-spin yaw. Deflecting the rudder opposite to the direction of yaw, therefore, must be our primary focus during spin recovery. All other factors being equal, the rudder's anti-spin contribution is strongest when a large, unshielded surface acts on a long moment arm, especially against a steeper spin. It's weakest when a small, mostly blanketed surface acts on a short moment arm, especially against a flatter spin.

Full opposite rudder is always recommended, but it may not always be sufficient by itself for recovery from developed spins (especially in airplanes certified in the Normal category). The opposite rudder's anti-spin effect often must be combined with other spin recovery actions to stop rotation. For example, the combined anti-spin effects associated with reducing the power, neutralising the ailerons, raising the flaps, and repositioning the elevator may be needed in addition to opposite rudder. Even so, the importance of applying the opposite rudder fully and briskly cannot be over-emphasised.

It's important to clarify that spin direction is always in the direction of yaw. References such as full rudder "against rotation", or "opposite to the spin", mean "*opposite to the direction of YAW*". In an upright left spin, for example, yaw and roll components appear to move in the same direction—left yaw and left roll. In an inverted left spin, these components appear to move in opposite directions—still left yaw, but right roll! Both cases are examples of left spins from the pilot's perspective, and right rudder is the rudder opposing the yaw.

Identifying the opposite rudder in an inadvertent spin is critical for recovery. The spin's roll component can adversely influence our perception of spin direction, which can lead to confusion when it's time to apply the opposite rudder. If you're not sure which way the airplane is spinning, implement the following strategies:

1. Look at the symbolic airplane of the turn coordinator or the needle of the turn and bank indicator. The symbolic airplane reliably leans in the direction of yaw during upright spins only; therefore, step in the opposite direction for recovery (i.e., toward the "high" wing). The needle, on the other hand, reliably shows the direction of yaw during both upright and inverted spins; step opposite to the direction of needle deflection. Keep in mind that the artificial horizon, heading indicator, and the slip/skid ball are **UNRELIABLE** during a spin, so ignore them.

2. Change your field of vision by sighting straight down the nose of the airplane. This action isolates the yaw component of the spin. Force yourself to look beyond the nose, observing the ground movement below; the ground will appear to "flow" past the nose like water in a river. Apply the rudder fully in the direction of this perceived movement. In other words, go with the flow! In a left spin, for instance, the ground moves in a blur to the right; so, step on the right rudder for recovery.

3. Sample the rudder pedals, feeling for the one that offers the most resistance. Press the "heavier" one all the way to the control stop. Unless you have a lot of experience spinning a particular airplane, this technique may be the most difficult of the three to implement during an unintentional spin. Subconsciously locking both feet on the rudder pedals is not uncommon when surprised by an unplanned spin entry. Subsequently, both pedals may feel like they're imbedded in concrete. Consciously relaxing your feet improves your sense of feel. It also reduces the tendency to oppose the application of full opposite rudder with your other leg.

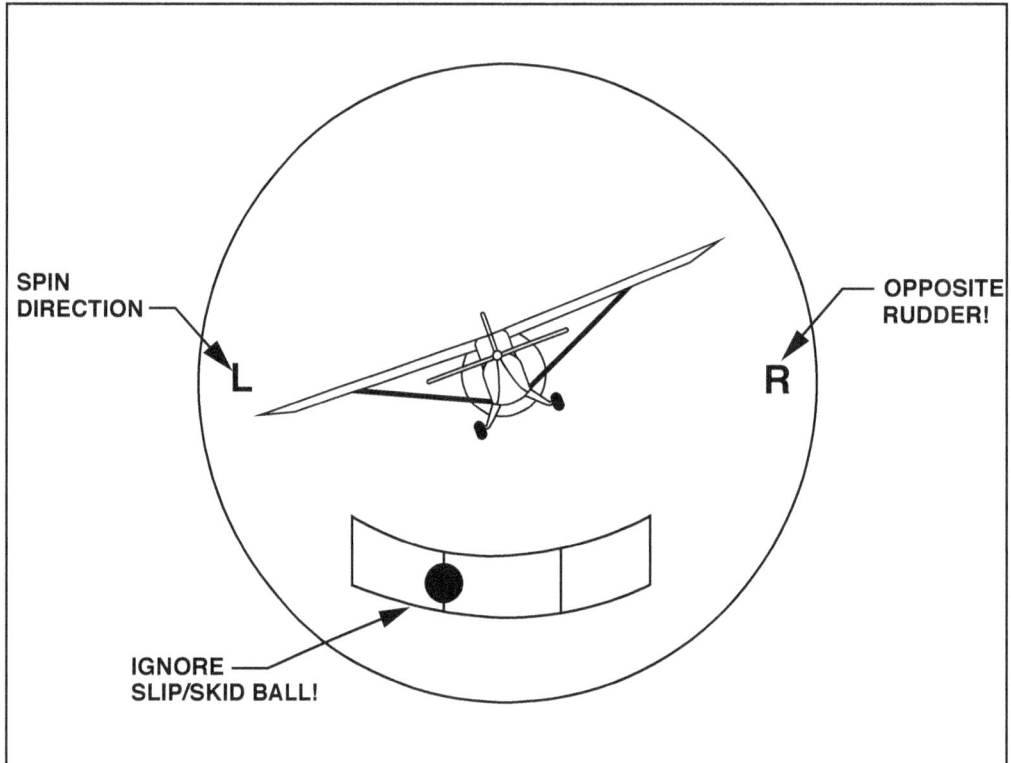

Figure 7-6: Turn Coordinator Indication during a Left Upright Spin

Elevator

We saw earlier how gyroscopic precession can contribute anti-spin yaw when applying forward elevator in an upright spin. Forward elevator can also lower our angle of attack and unstall the wing. Unfortunately, misapplying the elevator can result in an aggravated spin, a delayed recovery, or even a secondary spin. The timing of this input and the amount used are critical elements in the recovery process. As we'll soon discover, moving the elevator **AFTER** the rudder input is an important sequence of events.

The final position of the elevator control for spin recovery depends on the effectiveness of the opposite rudder. A definite relationship exists between these two inputs. For instance, if the application of opposite rudder significantly slows the rotation in an upright spin, then the elevator typically only has to move forward to its neutral position. Aerobatic airplanes, designed with increased control authority and proven spin recovery characteristics, usually follow this pattern. Non-aerobatic airplanes, on the other hand, typically have less effective rudders by design. They are not required to possess true spin recovery capability, either. Therefore, we should expect the elevator to play a greater role during recovery in these airplanes. If the opposite rudder has minimal effect on the spin, then move the elevator control through the neutral position, possibly all the way to the forward control stop.

In either case (aerobatic or non-aerobatic designs), the elevator control should be driven forward—**AFTER** the application of full opposite rudder—until either the spin stops, or you reach the forward control limit. Avoid randomly over-controlling the elevator, however. When spinning ceases, stop pushing. It's then time to recover from the dive. (Similarly, during an inverted spin, the elevator control should be pulled aft following the application of opposite rudder. When spinning ceases, stop pulling.)

Procedure vs. Technique

Recovery inputs must be applied in the proper sequence during an inadvertent spin. Knowing what to move, where to move it, and when to move it are the keys to successful spin recovery. Unfortunately, spin recovery actions don't follow a pilot's natural instincts, nor the reactions reinforced during primary training. Spin recovery is a learned response. It's a mechanical process, devoid of much of the usual sense of feel associated with Normal Flight.

Efficient spin recovery is predicated on the occurrence of the actions discussed so far, namely: Power—Off, Ailerons—Neutral (and Flaps—Up), Rudder—Full Opposite, and Elevator—Through Neutral. These actions form the essence of spin recovery procedure. They outline "what" needs to happen. "How" these actions are implemented define spin recovery technique. Maximising the probability of recovery certainly hinges on applying appropriate techniques to satisfy the intent of the procedure.

For the most part, the techniques used for spin recovery are straightforward. Closing the throttle (technique), for example, is how we satisfy Power—Off (procedure). Only one control position satisfies Ailerons—Neutral; likewise for Flaps—Up. Pressing the opposite rudder completely against the stop is the only way to satisfy Rudder—Full Opposite. Quantifying Elevator—Through Neutral, however, isn't as easy. Techniques abound concerning this one input. Words like "simultaneously", "let go of the stick", "far enough to break the stall", "full forward", and "briskly" are used to describe elevator actions that presumably will contribute to spin recovery. As discussed above, the elevator action depends on the airplane's response to the opposite rudder. Applying a measured amount of elevator, sequenced **AFTER** the rudder input, offers superior recovery potential. Otherwise, we increase the risk of encountering one of the following aggravated spins:

Accelerated Spin

Common to all airplanes, pushing the elevator forward during an upright spin speeds up the rotation (this phenomenon may even be observed temporarily during the normal recovery process). Forward elevator drives the airplane to a steeper spin attitude. The nose and tail move closer to the spin axis, decreasing the **RADIUS** of rotation, but increasing the **RATE** of rotation. The effect is analogous to figure skaters spinning on ice: rotation is slower with the arms outstretched; as they are drawn toward the body, rotational speed increases; maximum rpm occurs with the arms in and raised overhead, perfectly aligned with the spin axis.

Pushing the elevator forward may also increase the shielded area of the rudder, especially in conventional tail designs. Inherent damping in yaw from the aft fuselage may be reduced as well. These factors can further contribute to accelerated rotation and delayed recovery. Accelerating a spin magnifies the centrifugal effects trying to pull the nose and tail away from the spin axis. These centrifugal forces may actually pull some airplanes out of their accelerated spins into non-recoverable flat spins. Applying the opposite rudder first, **FOLLOWED BY** the elevator input, certainly minimises the probability of such aggravated characteristics.

Transition Spin

A nasty variant of the Accelerated spin, the Transition spin occurs when the airplane unexpectedly transitions from an upright spin into an inverted spin (or vice versa). Consider an upright spin, for example: Applying forward elevator either ahead of, or simultaneously with, the application of full opposite rudder steepens the attitude and accelerates the rotation. If too much elevator is applied, it could drive the wings from an upright stall straight through to an inverted stall. The opposite rudder input—relative to the upright spin—now becomes a pro-spin input driving an inverted spin. Rotation continues, often confusing and disorienting the pilot.

It's also possible to transition a spin without necessarily accelerating it first. In an upright spin, for instance, suppose too much forward elevator is added after applying full opposite rudder. Excessive forward elevator, held too long, could suddenly tuck the airplane into an inverted spin. Avoid over-controlling this input during recovery. Be deliberate with your elevator input, and apply a measured amount. Stop moving the elevator as soon as rotation stops.

Cross-Over Spin

Also known as a progressive spin, the Cross-over spin is a secondary spin in the opposite direction of initial rotation. A cross-over from a left, upright spin might happen something like this: Full right rudder is applied to stop the left spin, then forward elevator is added to break the stall; upon recovery, the elevator is immediately pulled back to recover from the dive, causing a secondary stall; the still-deflected right rudder input now kicks the airplane into a right spin. Oftentimes, the Cross-over spin rotates at a much higher speed compared to the original spin.

The sequence of events leading to a Cross-over spin is often identical to the inputs that started the spin in the first place. Full rudder followed by an aft elevator input is an efficient way to enter an upright spin. To avoid this scenario, we must exercise discipline over our control inputs throughout the recovery process. Once spinning ceases, neutralise the opposite rudder first to allay any chance of a secondary spin. We can then recover from the dive by pulling the elevator control aft.

(The term "cross-over spin" has a different meaning in competition aerobatics. It refers to an upright spin entered from an inverted attitude, or an inverted spin entered from an upright attitude; thus, it's actually closer to a Transition spin. The competition "cross-over spin" is a controlled manoeuvre, with a specified number of turns, with recovery on a pre-determined heading. Quite a bit different from the unintentional, aggravated spin described above.)

Don't forget the primary driving force behind Autorotation: yaw coupled with roll. As long as the left and right wings remain at different angles of attack, Autorotation will continue. We must address the differences between the wings first (using the rudder), before addressing the fact that they're stalled (using the elevator). Our primary defense against rotation is the opposite rudder. It directly attacks the yaw/roll couple, driving the wings toward a common angle of attack. Once rotation stops, neutralising the rudder reduces the probability of a secondary spin by eliminating excess yaw. Applying the rudder **BEFORE** the elevator, therefore, is a superior recovery technique.

Consolidating, simplifying, and prioritising the rudimentary spin recovery actions discussed so far yields the general, emergency spin recovery procedure. The preferred rudder-then-elevator sequence is included as well. As listed, the procedure is designed to achieve optimum anti-spin effect and is consistent with recommendations based on years of detailed spin research:

1. Power—Off.
2. Ailerons—Neutral (& flaps up).

3. Rudder—Full Opposite.
4. Elevator—Through Neutral.

   HOLD THESE INPUTS UNTIL ROTATION STOPS, THEN:

5. Rudder—Neutral.
6. Elevator—Recover to Straight and Level.

The first letter in each of the four primary recovery inputs spells out the acronym, PARE (pronounced "pair"). PARE is a convenient memory aid that points the way to spin recovery. The PARE format mimics the most docile spin configuration possible, affording the greatest response to recovery inputs. Errant control inputs that may aggravate the spin are avoided in the process. As a mental checklist, it forces you to focus on the appropriate recovery actions. Calling each item out loud also tends to reinforce the physical inputs.

The recovery process begins at the nose of the airplane and systematically moves aft to the tail. Perform the items in the checklist sequentially. As soon as one item is completed, the next one is initiated, and so on until the primary controls have been positioned according to PARE. The second step, Ailerons—Neutral (& flaps up), prepares the wing for Normal Flight. Rudder—Full Opposite means "opposite to the direction of yaw", using the spin direction cues presented earlier if necessary. The crucial rudder-then-elevator sequence appears twice: first to stop the spin, then after rotation has ceased. Reversing the order of these two inputs can aggravate the situation dramatically. It's also important to exercise control over your elevator input—when spinning stops, stop moving the elevator.

Pilot-Induced Flat Spin

The PARE procedure evolved from our analysis of spin dynamics. Its order minimises some of the factors that can lead to aggravated spins. Let's ride through a hypothetical spin sequence, assuming we're in an airplane that is recoverable from any spin mode. (The high performance, aerobatic Pitts is one such design, provided it's flown within weight and balance limits). Assume we enter an upright, left spin with idle power, the ailerons neutral, the rudder fully deflected to the left, and the elevator pulled fully aft.

Let's now add full power to increase the speed of rotation. Centrifugal and gyroscopic forces combine when spinning to the left, forcing the airplane into a flatter spin attitude. Applying full right aileron, opposite to the direction of roll, now levels the wings. Roll energy converts into additional left yaw, further increasing rotational speed. Pushing the elevator to the forward control stop now accelerates the spin even more. The push contributes additional left yaw in two ways: first, through the gyroscopic action of the propeller (review Chapter 3—Roll, Yaw, and Pitch); second, by reducing the damping effect of the tail. The airplane literally shudders in this Flat spin.

Look at our control configuration: full power, full aileron deflection opposite to the direction of roll, full rudder deflection in the direction of yaw, and full forward elevator. Even though the elevator is forward, we're in an upright spin, with the nose tracking almost level along the horizon! We're generating maximum pro-spin force now. The only chance we have of recovering is to undo the inputs that helped to create this monster. We can only hope this will generate anti-spin yawing moments sufficient to overcome the strong inertial and yaw/roll couples sustaining Autorotation.

Let's now eliminate the offending inputs. Since we've misapplied the elevator ahead of schedule according to PARE, we'll start by returning it to the aft position. This exposes more of the rudder to the relative wind and increases damping in yaw. Now continue with the PARE procedure: Power—Off, Ailerons—Neutral, Rudder—Full Opposite, Elevator—Through Neutral (push forward in this case). When rotation stops, neutralise the rudder, then pull out of the dive to straight and level flight.

If you're confused by the control configuration in a spin, reduce the power to idle and release the stick or control wheel. In our Flat spin example, aerodynamic forces would cause the elevator to move aft (stick back) and the ailerons slightly in the direction of roll (ailerons in-spin). We now have known control positions from which to continue with the PARE procedure. Look at the controls as you proceed: Ailerons—Neutral, Rudder—Full Opposite, Elevator—Through Neutral (push in this case).

(The PARE format is applicable to recovery from inverted spins as well. The only difference will be the direction in which the elevator moves to satisfy the step, Elevator—Through Neutral. Upright spins require a **PUSH** to move the elevator control through neutral, whereas inverted spins require a **PULL**.)

Obviously, prevention is the most effective course of action against spinning. If you inadvertently enter a spin in airplanes placarded against it (i.e.: all Normal and some Utility category designs), you have a slim, one-turn margin of safety in which to recover. Recovery may be impossible beyond this, regardless of your recovery actions. Twin engine airplanes have **ZERO** margin of safety in this realm. The key is to stay coordinated during high angle of attack flight. At the first sign of spin entry, react with PARE for maximum effect.

Occasionally sit in your airplane and rehearse your recovery actions before starting the engine. Talk out loud as you go. Mentally run through the PARE procedure until it becomes automatic. Better yet, take some hands-on spin training with a qualified instructor. Also, spend some time getting comfortable in your seat. Make sure the full range of control movement is available to you before starting each flight. Adjust the seat accordingly, padding it with extra cushions if needed. And keep your seat belts snug.

We've developed three unique recovery strategies in the last three Chapters, each one applicable to a specific manoeuvre: the spiral, the stall, and the spin. The driving force behind each of these is different; consequently, so is our primary recovery action. Each configuration has its own characteristic look, sound, and feel, as illustrated in Table 7-2. Notice how our control emphasis changes from the ailerons during spirals to the elevator during stalls to the rudder during spins. We must identify the specific manoeuvre, understand the reason it's happening, and then initiate the correct sequence of events.

CHARACTERISTICS	MANOEUVRE		
	SPIRALS	STALLS	SPINS
ANGLE OF ATTACK	BELOW CRITICAL	ABOVE CRITICAL	ABOVE CRITICAL
AIRSPEED	INCREASING	LOW & CONSTANT	LOW & CONSTANT
ALTIMETER	UNWINDING	UNWINDING	UNWINDING
G-LOAD	INCREASING	ESSENTIALLY +1.0g	ESSENTIALLY +1.0g
PRIMARY CAUSE	EXCESSIVE BANK	EXCESSIVE AOA	YAW & ROLL COUPLED
PRIMARY REMEDY	AILERONS	ELEVATOR	RUDDER
RECOVERY ACTIONS	POWER-PUSH-ROLL	ELEVATOR FORWARD	PARE

Table 7-2: Comparison of Upright Spiral, Stall, & Spin Characteristics

Whereas this chapter focused on yaw and its relationship to spins, the next chapter focuses on roll and its relationship to unusual attitudes resulting from excessive bank angles. We'll expand on the Power-Push-Roll strategy developed for spiral recovery to address other overbanked scenarios.

8
Overbanked

Three distinct emergency recovery procedures have evolved in the last few chapters to cope with different types of unusual attitudes. Each requires focusing on a different control input: ailerons during spiral recovery, elevator during stall recovery, rudder during spin recovery. This chapter expands on the Power-Push-Roll procedure for spiral recovery introduced in Chapter 5—Curved Flight.

As pointed out earlier, the driving force behind spirals is a rolling moment that continuously overbanks the wings. Spirals are one of a set of attitudes possessing a common trait: excessive bank angles. Improperly executed aerobatic manoeuvres, encounters with wingtip vortices (wake turbulence), and poorly managed turns can propel the airplane into an overbanked attitude. Regardless of the cause, however, recovery depends on efficient use of the ailerons.

A common theme regarding in-flight emergencies and unusual attitudes peppers this book: Don't react with premature elevator inputs, especially those of the **PULL** variety! We've seen how additional back pressure during upright stalls aggravates stall characteristics. Pulling during poorly executed turns only magnifies the rate of descent and increases the g-load. Near inverted, pulling incites a rapid conversion of precious altitude into lots of airspeed.

Most pilots react to their first inverted attitude by hauling back on the elevator control. This natural reflex is ingrained in us. Let's face it, being upside down is not a normal experience; so, the typical response is to withdraw from the situation. Clutching the stick or yoke to keep from falling out of the seat, coupled with the erroneous perception that "pull-equals-up", certainly compound a pilot's propensity to pull when in an unusual attitude.

It takes a conscious effort to modify such involuntary behavior. Our normal reaction must be replaced with instincts and control inputs specific to overbanked attitudes. Our top priority near inverted is to rectify the excessive bank angle, not to overreact to the pitch attitude. We can modify bank angle one of two ways: by rolling—which directly, efficiently controls bank angle, or by pitching (pulling)—which indirectly affects bank angle when moving in the vertical plane (review Chapter 5—Curved Flight).

A roll input offers the shortest route back to wings level. Rolling doesn't increase the g-load either. On the other hand, pulling forces the airplane into a half loop earthward—called a Split-S. Pulling traps us in a Catch-22: the diving half loop rapidly consumes altitude, resulting in a dramatic increase in airspeed, causing the loop's radius to grow exponentially, necessitating higher g's to bend the airplane around in an arc, demanding a progressively harder pull to minimise altitude loss and airspeed build-up.

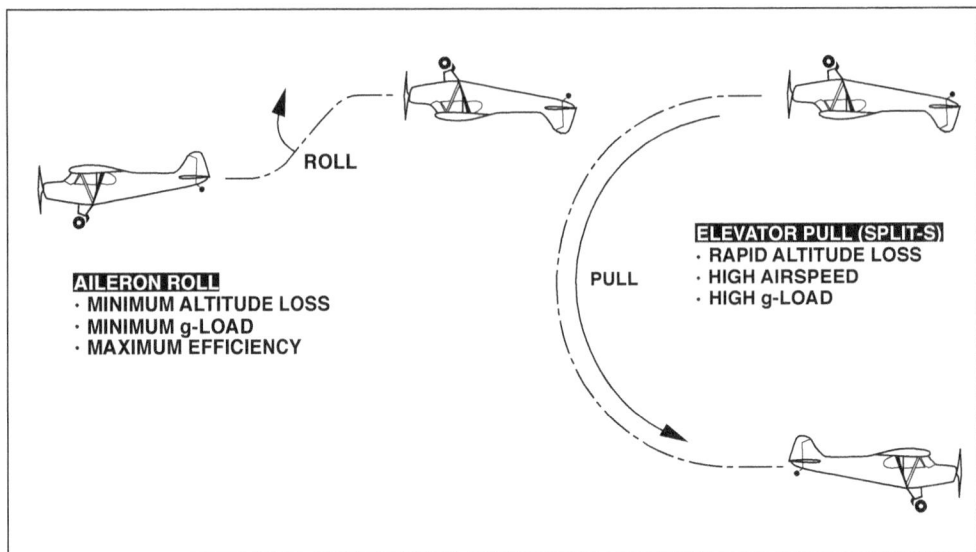

Figure 8-1: Comparing a Roll vs. a Pull Recovery from Inverted

Without a doubt, pulling during an overbanked attitude quickly compounds our problems. Yanking back on the stick or yoke pitches three strikes against the pilot:

Strike One—You could pull the airplane into the ground, especially if starting from low altitude.

Strike Two—The increasing g-load needed to bend the flight path around in a half loop may bend the airplane structure instead. The design limits prescribed by the V-g diagram clearly portray the danger of high g's coupled with high airspeed.

Strike Three—You're out! The magnitude of the g's experienced by a pilot, and the duration of exposure to the g's during a Split-S manoeuvre may facilitate the onset of g-induced loss of consciousness (G-LOC). Even with recent exposure to g's through aerobatic training, pilots can still be susceptible to the physiological effects of high g's during such a manoeuvre.

Aircraft design can also contribute to the Split-S phenomenon. Normal, Utility, and even Acrobatic category airplanes fly at peak efficiency close to level, upright flight. Airfoil shape, the design of the fuel and oil systems, and elevator control authority and trim settings typically favor positive g flight. As bank angle approaches 180 degrees, airplanes display a natural pitching tendency toward the ground, even if the pilot isn't pulling. This pitching moment becomes stronger above the trim speed.

Sustained inverted flight actually requires a push on the elevator control. Inverted flight entails transitioning from a positive angle of attack, positive g, pull-on-the-elevator environment to a negative angle of attack, negative g, push-on-the-elevator environment. A negative angle of attack is needed to generate Lift when upside-down. Pushing points our Lift force skyward so as to offset the airplane's Weight. Forward elevator pressure also retards the rate at which the nose pitches earthward and reduces the positive g-loading. Used properly, slight forward pressure improves roll performance. Although pushing is contrary to our innate reaction, it's a survival reflex that must be learned.

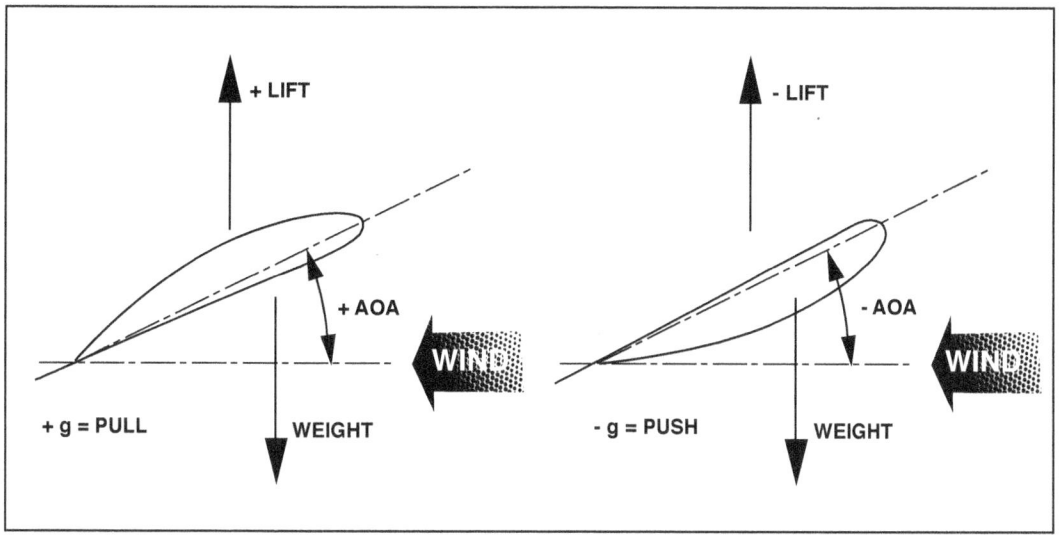

Figure 8-2: Flying an Airfoil Upright and Inverted

Suppressing the urge to pull near inverted, let's analyse the elements of the Power-Push-Roll recovery strategy. Our foremost concern is to return the wings to level, upright flight quickly and efficiently. The emphasis is on aileron inputs. Spirals and inverted attitudes can deteriorate quite rapidly; it's imperative, therefore, to roll to shallower bank angles without hesitation.

Roll Dynamics

The ability of the ailerons to generate rolling moments is our primary focus in the Power-Push-Roll procedure. Unfortunately, most light airplanes display less-than-invigorating roll performance, especially at low airspeeds. Although some aerobatic aircraft are capable of roll rates on the order of 360 degrees per second, the typical light airplane rolls considerably slower and with much effort. Roll rate may drop off to a lethargic 30-40 degrees per second at traffic pattern speeds, even with full aileron. Since optimum roll performance is essential for inverted attitude recovery, let's review the variables influencing an airplane's roll response.

Rate of roll is a function of aileron deflection and airspeed in a given airplane. Lower airspeeds and small aileron deflection yield slower rolls. Higher airspeeds and greater aileron deflection generate faster rolls. Aileron inputs change the shape of the airfoil along the length of the ailerons, altering the local chord of the wing. The upward deflected aileron reduces the local angle of attack, effectively decreasing the local Lift force at angles of attack below critical. On the other side, the downward-deflected aileron increases the local angle of attack; consequently, the local Lift force increases. The unequal Lift forces rapidly accelerate the airplane in roll.

A rolling moment opposite to the direction of roll develops as soon as the aileron input takes effect. The opposing moment brings the airplane to equilibrium (constant roll rate) very quickly. This reaction, known as "damping in roll", stems from subtle changes in the relative wind as the airplane rolls (review Chapter 3—Roll, Yaw, and Pitch).

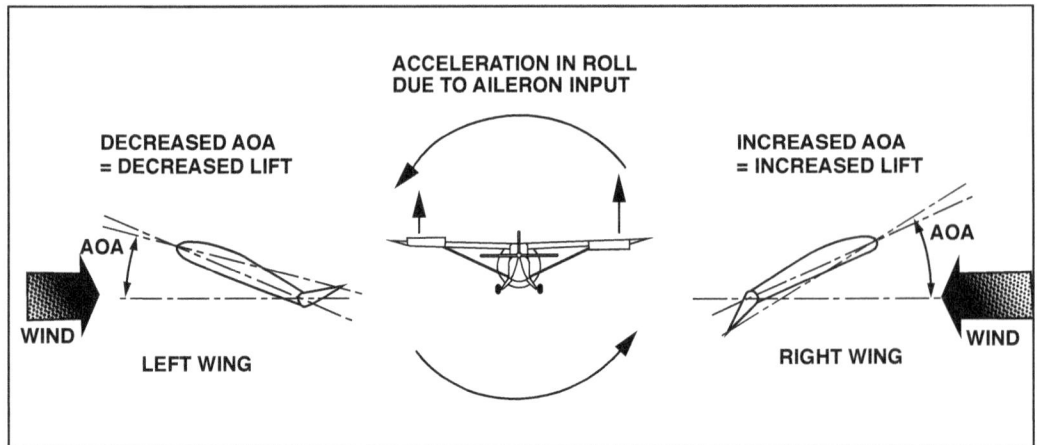

Figure 8-3: Generating Roll Rate by Changing the Local Angle of Attack

The wing descending in roll experiences an upward relative wind component while the ascending wing experiences a downward relative wind component. Combining these components with the relative wind associated with our forward motion results in new relative winds that now meet the left and right wings at different angles of attack. The descending wing operates at a higher angle of attack, therefore generating more Lift. Meanwhile, the ascending wing operates at a lower angle of attack, generating less Lift. Roll rate stabilises as soon as these aerodynamic changes in Lift offset our aileron-induced changes.

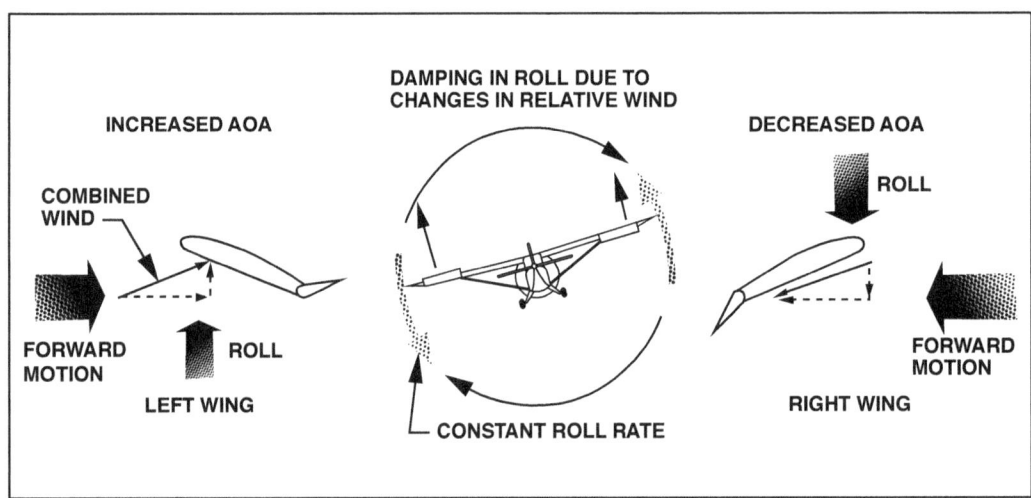

Figure 8-4: Roll Rate Stabilises due to Changes in the Local Relative Wind

The roll actions and reactions just described are predicated on an angle of attack less than critical. Otherwise, as demonstrated in Chapter 6—Stalls, all bets are off. Aileron movements near or above critical angle of attack could result in a roll response that's contrary to our expectation (e.g.: left aileron suddenly causing a right roll). The aileron reversal phenomenon accompanying high angle of attack flight highlights the importance of reducing back elevator pressure prior to rolling. A slight Push on the elevator control lowers the angle of attack, clearing the path for the Roll input.

All other things being equal, longer wings exhibit greater lateral damping than shorter wings. Longer wings have more surface area exposed to the air when rolling, thereby slowing the roll rate. The adverse yaw that accompanies aileron inputs also diminishes roll rate. Adverse yaw produces a dihedral effect that tries to roll the airplane opposite to the aileron input. Left aileron, for example, produces right adverse yaw. Uncorrected, this right yaw induces a small amount of right roll, which impedes the left roll.

The wing's inherent lateral damping effect is beyond our control. However, we can certainly improve roll rate by minimising adverse yaw. The small Push action in the recovery procedure tends to reduce adverse yaw by lowering the wing's angle of attack; thus, less rudder is needed to cancel it. Nevertheless, it's important to apply coordinated aileron and rudder inputs when rolling, as you should whenever making aileron inputs.

Many elements work against us near inverted. We must not exacerbate the situation with timid aileron inputs. Actual experience with inverted attitudes—in a controlled, dual environment—can instill the confidence and discipline necessary to isolate, input, and hold all of the aileron available. Our roll rate, and thus the amount of time it takes to level the wings, rests on the amount of aileron deflection obtained at a given airspeed. Maximum aileron deflection minimises the length of exposure to the overbanked attitude. Since aileron deflection and airspeed determine roll rate, the significance of obtaining full aileron at any speed should be obvious. Full deflection is especially important during a vortex encounter on final approach, where we're low on airspeed and altitude.

V-p & V-g Diagrams

Roll performance is often portrayed on a V-p diagram by plotting roll rate (p) as a function of airspeed (V) for various degrees of aileron deflection. Many light airplanes display marginal roll performance by design, even with full aileron. Striving to deflect the ailerons fully, especially at slow speeds, will help to return the airplane to upright flight in the least amount of time, with the least amount of altitude lost.

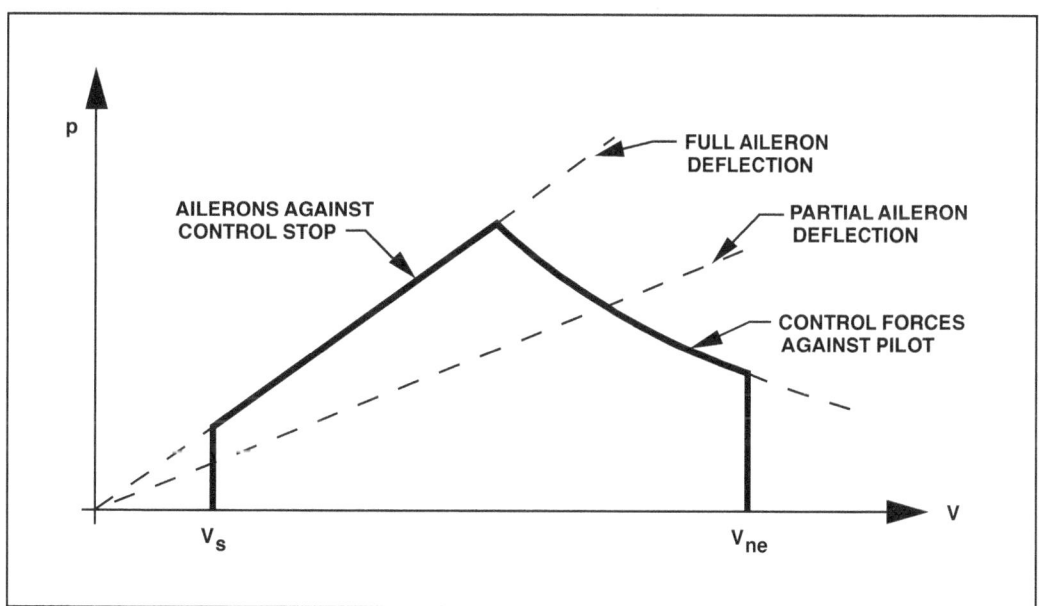

Figure 8-5: The V-p Diagram

As the V-p diagram reveals, rate of roll increases linearly to a maximum point. It then tapers off as aerodynamic pressure on the ailerons becomes too great for pilots of average strength to maintain full deflection. Roll rate becomes a function of the control force exerted against the pilot in high speed flight. Even so, conceding anything less than ailerons-against-the-stops when recovering from spirals, botched turns, vortex encounters, or bungled aerobatic manoeuvre reduces recovery time. Hence, apply and hold as much aileron deflection as physically possible.

Aileron inputs also generate twisting moments on the wing. Deflecting the ailerons at low speeds cannot create torsional loads significant enough to affect the airplane's structural integrity. Aileron inputs at higher speeds, however, can twist the wings sufficiently to cause structural damage, especially if the airplane is experiencing g-load from a simultaneous pull on the elevator control. Such rolling pull-outs compress our V-g operating envelope. In fact, asymmetric loads imposed during a rolling pull-out can reduce limit load factors by as much as thirty-three percent.

A rolling pull-out during Normal category operation, for instance, squashes the design limit load down to just +2.5 g's (+3.8 x 2/3). Under the same conditions, Utility category operation shrinks to +2.9 g's (+4.4 x 2/3); Acrobatic category operation, to +4.0 g's (+6.0 x 2/3). Also, extreme twisting and bending at speeds exceeding Vne can cause aileron reversal (left aileron = right roll, right aileron = left roll), just before the wings depart from the airplane!

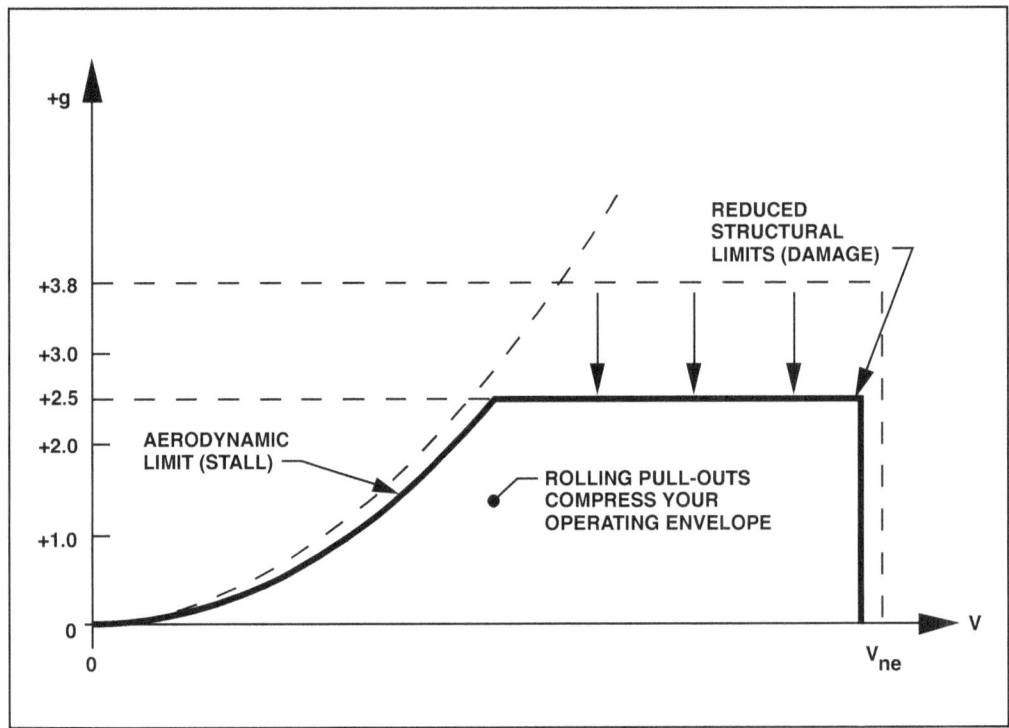

Figure 8-6: Illustrating the Effect of Rolling Pull-Outs on the V-g Diagram

Once again we see how a pull reaction compounds an emergency. Concentrate on pure aileron inputs only; don't contaminate them with a simultaneous pull on the stick or wheel. Errantly applying back pressure when rolling often results in a relaxation of the aileron input as well. Of course, this slows the roll rate and diverts energy away from the primary objective. We must reduce our bank angle **FIRST**, then worry about returning to a level flight attitude. Slightly pushing instead allows the Roll to occur in a lower g environment and ensures a greater margin from structural design limits.

Based on the above points, we can appreciate the utility and efficiency of the Power-Push-Roll procedure. The significance of developing the disciplined reactions and the confidence to cope with spirals and inverted attitudes should be apparent as well. Let's now highlight the different actions prescribed in the Power-Push-Roll procedure:

Power

The Power action for overbanked attitudes isn't a steadfast rule like it is for spin recovery (where power is **ALWAYS** reduced to idle immediately, no ifs, ands, or buts about it). Our throttle response when overbanked depends on a number of factors: altitude, attitude, configuration, and airspeed trend. Since time is not on our side, we should not waste it evaluating what to do with the power once an actual emergency erupts. We need to act, and act fast. In the pattern, for instance, expect to add power; at altitude, expect to reduce it.

Flight around an airport where wake turbulence is a factor, for example, involves these known quantities: low altitude, low airspeed, low power settings, and a dirty configuration (flaps and gear extended). The airplane is low on energy, is close to the ground, and is experiencing high Drag. Adding full power could help to conserve our limited altitude. As part of preflight planning for such operations, review the Power-Push-Roll strategy considering a Power-On reaction.

On the other hand, if flying at altitude performing turns, or perhaps practicing aerobatic manoeuvres, or cruising along an airway frequented by airliners, anticipate reducing the power if you encounter an unplanned, overbanked attitude. Also, reduce the power to idle any time the wind-screen is filled with more ground than sky—like during a steep spiral. If you're uncertain about the attitude, close the throttle. However, don't labor indecisively over this step. Move on and get the airplane upright as quickly as possible, without pulling on the elevator.

Push

The Push input is important for several reasons: it reduces the wing's angle of attack, it reduces the g-load, it counters the earthward pitching tendency of the airplane, and it reduces the adverse yaw effect of the ensuing aileron input. Although some forward elevator movement is necessary, we shouldn't push ourselves through the roof! Nor should we try to return the nose to level, inverted flight. Sustained inverted flight in most airplanes is impractical, if not impossible. The Push input is intended only to freeze the attitude momentarily as the primary Roll input is initiated. Practice in a dual environment is the only way to develop the discipline needed to release back elevator pressure.

The exact amount of forward pressure required depends on the airplane's attitude. Progressively more Push is needed as the airplane approaches inverted flight. Spirals and botched turns generally require merely relaxing back elevator pressure. A fully inverted dive, on the other hand, requires slightly more forward pressure, perhaps briefly placing us in a near-zero g environment. Regardless of the severity of the attitude, a definite change is required in elevator pressure. Avoid reacting with more back pressure. Instead, Push forward a little bit.

As with the Power step, don't waste time exactly positioning the stick or yoke for inverted flight. We need to get rolling. With the back pressure released, we now can make coordinated Roll inputs with minimal danger of an accelerated stall or structural damage. Don't become over zealous with your Push, either; it's a small input. Use the Push as a safeguard against the dangerous pull reaction, then quickly move on. Push and Roll, Push and Roll.

Roll

Achieving a full aileron input is the primary focus of the whole procedure. Get the airplane rolling as soon as possible. To increase the Roll's efficiency, add more and more rudder pressure, in the direction of Roll, as you proceed toward zero angle of bank. Be conscious of any increase in g's as well, which means you're applying back elevator pressure too soon. Stop pulling if necessary, and keep pressing the ailerons against their stops. Don't quit until you're upright again.

Follow the shortest path to upright flight whenever possible. In spirals, defective turns, and blown aerobatic manoeuvres, for example, Roll toward the big blue sky. If the ground fills the wind-screen, reduce Power, Push a little, and get Rolling either way—pronto! In the vicinity of large, heavy aircraft and their accompanying wake turbulence, react with full Roll inputs in the same direction as the vortex roll if the vortex has flipped the airplane nearly inverted. Once you fall prey to these horizontal tornadoes, it may be better to take advantage of their energy to return to upright flight.

Once you've committed full Roll inputs, stick with it. Don't become tentative in mid-stream. Neutralise your aileron and rudder pressures once you've returned to level flight—not before. Reduce the unusual attitude to a straightforward matter of recovering the pitch attitude. Focus on modifying the bank angle first, then worry about pulling to level flight. The appropriate time for back elevator pressure is **AFTER** the airplane is upright again.

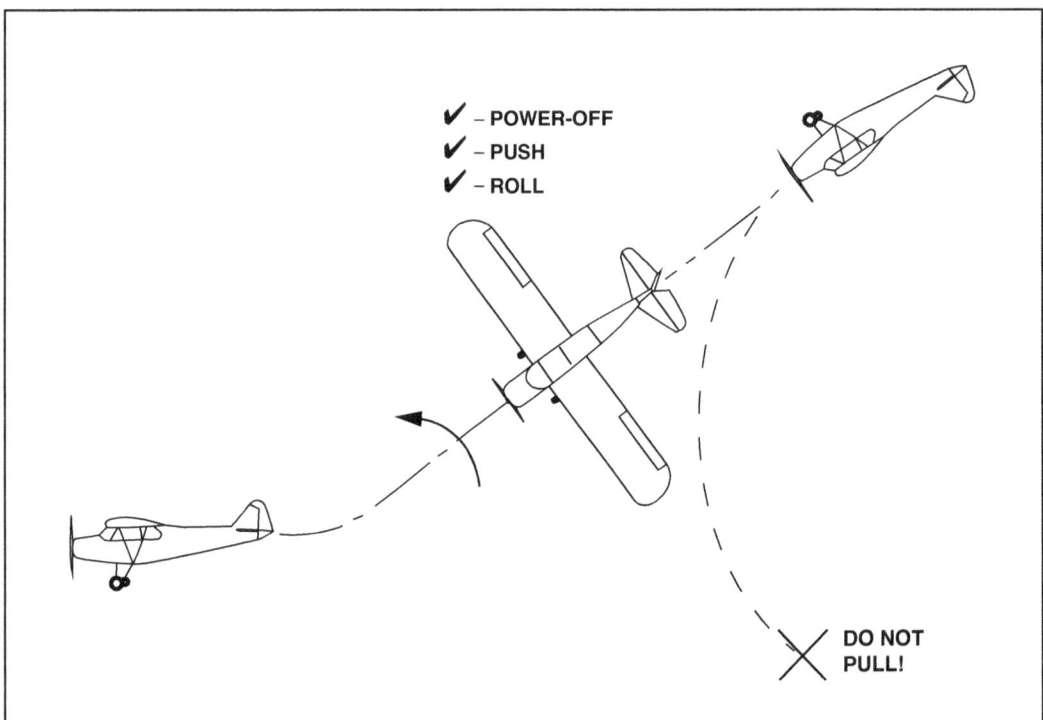

Figure 8-7: Illustrating Power-Push-Roll Actions

Managing The Airspeed

One hazard associated with recoveries from inverted attitudes is the potential for unhealthy increases in airspeed. Spirals and flubbed aerobatic manoeuvres are particularly susceptible to rapid gains in speed as altitude is lost. As in any emergency, prompt corrective actions increase the efficiency of unusual attitude recovery inputs and minimise adverse side effects. Applying the Power-Push-Roll strategy as soon as a steep turn goes astray, or as soon as a manoeuvre decays into an inverted dive, reduces the probability of extreme increases in airspeed.

Don't panic if the airspeed is near or above Vne as you reach upright flight. Maintaining your composure is particularly crucial in this case. The airplane is intolerant of high g's at high airspeeds, as illustrated on the V-g diagram. Don't be shocked into reacting with a sudden pull to bleed off excess airspeed. As long as the airplane is still intact, it doesn't matter what the airspeed indicator reads, or how loud the cockpit becomes—**FLY THE AIRPLANE**. That means go easy—very easy—with your elevator inputs if near red line.

Avoid executing a rolling pull-out as well. Roll **FIRST**, before pulling. This places the airplane's inherent stabilising tendency back in our favor. Once we've rolled upright, the airplane will naturally seek its trim airspeed. Next, establish a level flight attitude with back elevator pressure. At speeds below Va (in the green arc), apply sufficient back pressure to stabilise the attitude without stalling. Between Va and Vne (in the yellow arc), manage the pull to avoid exceeding the design structural limit of the airplane (+3.8 g's in the Normal category—provided you're not rolling at the same time). Near and above Vne (red line), be gentle with your elevator input. Gingerly coax the airplane away from Vne. In fact, slight forward resistance may be required to prevent trim pressure from decelerating the airplane too abruptly, thus imposing unacceptable loads on the airframe.

In The Pattern

Perhaps the least opportune time for an encounter with an inverted attitude is in the traffic pattern. Here, the odds for recovery are stacked against the pilot: we're low on altitude, low on airspeed, marginal on roll authority, high on Drag, and high on pilot work load. Even though dealing with an inverted attitude will be formidable under these conditions, a little advanced planning and heads-up flying in the pattern can avert the need to implement Power-Push-Roll actions. The best method for coping with in-flight emergencies is to heed the warning signs preceding an all-out emergency. Avoidance, after all, is the most powerful strategy at our disposal.

The rest of this chapter addresses wake turbulence avoidance in the traffic pattern. Regardless of requests received from air traffic control (ATC), or whether you've been cautioned about this potential menace or not, the responsibility is yours—and yours alone—to steer well clear of wake turbulence. The *Flight Training Handbook* and the *Airman's Information Manual* (AIM) are explicitly clear on this particular point:

"Whether or not a warning has been given, however, THE PILOT IS EXPECTED TO ADJUST THE FLIGHT-PATH AS NECESSARY TO AVOID WAKE ENCOUNTERS.*"—Flight Training Handbook, AC 61-21A, p. 79.*

"Pilots are reminded that in operations conducted behind all aircraft, acceptance of instructions from ATC ... is an acknowledgment that the pilot will ensure safe takeoff and landing intervals and accepts the responsibility of providing his own wake turbulence separation."—Airman's Information Manual, Chapter 7., Section 3., Paragraph 7-57.c. This same wording also appears in Advisory Circular 90-23E, "Wake Turbulence Avoidance", p. 15.

Moreover, the last statement appearing at the end of AIM Section 3 reiterates Federal Aviation Regulation Section 91.3, Responsibility and authority of the pilot in command:

NOTE—FAR 91.3(a) states: 'The pilot in command of an aircraft is directly responsible for and is the final authority as to the operation of that aircraft.'

So, do whatever **YOU** feel is necessary to evade another airplane's wake, no matter what ATC tells you, or doesn't tell you to do. Your safety is at stake. To formulate guidelines that minimise the risk of wake turbulence encounters, it's important to understand the nature of this beast, and to respect its power.

Invisible Tornadoes

Just like a boat moving through water, an airplane upsets the air as it passes through it. Consequently, air is left tumbling and churning in the wake behind a moving airplane. The strongest component of this wake turbulence is a vortex left over from the lifting process. In essence, higher pressure air on the bottom of the wing tries to flow toward the lower pressure on top of the wing (Chapter 2—Basic Aerodynamics). Air trying to curl around the wingtip is swept aft by the local relative wind flowing past the wing.

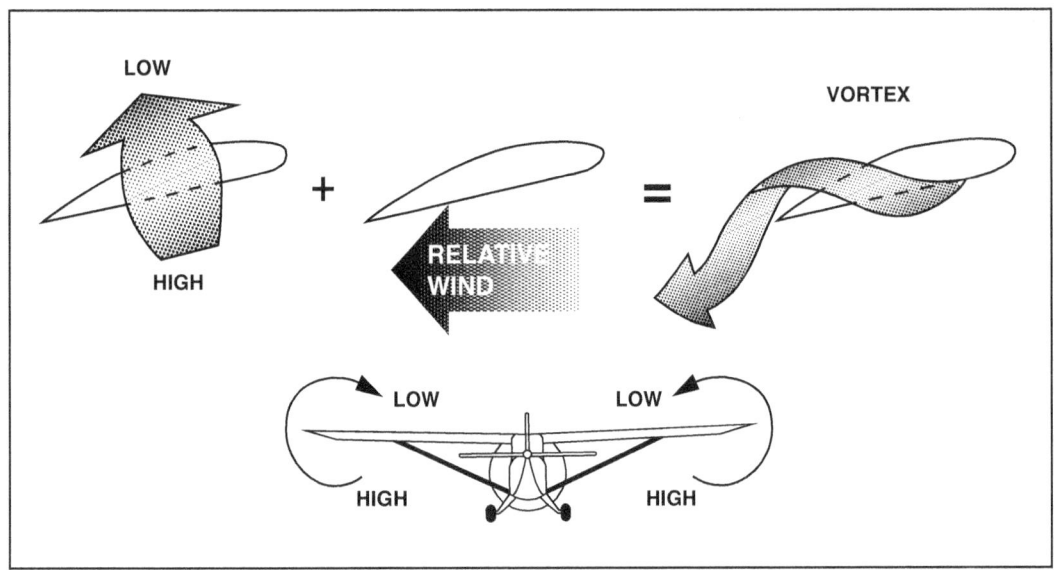

Figure 8-8: Generating Wingtip Vortices

A corkscrew of swirling wind evolves approximately 2 to 4 wingspans downstream, centered near the 80 percent point of the wing span. Viewed from behind, the left wing generates a clockwise vortex; the right wing, a counterclockwise vortex. Sheets of air sliding off the trailing edge tend to flow downward and outward as well, eventually rolling up into the vortex trail.

Vortices are by-products of wings producing Lift. Energy expended generating vortices reduces the efficiency of our wing and diminishes its lifting ability. Vortices are, therefore, a physical manifestation of Induced Drag. Their strength is related to the magnitude of the Drag induced when manipulating Lift.

With all other variables equal, Induced Drag varies as a function of the square of aircraft Weight [$D2/D1 = (W2/W1)^2$]. Doubling the Weight, for example, increases the Induced Drag fourfold. Also, hitting your own vortex at the end of a 360 degree turn with 45 degrees of bank "thumps" the airplane harder than after a 360 degree turn with only 10 degrees of bank. A 45 degree bank requires +1.41 g's for steady flight, whereas a 10 degree bank requires only +1.02 g's. The increased g-load—a 38 percent increase in effective Weight—almost doubles the Induced Drag. The resulting vortices gain strength, too.

With Weight constant, Induced Drag varies inversely as the square of the airspeed [$D2/D1 = (V1/V2)^2$]. Slowing down from a cruise speed of 140 mph to 70 mph in the traffic pattern quadruples the Induced Drag. Therefore, wingtip vortices will definitely pack more energy at slower airspeeds. Now roll into a 45 degree bank at 70 mph and load the wings with +1.41 g's for a level turn. The added Weight component, which almost doubles Induced Drag by itself, compounds the increased Drag associated with the lower airspeed. As a result, Induced Drag is amplified nearly **EIGHT TIMES** compared to level flight at 140 mph.

Aircraft Configuration Effects

Flight operations around an airport can spawn strong vortices. The relative strength of these swirling air masses is affected by wing shape, angle of attack, weight, airspeed, and configuration. Slow, heavy aircraft tend to shed more potent vortices, especially in the clean configuration (gear and flaps up). Although vortices can still be quite strong with the flaps deployed, secondary vortices spun off at the edges of the flaps can weaken the primary vortices. Exhaust from wing-mounted engines can weaken vortices, too. Unfortunately, warm exhaust temperatures may also buoy the vortices up.

Once formed, vortex trails generally force each other downward and behind the generating aircraft, often descending 150-350 feet per minute. Settling near the ground, they tend to move outward, away from each other. The downwash area between vortices can descend at 600 to 1,400 feet per minute—often exceeding the climb capability of the typical, light airplane. Tangential velocities near the vortex core can surpass 200 miles per hour.

Although rotational energy does decay with time, vortices retain most of their energy up to the very end. If the airplane enters a vortex trail at a right angle, it could experience sudden, rapid changes in pitch and g-load. Structural damage is possible, especially if the pilot tries to compensate by over-controlling the elevator. If the airplane flies parallel into the vortex trail, one of two reactions is possible: near the vortex core, the airplane may roll sharply; in the downwash area between vortex cores, the airplane may become trapped in an uncontrolled descent.

Atmospheric Effects

Vortices are influenced by such atmospheric conditions as air density, temperature, turbulence, and wind. The lower air densities associated with higher altitudes, for example, offer less resistance against vortex rotation; consequently, vortices tend to endure longer. Vortex strength and longevity also tends to be strongly dependent upon temperature gradient (the rate of temperature change in the atmosphere).

As a vortex loses altitude, the surrounding atmospheric pressure increases. The mounting pressure compresses the vortex, causing its temperature to rise. As the vortex warms up, it becomes more buoyant and its rate of descent slows. It may eventually level off at a constant altitude, churning in place until its energy dissipates. Temperature inversions tend to impede vortex movement downward and tend to hasten the vortex's demise. Turbulence also helps to break up vortices quicker.

Wind affects vortex movement, too. Crosswinds can push vortices trailing from aircraft on intersecting or parallel runways onto the runway you're using. Light winds, especially light cross winds, can cause vortices to linger close to the runway. Light quartering tailwinds can cause vortex trails to drift farther down the runway. Therefore, awareness of surface winds is important. Monitor ATIS for wind direction and strength, and make it a habit to look at airport wind indicators before taking off and landing. Additionally, we must remain acutely aware of the type of traffic operating directly ahead of us, including traffic using parallel and intersecting runways.

Even ground effect can influence vortex behavior. In fact, vortices generated in ground effect, or those descending into it, have been observed to rebound skyward as high as twice the generating aircraft's wing span. It's possible, then, for vortices to exist **ABOVE** the generating aircraft's flight path near the ground.

When significant size, weight, and speed discrepancies are anticipated between aircraft in the pattern, lighter aircraft are always at a disadvantage against the invisible rotational energy discharged by heavier traffic. Covering all the permutations of possible vortex encounters is cumbersome, and often leads to confusion. Instead, applying a simple spacing formula—**SEPARATION + ELEVATION**—can minimise the risk of a confrontation with wake turbulence.

Separation

Since vortex strength declines over time, give yourself plenty of room behind large aircraft. This way, you'll be dealing with relatively looser, weaker masses of rotating air, instead of the tighter, higher energy tornadoes spun off close behind the generating aircraft.

Wherever possible, position yourself on the upwind side of heavier traffic. This action takes advantage of wind effects that tend to retard vortex movement in your direction. Placing yourself upwind essentially increases your Separation. Use time, distance, and wind effects to your advantage. If you choose to skimp on Separation, however, you better have an abundance of the other key ingredient.

Elevation

Based on the general movements of vortex trails, it's always best to keep your flight path above the flight paths of heavy traffic ahead of you. Simply don't permit your paths to cross. And, without exception, don't get caught in the airspace below the flight path of heavy traffic, as this may be the sovereign domain of some serious vortices.

Imagine the flight paths of heavy traffic in front of, or parallel to you to be hard boundaries, impenetrable. Note the touchdown and rotation points of heavy aircraft ahead of you as well. These points help to define zones of minimum and maximum vortex risk. Of course, we want to operate in zones of minimum risk, using the Separation-plus-Elevation formula adjusted for wind effects.

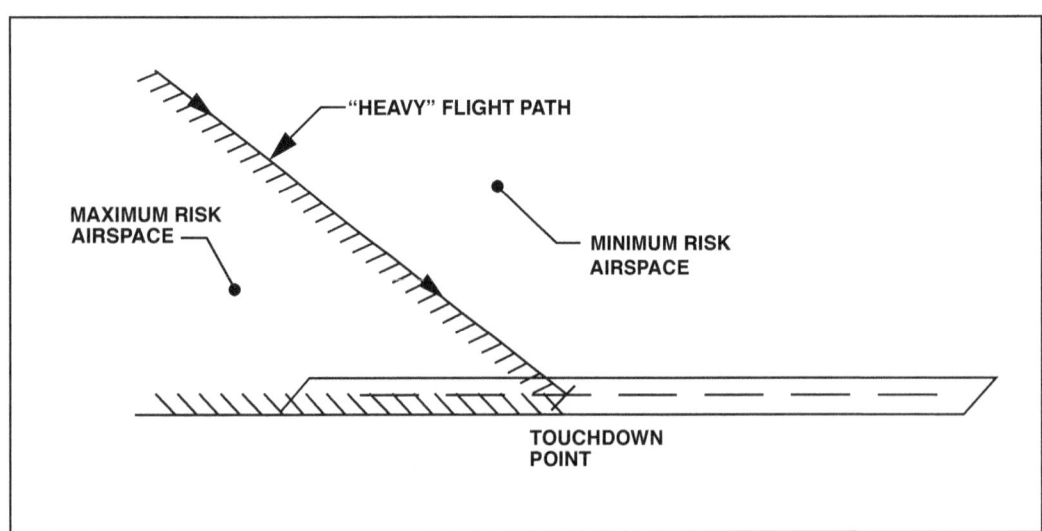

Figure 8-9: Assessing Vortex Risk—"Heavy" Traffic Landing

For instance, you have two options when landing behind heavy traffic that is also landing: either go around (Separation), or remain above the heavy's flight path and land beyond its point of touchdown (Elevation). You have two options if you're taking off: either wait for the heavy's vortices to dissipate (Separation), or rotate beyond its point of touchdown (Elevation). Visualise your minimum risk envelope and fly within it.

Similar options are available when landing behind heavy traffic that is taking off: either go around, staying above the heavy's flight path (Separation-plus-Elevation); or land well before its point of rotation (Separation). If you're departing also, your options include waiting (Separation), or rotating well before the heavy's point of rotation and remaining above its flight path (Separation-plus-Elevation).

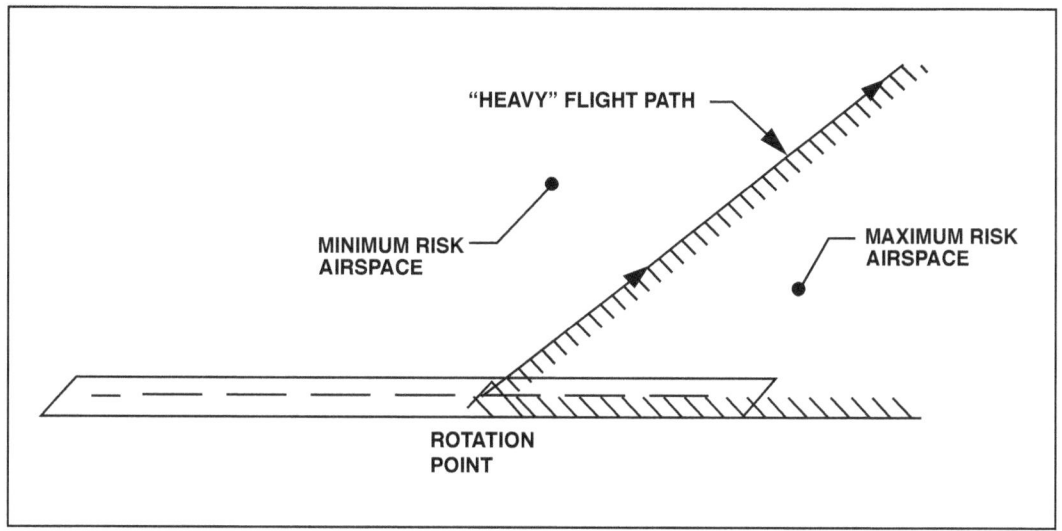

Figure 8-10: Assessing Vortex Risk—"Heavy" Traffic Taking Off

When heavier traffic is performing touch-and-go's, touchdown and rotation points occur on the runway within a relatively short time interval. This scenario reduces our minimum risk area, especially near the runway. Emphasising Separation in this case allows more time for vortices to dissipate. Greater Separation effectively expands our minimum risk envelope.

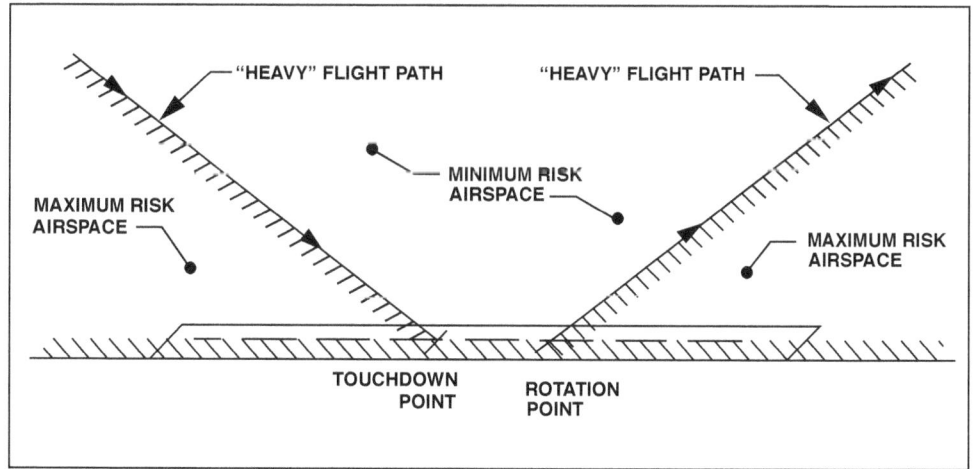

Figure 8-11: Assessing Vortex Risk—"Heavy" Traffic Executing a Touch-and-Go

Proceed with extreme caution if the heavy traffic executes a go-around or a missed approach. The entire runway may be under a blanket of maximum risk airspace; so, be patient. If you're on the ground holding short, wait it out. If you're on final behind heavy traffic, consider going around, too, while you're still above the heavy's flight path. And displace your airplane to the upwind side whenever possible.

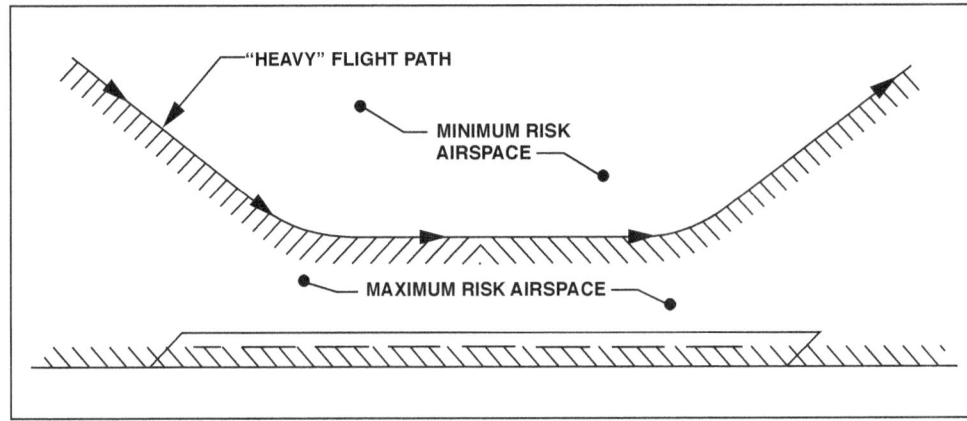

Figure 8-12: Assessing Vortex Risk—"Heavy" Traffic Executing a Missed Approach

Fly defensively to maintain a healthy balance between Separation and Elevation. If it appears that your flight path will cross the path of conflicting, heavy traffic, take immediate evasive action. Execute go-around procedures, or abort your takeoff roll, or exercise your right to hold short for as long as you deem prudent. It's far better to let the Hobbs meter turn another digit or two during an extra trip around the pattern, or to sit firmly planted on the ground waiting for the air to clear, than it is to wrestle with a tornado.

Be Prepared

Planning ahead can minimise your exposure to the hazards of wingtip vortices. Wake turbulence avoidance begins when you decide to mix your small airplane with larger, heavier traffic. Reviewing avoidance procedures before the flight even begins and remaining situationally aware in the pattern will reduce the probability of an inadvertent vortex encounter. They'll also minimise the element of surprise should a vortex flip your aircraft onto its back.

Unlike the mechanical, step-by-step process required for spin recovery, overbanked attitudes demand dynamic interaction between pilot and airplane throughout the recovery process. We must react instinctively if the airplane rolls inverted, especially near the ground. Investing a small amount of time reviewing avoidance and recovery strategies beforehand helps to minimise delayed reaction time. In the pattern, Separation-plus-Elevation is our first line of defense against wake turbulence. Failing that, we have Power-Push-Roll actions. Of course, precautions taken to avoid an emergency are far more effective, and thus less stressful, than actions taken to recover from a full-blown, unusual attitude. It's also a good idea to secure loose objects and tighten your seat belt an extra notch in the pattern.

Too many variables are stacked against an inverted airplane close to the ground. No amount of aerobatic training can ensure a flawless roll upright to a perfect landing after tangling with a vortex. The airplane will probably contact the ground prematurely. Even so, Power-Push-Roll actions are our only hope. Rolling moves the airplane toward the landing attitude, thus improving our chances of surviving the impact (crash survivability is maximised when contacting the ground wheels-first; it's near zero when contacting the ground canopy-first). Consider rolling with the vortex energy if the bank is already near inverted.

Whether you find yourself in a spiral, falling out of an aerobatic manoeuvre inverted, or caught in a wingtip vortex, address the excessive bank angle first—without pulling prematurely on the elevator control! Implementing emergency procedures demands presence of mind and discipline with your inputs. Airspeed, altitude, and structural design safety factors dissolve quickly as spirals and inverted attitudes progress. React with Power-Push-Roll, focusing on positive aileron deflection until the wings reach zero angle of bank. The next chapter also draws on elements of the Power-Push-Roll procedure to manage various in-flight control failures.

9

Control Failures

As we've emphasised throughout this book, successfully coping with an emergency depends on preparedness, early recognition, and prompt, positive action. Emergency procedures are more effective the earlier we perceive a potential problem and take corrective steps. This chapter reviews various control failure scenarios that may hinder our ability to control an airplane. Some of the tools we'll use to contend with these failures include the Power-Push-Roll strategy studied in the last chapter, as well as slips and slipping turns.

Our first course of action, regardless of the emergency, is always to **FLY THE AIRPLANE**. Whenever control unexpectedly becomes limited, restrict your operating envelope to a narrow, closely monitored window. In other words, avoid making large inputs once you've regained control over the situation. Don't allow gross deviations to occur before acknowledging that you have a problem, either. Always have a bank angle, pitch attitude, and heading in mind before executing a manoeuvre. Should the airplane wander beyond the parameters you've consciously (or subconsciously) defined, immediately abort the manoeuvre and address the problem. Pay attention, and respond as soon as you sense trouble.

Control failures, although rare, are usually manageable if corrective actions are initiated before the airplane progresses into an unusual attitude. Unfortunately, warning signs may not precede a control problem. The first hint of a problem may come while right in the middle of a critical manoeuvre, like a base-to-final turn. It's important, therefore, for the pilot to identify the nature of the problem quickly and to apply appropriate counter measures. Let's map out some strategies for dealing with various control failures.

Ailerons

During aileron control failures, we must enlist the secondary roll effects associated with rudder inputs to counter roll forces (review Chapter 3—Roll, Yaw, and Pitch). It's also best to limit subsequent bank angles to less than 15 degrees, since shallower banks will minimise yaw arising from our rudder inputs. For example, small, controlled rudder movements could be used to bank or level the wings if the ailerons fail in the neutral position. (Asymmetric use of power in twin engine airplanes could help to control the bank, too.)

If the ailerons should jam in a deflected position, apply the rudder opposite to the direction of roll. Avoid being overly aggressive with your corrective input, however. Instead, smoothly step skyward, using just enough rudder to transition into a slip. Remember that your heading (where the nose points) will be different from your track (where the airplane actually goes) when slipping. Keep the desired flight path somewhere between the nose and the low wing by continuously adjusting the amount of rudder used. Perform slipping turns in the direction of the low wing to change your direction of flight. To turn, relax some of your rudder pressure while applying easy back elevator pressure. To stop turning, relax the elevator pressure and re-apply some rudder pressure to stabilise the slip.

Imagine, for instance, initiating a right turn with 30 degrees of bank. Assume the airplane continues rolling beyond 30 degrees, with the aileron control suddenly frozen in place. **DO NOT PULL** on the elevator control. Instead, recall the Power-Push-Roll procedure. Reduce power if appropriate and relax back elevator pressure to lower the angle of attack. In this case, rudder inputs are used to neutralise the roll stemming from the jammed aileron. Feed in enough left rudder—step toward the sky—to establish a stabilised slip. Don't let the nose pitch up above the horizon during the process.

Once the airplane is under control again, we can attempt to free the ailerons. A momentary flick of the aileron control in the same direction as the low wing may dislodge a foreign object. If aileron control cannot be regained, make preparations to land in a slip. Review your flight manual for recommendations concerning the use of flaps during slips. In some airplanes, extending flaps when slipping can disrupt airflow over the tail section, resulting in loss of elevator and rudder control authority. Determine the maximum degree of flaps allowed, as well as the corresponding approach speed.

Landing in a slip may result in the loss of directional control; nevertheless, fly the airplane all the way to touchdown. Don't give up your control over the airplane. Try to land as slowly as possible, as close to the normal landing attitude as possible. This will reduce the probability of serious injury. If a crosswind runway is available, use the wind against your slip. Let someone know about your predicament, too. All turns will be slipping turns in the direction of the low wing only. A 270 degree slipping turn to the right, for instance, will eventually end up in the same place as a 90 degree, left turn.

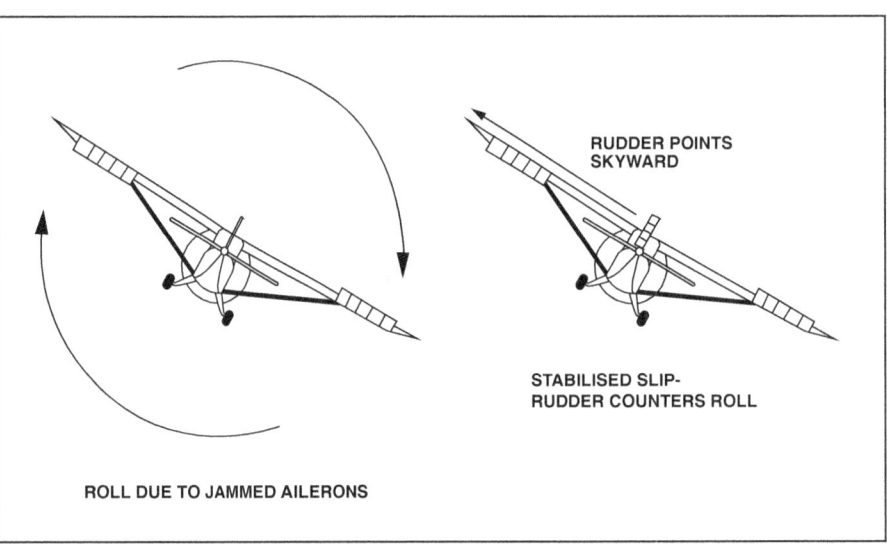

Figure 9-1: Using Slip Inputs to Counter Jammed Ailerons

Rudder

Rudder problems have the potential to be more serious than aileron failures since yaw control, and therefore spin prevention, is compromised. In this situation, we cannot allow large excesses of yaw to develop. Should the rudder fail in the neutral position, for example, avoid maximum performance climbing turns. Make smooth power changes and small, controlled aileron inputs. Restrict your operating envelope to no more than 15 degrees of bank and 10-15 degrees of pitch. Realise that any excess yaw can excite a spin near critical angle of attack, so strive to keep yaw to a minimum.

If the rudder ever jams in a deflected position, apply opposite aileron to transition into a slip. You'll be rolling the deflected rudder skyward in the process. As with any control problem, don't waste time fighting with the rudder. And don't be lured into pulling on the elevator control prematurely; otherwise, you might pull the airplane into the skid/spin discussed in Chapter 6—Stalls. The order in which we apply aileron and elevator inputs can be the difference between an unusual attitude and a controlled slip.

It's critical to roll at a low angle of attack, regardless of the pitch attitude. Transition into the slip with Power-Push-Roll actions. Adjust the throttle if needed, relax your back elevator pressure, and use the ailerons to counteract the yaw/roll couple caused by the deflected rudder. Once the slip is stabilised, use slipping turns to change your direction of flight. Always perform slipping turns toward the low wing by adding more aileron pressure and applying easy back elevator pressure. Stop the turn by relaxing the additional elevator and aileron pressures, but remain in the slip.

To illustrate the correct response to a jammed rudder, imagine starting a right turn with 30 degrees of bank. Assume the airplane continues to yaw and roll, skidding beyond 30 degrees. The rudder is now frozen in place as the nose slices through the horizon. **DO NOT PULL** on the elevator! Instead, move the elevator forward a little, relaxing your back pressure. Smoothly apply left aileron. Roll the right wing, and the jammed right rudder, skyward. Don't stop until the right wing points to the sky. Recover the pitch attitude only after the slip is established.

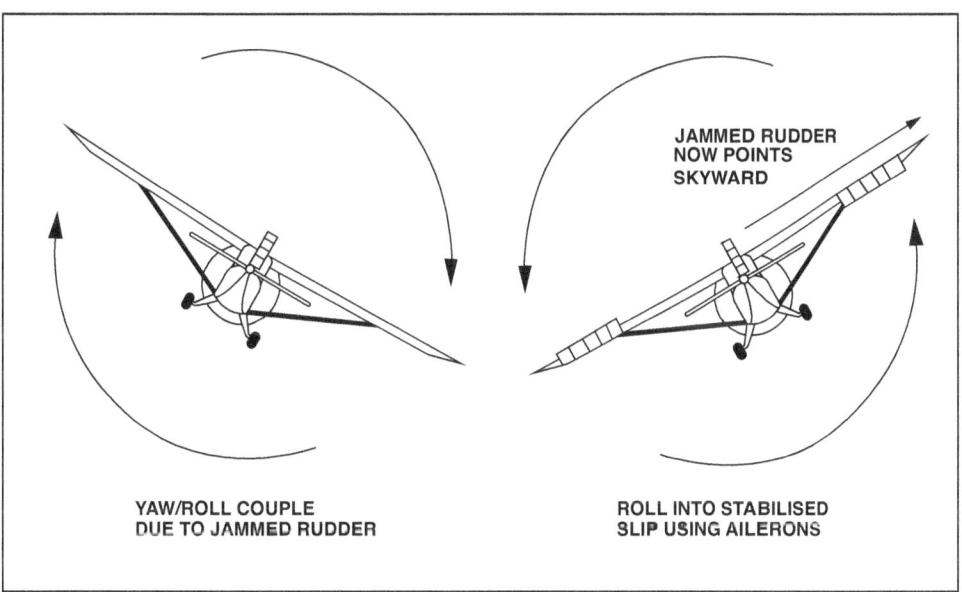

Figure 9-2: Using Slip Inputs to Counter a Jammed Rudder

Once the airplane is under control, try a quick jab in the direction of the stuck rudder. If this doesn't free it, plan to land in a slip. The same rules apply as when landing in a slip with jammed ailerons: discern the proper flap setting and corresponding airspeed to use in the slip, fly the airplane all the way to touchdown, land as slowly and as close to the normal landing attitude as possible, and use available crosswinds to your advantage. Keep excessive yawing to a minimum in the traffic pattern. If you must execute a go-around, apply power smoothly and maintain control over the slip.

Elevator

Since elevator position ultimately determines how the airplane contacts the ground, elevator control failures can be the most serious of the primary control surfaces. We can make use of the secondary pitch effects associated with power changes, elevator trim tab setting, and center of gravity location to counter such problems. As we saw earlier, we tackle the root of the problem only **AFTER** regaining positive control of the airplane, not on the way to an unusual attitude.

The combined effect of adding power and shifting passengers and baggage aft tends to raise the nose in the typical, single engine airplane. Reducing power and shifting passengers and baggage forward tends to lower the nose. As long as the elevator control problem doesn't interfere with the elevator trim system, trim may offer an effective means of secondary pitch control, too. A design criterion for modern light singles is that they be landable without the use of the primary pitch control. Power and elevator trim combined must be effective enough to control the airplane through touchdown.

For example, if an elevator cable snaps, but the elevator is still able to float with the relative wind, elevator trim should work in the normal sense. Deflecting the trim surface should move the elevator into the appropriate position: "nose up" trim yields nose up, "nose down" trim yields nose down. On the other hand, if the elevator is jammed in a particular position and the trim is hinged to its trailing edge, the trim tab itself becomes your elevator. The tab, however, moves opposite to the elevator's intended direction of movement; hence, expect the airplane now to respond in reverse: "nose down" trim should raise the nose, "nose up" trim should lower the nose.

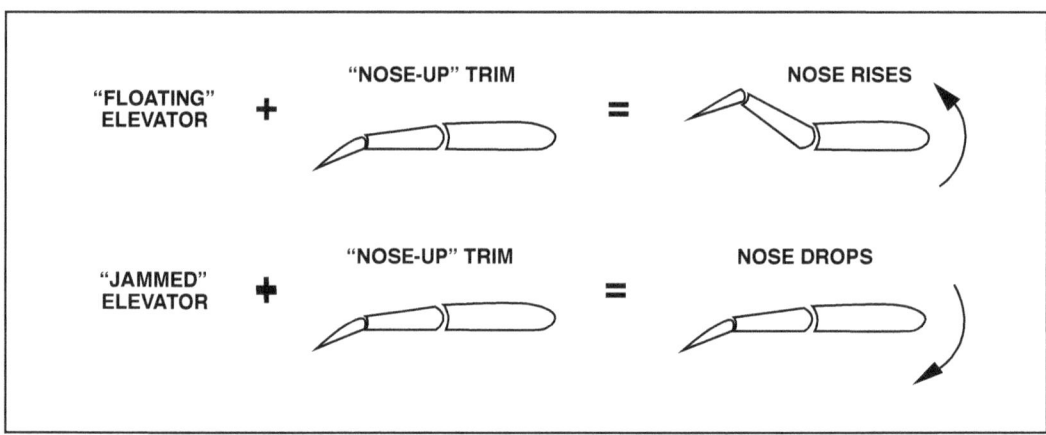

Figure 9-3: Using Trim as the Pitch Control when Experiencing Elevator Problems

If the elevator jams in a nose-up position, reduce power, try adjusting the trim "nose-up", and shift passengers and baggage forward to lower the nose. Since the gyroscopic properties of a clockwise-rotating propeller (review Chapter 3—Roll, Yaw, and Pitch) may also help to lower the nose in some single engine airplanes, try introducing a small amount of right yaw. Do this by placing the airplane into a right rudder/left aileron slip. Smoothly add power, re-adjust the trim, or reduce the amount of slip if you need to raise the nose.

Attempt to unjam the elevator control by briefly applying some back elevator pressure. If you cannot free it, a short field landing technique will be required. Use power to control rate of descent as well as pitch attitude. Fly the airplane all the way to touchdown, striking a balance between a safe airspeed and a low rate of descent. Also, ground effect creates a nose-down pitching tendency, so expect the nose to drop during the flare. Use small power changes to cushion the landing.

Should the elevator fail in a nose-down position, add power, try adjusting the trim "nose-down", and shift passengers and baggage aft to raise the nose. Gyroscopic effects may be of assistance here as well. Placing the airplane in a shallow, left rudder/right aileron slip may help to raise the nose. Smoothly reduce power, re-adjust the trim, or reduce the amount of slip if you need to lower the nose.

Opening the throttle while descending may seem contrary to your natural instinct. Recall, however, that adding power tends to raise the nose, thus shallowing the descent. As we saw in Chapter 4—Pitch and Power, power also permits more airspeed to be gained per foot of altitude lost. Power converts fuel into airspeed, ultimately conserving altitude. An increase in airspeed also increases the downwash on a conventional tail configuration, which may contribute to raising the nose.

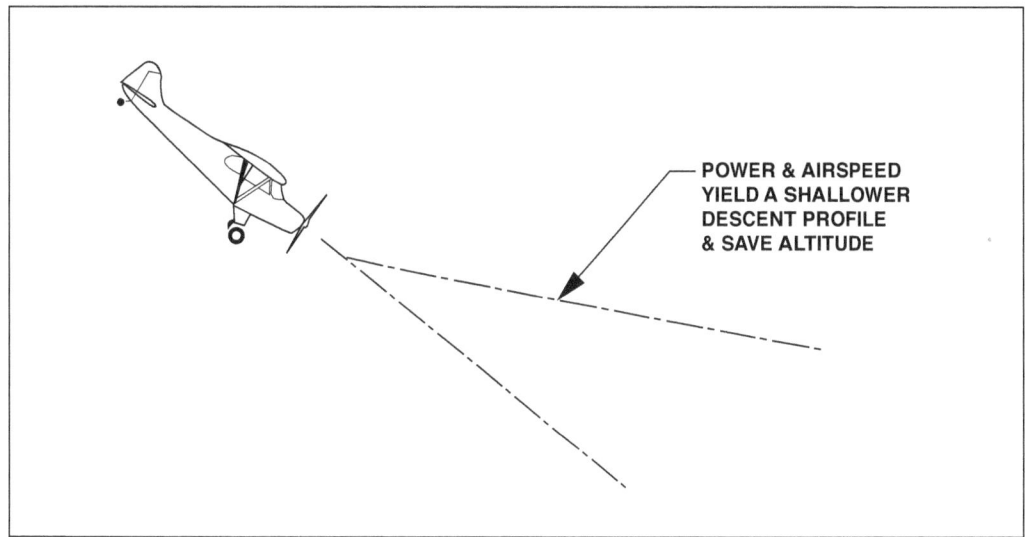

Figure 9-4: Using Power to Control Pitch when Experiencing Elevator Problems

If the combination of these secondary pitch effects cannot return the airplane to level flight, maintain the shallowest descent profile at the slowest possible airspeed. Adjust the throttle as necessary. Try to free the elevator control by momentarily applying forward elevator pressure. Otherwise, prepare for an extended approach to a long runway, or some other nearby landing site. You may need plenty of room to dissipate excess airspeed. Also, expect ground effect to pitch the nose down even farther.

An extreme nose-down elevator failure could present quite a precarious dilemma. If a shallower pitch attitude cannot be attained, the airplane will hit the ground fast, in a steep, nose low attitude. A half roll to an inverted crash landing, contacting the ground tail first, **MAY** offer slightly better odds for survival instead; only the pilot-in-command can determine if this is a viable course of action. Here's an ideal situation in which to exit the airplane if you have a parachute on board. Fortunately, such an extreme scenario isn't likely in the normal flight environment.

Should an elevator cable break, leaving pitch control in one direction only, adjust the trim tab in the opposite direction. Pitch is then controlled by relaxing elevator pressure in one direction and applying heavier elevator pressure in the other. For instance, assume the "down" elevator cable snaps. Trim the airplane nose-down. You'll need to hold back elevator pressure to maintain level flight. Relaxing your control pressure allows the trim setting to lower the nose. Applying more back pressure, against the nose-down trim pressure, raises the nose.

Flaps

Flap problems come in three varieties: they can fail to deploy, they can fail to retract, or they can move asymmetrically, which is called a split flap. First, be wary of flap position indicators. Adopt the practice of visually monitoring flap movements whenever possible. Also, deploy and retract flaps incrementally, especially during go-arounds. Incremental flap inputs reduce the magnitude of pitch changes induced by flap movements. They also prevent a sudden settling of the airplane during an aborted landing and they will limit the degree of asymmetry should a split flap occur.

As part of preflight planning, consider how you'll respond, and to what airport you'll divert, should you experience flap problems. Determine the maximum degree of flaps you'll extend given the conditions at your destination. The decision is easier if you assume the flaps will be locked in place once set. Depending on airplane weight, engine horsepower, density altitude, and obstacles, climb performance with full flaps could be marginal, or even nonexistent. If you don't think your airplane can hobble around the pattern at a high airport, on a hot day, with 40 degrees of flaps dangling from the wings, consider 30 degrees, or 20 degrees, or no flaps. And don't forget to review the corresponding approach speed for the intended flap setting.

Flaps that fail to deploy simply require the use of the airplane's no-flap landing procedure, which includes a higher approach speed and a longer landing roll-out. If runways at your destination aren't long enough to accommodate a no-flap landing, divert to a suitable alternate.

The least opportune time for flap retraction problems would be during a go-around. During certification, Normal, Utility, and Acrobatic category airplanes demonstrated a nominal 2 degree climb angle during go-arounds at sea level, with takeoff power applied, full flaps deployed, and the gear extended. Although a high-time rental airplane with an oil-coated belly may be hard pressed to duplicate such factory-new performance on a hot day, it's likely that it'll be able to at least arrest the descent under most circumstances. Smoothly add power while pitching for airspeed. Maintaining control over the airplane, begin retracting the flaps one notch at a time. Should they not respond at any stage, fly the pattern at or below the recommended flap extension speed, Vfe. Fly the next approach at the airspeed corresponding to the current flap setting. If you cannot see the flaps, or cannot tell how far they're deployed, use the recommended speed assuming the least amount of flaps.

A split flap occurs when only one flap deploys or retracts, leaving the left and right flaps at different settings. Aerodynamically, the net effect is similar to a depressed aileron: The wing with the **LOWER** flap experiences a greater local angle of attack. The increase in local angle of attack generates more Lift and more Drag compared to the opposite wing, resulting in roll and yaw moments that could lead to an overbanked attitude or a spin if left uncorrected.

Flap-induced roll and yaw rates increase as the degree of flap asymmetry increases. Again, incremental inputs will minimise the difference between the two flaps. The airplane will roll away from the lower flap; it will yaw, however, toward the lower flap. This action is identical to the roll and adverse yaw motions associated with a downward-deflected aileron.

React with Power-Push-Roll once again. Focus on smoothly applying ailerons opposite to the roll and rudder opposite to the yaw. Use the same cross-controlled inputs as in a slip, but don't be overzealous with your corrective actions. And don't yank on the elevator control! Apply sufficient aileron and rudder to counter the split flap-induced movements. Using asymmetric power in twins may help, too. Try neutralising the asymmetry by reversing your previous flap input. If this works, fly your next approach at the airspeed corresponding to the given flap setting.

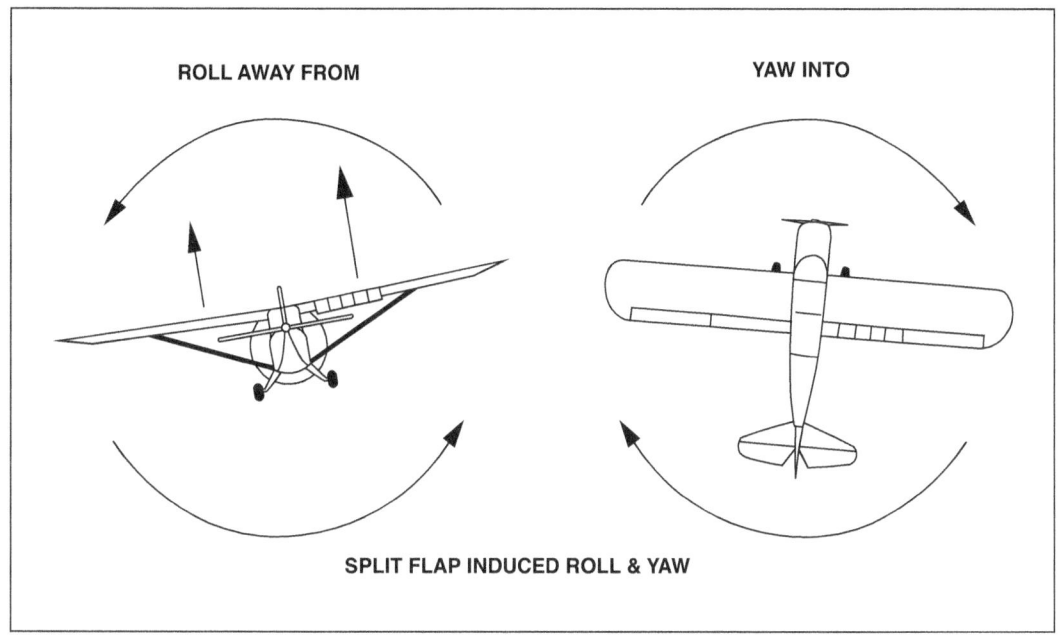

Figure 9-5: Airplane's Reaction to a Split Flap on the Right

If you cannot equalise the flaps, fly the approach at the airspeed recommended for the least deployed flap. For example, suppose one flap is jammed at 10 degrees; the other, at 30 degrees. The wing with 10 degrees of deflection will stall at a higher airspeed than the wing with 30 degrees of flaps. Therefore on final approach, use the airspeed listed for a flap setting of 10 degrees.

WEIGHT (LBS)	FLAP SETTING	ANGLE OF BANK (G-LOAD)				
		0° (+1.0 g)	30° (+1.15 g)	45° (+1.41 g)	60° (+2.0 g)	
1600	UP	36	39	43	51	
	10°	36	39	43	51	CRITICAL WING
	30°	31	33	37	44	

Figure 9-6: Identifying the Critical Wing with Split Flaps

Flutter

Flutter can occur whenever one of the airplane's natural, resonant frequencies is excited. The accompanying high frequency vibration can cause the catastrophic failure of major airplane components, literally in a matter of seconds. Flutter can be induced by a loose control or trim surface, or by high speed flight. It can also be triggered if a control surface departs the airplane.

Loose control surfaces vibrating at the right frequency, particularly trim tabs with worn hinges, can cause the entire airplane to oscillate uncontrollably. The best prevention against flutter is to preflight the primary and secondary control surfaces carefully. Scrutinise trim tabs and their hinges for wear and cracks. Learn what amount of play is acceptable in the ailerons, rudder, elevator, and flaps from a reputable mechanic. In the air, don't fly at or above Vne intentionally. Should you encounter flutter, or even a high frequency buzzing in the control surfaces, **SLOW DOWN IMMEDIATELY**. Close the throttle and bleed off airspeed until the vibration ceases.

After addressing any control failure, take whatever time is available to evaluate your landing options. If possible, play out a number of scenarios. Select the one best suited to the occasion and focus on flying the airplane. Land slowly, controlled, and in the proper attitude. Don't rush to the ground; regroup, think, and work within the limits of the airplane's controllability.

This chapter addressed some of the less common problems encountered during flight. Our ability to cope with control failures often hinges on our ability to perform slips and slipping turns—flying the airplane cross-controlled. Generally, we apply Power-Push-Roll actions first, which allow us to regain some control by transitioning into a slip. This is especially crucial with aileron, rudder, or split flap failures. Slips offer far more utility than simply a way to lose altitude on final approach. Practice them regularly, until you can control them precisely and comfortably.

10
Glides

Like it or not, pilots haven't been able to contradict the theorem, "What goes up, must come down." Gravity always wins. How well we cooperate with it plays a major role in determining the airplane's attitude and energy when it contacts the ground. Should our man-made engine fail, mother nature's powerplant will take over without skipping a beat. Although gravity may not pull us to the preferred landing site, we should learn to make efficient use of it nonetheless. Power-off glides are maximum performance manoeuvres requiring precise airspeed control, proper coordination, good planning, and an understanding of glide dynamics.

We can draw some interesting parallels between mother nature's powerplant and our mechanical engine. In a glide, gravity is the engine. Its pull provides the necessary Thrust to offset Drag while generating Lift. Altitude is the fuel—natural avgas—burned in exchange for airspeed; therefore, the altimeter is a fuel gage of sorts. The vertical speed indicator (VSI) is akin to a fuel flow meter; it registers the rate of fuel consumption. The airspeed indicator is analogous to a tachometer; it measures the power output of our gravity engine.

The aerodynamics review in Chapter 2 included a graph displaying the ratio of Lift-to-Drag (L/D) versus angle of attack for a given airfoil. The peak on this curve depicts a significant aerodynamic property: (L/D)max. This point represents our best glide ratio. Flight at (L/D)max results in a minimum angle of descent and maximum glide range (in no wind conditions). From a practical standpoint, think of L/D as your Length-to-Drop ratio. For instance, an L/D of 10:1 means the airplane travels 10 units horizontally while dropping 1 unit vertically in a glide. The units can be feet, miles, or any other convenient measure of distance.

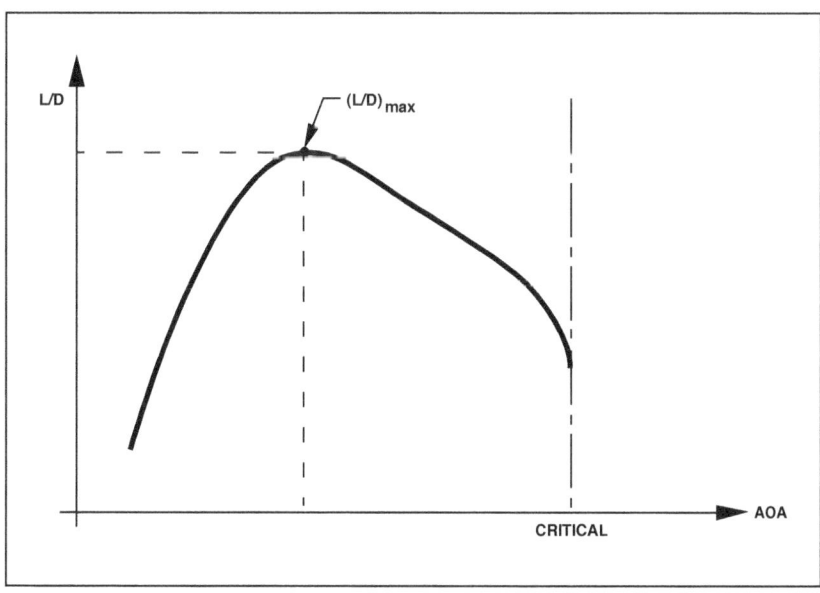

Figure 10-1: Lift-to-Drag Ratio vs. Angle of Attack

(L/D)max occurs at a specific angle of attack for a given wing. Gliding at angles of attack above or below this value results in shorter glide distances. This phenomenon was demonstrated during our quest to identify airspeed and altitude controls in Chapter 4—Pitch and Power. Our glide tests revealed that both high angle of attack (low speed) and low angle of attack (high speed) flight had steep flight paths; intermediate angles of attack had shallower flight paths; best glide angle of attack provided the shallowest descent profile and covered the most ground.

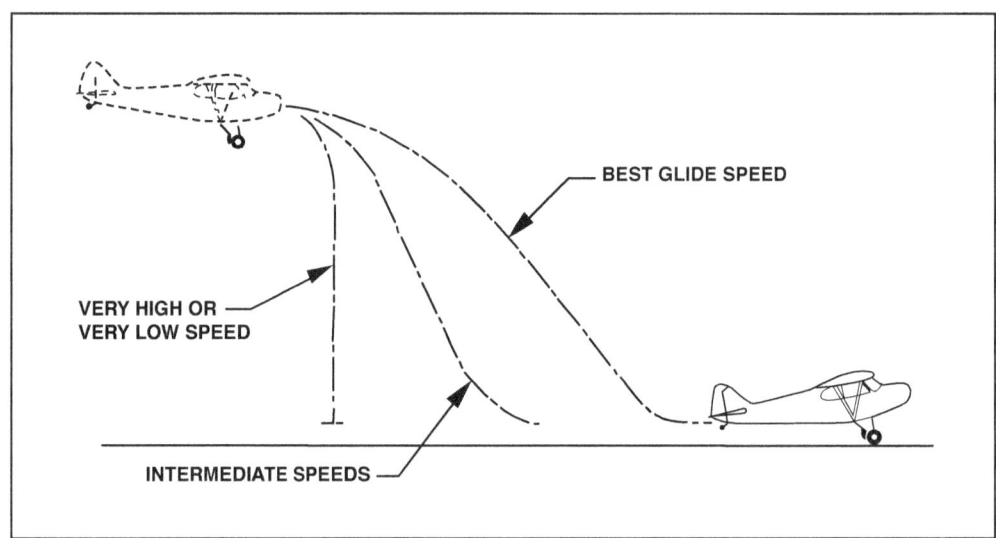

Figure 10-2: Converting Altitude into Airspeed during a Glide

Flight at high angles of attack is plagued with large amounts of Induced Drag. Low angle of attack flight suffers from large Parasite Drag penalties. These increases in Drag reduce glide performance. (L/D)max, however, splits the total Drag equally between its two components—half of it is Induced Drag; the other half, Parasite Drag. Maintaining this delicate balance yields maximum glide range in no-wind conditions.

Unfortunately, most light airplanes are equipped to measure airspeed only, not angle of attack. How do we achieve (L/D)max, then? Both angle of attack and airspeed are controlled through elevator inputs; therefore, changes in airspeed correspond directly to changes in angle of attack. Changing our elevator position alters the proportion of angle of attack and airspeed as Lift struggles to balance Weight. For steady flight at a specific Weight, each angle of attack comes packaged with a unique airspeed, and vice versa.

The airplane's best glide speed, Vbg, corresponds to the angle of attack for (L/D)max. Relatively speaking, gravity merely sips on altitude when at Vbg, efficiently converting potential energy into as much glide distance as possible. As speed moves farther away from Vbg, gravity gulps down the altitude, reducing our horizontal progress in a glide. But as with most flight parameters, Vbg is not a single, rigid value. Best glide speed and glide distance are influenced by factors like weight, wind, turning flight, and airplane configuration. Let's see how these elements combine to affect glide performance:

Weight

The value of (L/D)max and the angle at which it occurs are constant for a given wing. With a fixed angle of attack, only airspeed can vary to achieve steady flight. The force balance presented in Chapter 4—Pitch and Power for descents included a component of

Weight acting like Thrust to accelerate the airplane earthward. The more the configuration weighs, the greater this Thrust component becomes; hence, a higher airspeed is attained before Lift and Drag balance Weight. Conversely, the less the configuration weighs, the lower the airspeed is to reach equilibrium.

Other things being equal, flying at (L/D)max always yields the same glide ratio, and hence glide range, regardless of Weight. Whether the airplane is lightly or heavily loaded, **IT WILL REACH THE SAME SPOT** in a glide at its (L/D)max. For example, suppose our airplane's operating handbook lists the following information: Glide ratio, 10:1; Vbg, 65 mph; maximum gross Weight, 1600 pounds. Assume the engine quits 2000 feet above the ground, in light winds, with almost full fuel, maximum baggage, and each seat occupied. At 65 mph and 10:1, the airplane glides horizontally about 3-3/4 miles before losing 2000 feet, reaching the ground in less than 3-1/2 minutes.

Next, assume the airplane runs out of fuel during a solo flight (which is inexcusable), starting from the same altitude and with the same wind as above. The airplane is lighter now, weighing just 1200 pounds without fuel and passengers. For steady flight, the wing needs to generate 1200 pounds of Lift, instead of 1600 pounds. Slowing the airplane to a speed of 56 mph generates the required Lift and preserves the 10:1 glide ratio. The airplane glides to the same spot 3-3/4 miles ahead, only it takes a little longer—4 minutes en route in this case.

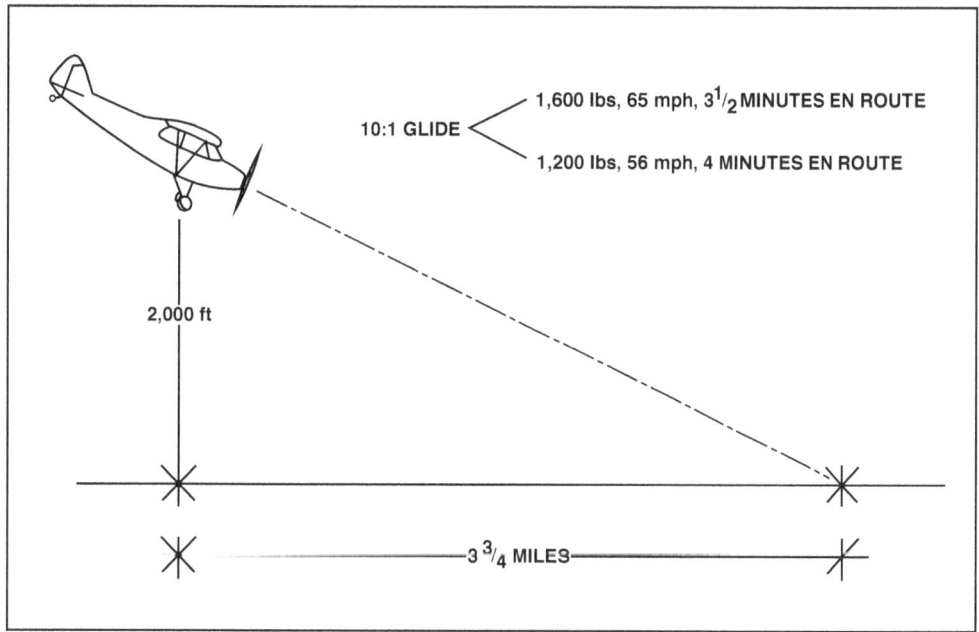

Figure 10-3: Glide Range is Independent of Weight when Operating at (L/D)max

Holding the airspeed constant at 65 mph, on the other hand, requires an adjustment in angle of attack to balance Lift and Weight. In this case, L/D moves away from its peak value. The airplane experiences a deterioration in glide range as a result, falling short of the spot 3-3/4 miles ahead.

Wind

Wind speeds in excess of 10 mph can influence glide performance. Strong headwinds retard the airplane's upwind progress, whereas strong tailwinds can assist the glide. Even though flight at speeds other than Vbg result in lower glide ratios, our glide range in windy conditions can be enhanced through moderate changes in glide speed. To illustrate this, suppose the theoretical best glide speed is 65 mph, but we encounter a 65 mph headwind. Glide range is zero into the wind; our flight path is vertical! Increasing the speed to 95 mph reduces our L/D, but it allows the airplane to penetrate upwind, thus achieving at least some glide range. Regardless of airspeed, however, we will not glide as far into a strong headwind as we would in zero wind conditions.

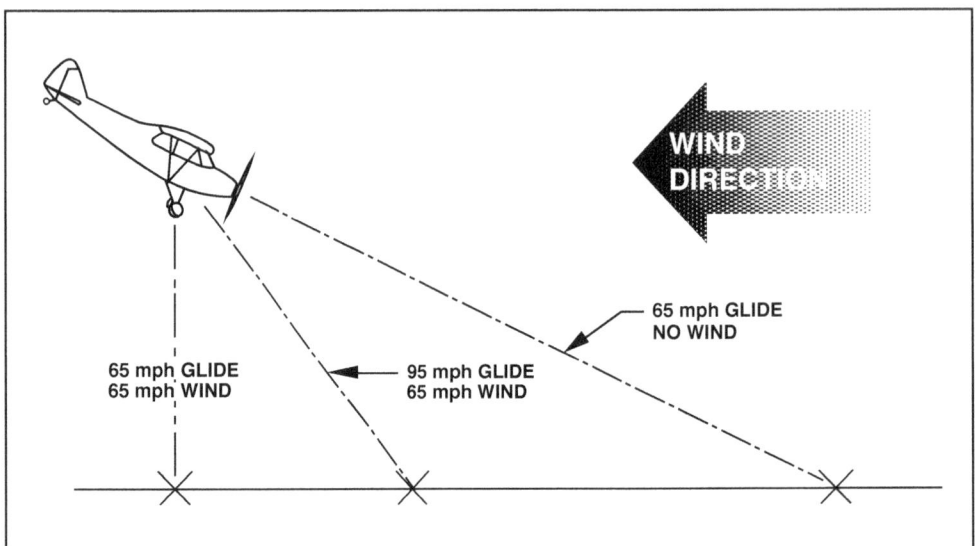

Figure 10-4: Effect of Strong Headwind on Glide Performance

By contrast, strong tailwinds can boost glide performance if we reduce our speed slightly below Vbg. A slower airspeed gives the airplane more time to drift with the moving air mass. The aerodynamic penalty for gliding at a lower L/D is offset by an additional horizontal push added by the strong tailwind. The net result can be an increase in glide range.

Several rules of thumb are available to correct best glide speed for the effects of weight and wind. Given the relatively small range of operating weights for most light singles, and for glides in winds not exceeding 20 mph, best glide speed does not vary appreciably. Typically, an adjustment of only 5 units (knots or mph) up or down is all that's needed to improve glide performance.

The value of adjusting Vbg becomes apparent during extended wings-level glides in strong winds. Modifying Vbg is beneficial during the approach to landing as well, particularly as the airplane turns into the wind on final. Reducing speed 5 units below Vbg when lightly loaded, in light winds, decreases the amount of energy to be dissipated and the landing distance. Increasing speed 5 units above Vbg when heavily loaded, with strong headwinds, helps the airplane cut through the wind to reach the landing spot. The additional speed gives the wind less time to push the airplane away from the landing site.

Turning Flight

Manoeuvring during glides always shortens glide range. We found above that an airplane with a 10:1 glide ratio at 65 mph would glide almost 3-3/4 miles, starting from 2000 feet with no wind and the wings level. Picture the glide path as a stiff piece of wire stretching all the way to the ground. Bending the flight path into a series of S-turns drags the end of the wire closer to the airplane. Coiling the flight path into a spiral brings the end of the wire directly beneath the airplane.

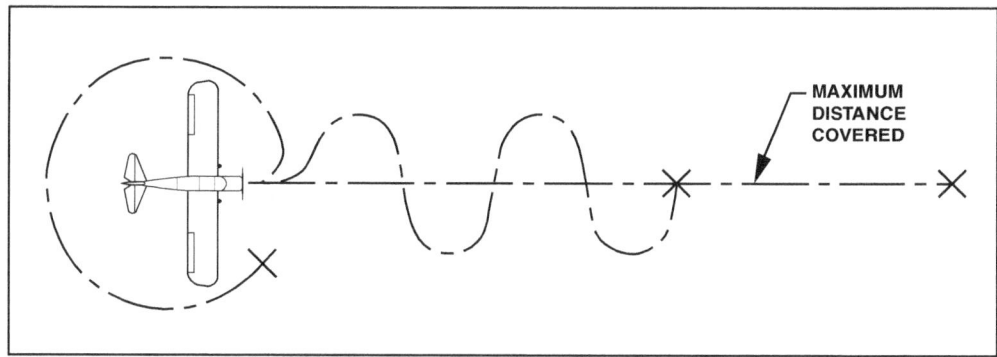

Figure 10-5: Effect of Manoeuvring on Glide Performance

Although gliding turns reduce glide range, they generally form an essential part of the forced landing process. The strength of gliding turns lies in their ability to change our heading. They point the airplane in the direction of a suitable landing site, or position it for the approach upon reaching the site. On the other hand, the strength of wings-level glides lies in their ability to move us from A to B efficiently. Tapping into these strengths allows us to get the most utility from our glide. Naturally, the assortment of turns mixed with wings-level gliding depends on the situation at hand.

For example, more suitable landing sites may be behind us following an engine failure at altitude. An 180 degree turn will point the airplane in the desired direction, no matter what bank angle is employed. But by conserving altitude during the turnaround, more altitude can be converted into glide range afterwards. We can formulate some general guidelines to reduce altitude loss in a gliding turn using information presented in Chapter 5—Curved Flight. The most important guideline, of course, is to maintain control of the airplane. Remember, the elevator cannot hold the airplane "up". We must use elevator inputs to maintain airspeed as the flight path curves around to a new heading.

As soon as we bank and turn, stall speed, g-load, angle of attack, and the power required for steady flight all increase. They continue to increase as bank angle steepens. These trends can be illustrated on diagrams similar to those examined in earlier chapters. Since power is not available following an engine failure, the familiar power required curves now represent rate of descent curves. Increases in g-load, stall speed, and best glide speed inherent in turning flight combine to shift these curves upward and to the right. Rate of descent is also affected when varying the airspeed while at a set bank angle.

We could analyse gliding turns in absolute terms, seeking the one bank angle and airspeed combination that conserves the most altitude (around 45 degrees of bank). Restricting our manoeuvring to this one bank, though, may not be practical. It would place additional demands on pilot performance during the forced landing process as well. Since the primary objective of a gliding turn is to change heading, let's strive for altitude conservation in relative terms, balancing speed, rate of descent, g-load, and pilot proficiency for a range of bank angles.

Shallower turns, for instance, experience smaller increases in rate of descent compared to steeper banks. Changes in g-load and operating speeds become less significant as bank angles become shallower. The drawback is that shallow turns exhibit much larger turn radii. They also take longer to complete, thus smaller increases in rate of descent are overpowered by disproportionately longer times to complete heading changes. The net effect is greater altitude losses during shallow turns.

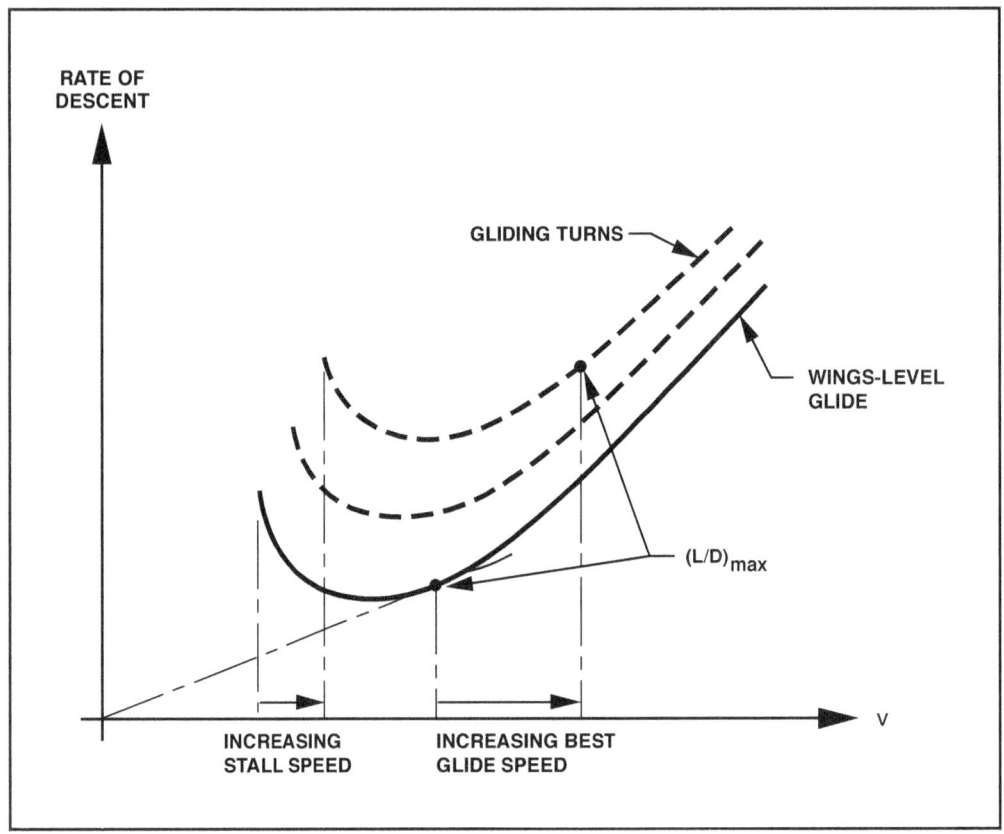

Figure 10-6: Rate of Descent Curves

Steepening the bank angle results in larger increases in g-load, rate of descent, and stall speed, but dramatically reduced turn radii and turn times compared to shallow turns. Further reductions in turn radius and time become less significant as bank angle exceeds about 40 degrees. Increases in g-load, stall speed, and rate of descent, however, become more significant. Eventually, an accelerated stall is likely if the airspeed is held constant while continually increasing the bank. The progressively higher rates of descent associated with steep gliding turns result in greater altitude losses.

TYPE OF TURN	SHALLOW			MEDIUM						STEEP		
BANK ANGLE	5°	10°	15°	20°	25°	30°	35°	40°	45°	50°	55°	60°
+G-LOAD	1.00	1.02	1.04	1.06	1.10	1.15	1.22	1.30	1.41	1.56	1.74	2.00
% INCREASE IN STALL SPEED	0%	1%	2%	3%	5%	7%	10%	14%	19%	25%	32%	41%
% DECREASE IN TURN TIME VS. BANK	0%	50%	67%	76%	81%	85%	88%	90%	91%	93%	94%	95%

Table 10-1: Effect of Bank Angle on Turn Performance

To illustrate these trends, doubling bank angle from 15 to 30 degrees only adds 0.11 g to our effective Weight. Stall speed creeps up 7 percent. The corresponding increase in rate of descent is small as well, but turn time is reduced an additional 54 percent. Doubling bank angle again, this time to 60 degrees, almost doubles the g-load felt at 15 degrees. Stall speed increases markedly, now up 41 percent. The increase in rate of descent is equally as significant. Turn time, however, does not experience a comparable decrease, down only another 30 percent compared to the 30 degree bank (provided the increased stall speed does not coincide now with best glide speed).

Medium banked turns offer superior altitude conservation potential compared to shallow or steep turns. They represent the best compromise between all of the variables involved in turning flight: substantial savings in turn times over shallow banks, without the exaggerated g-loads, stall speeds, and rates of descent associated with steep turns. Another advantage when using medium banks is increased stability, making airspeed control easier. Medium banks tend to stay where they are, unlike the inherent underbanking and overbanking tendencies displayed during shallow and steep turns (review Chapter 5—Curved Flight).

Since best glide speeds typically range from 1.2 to 1.4 times 1-g stall speeds, holding airspeed constant at Vbg for banks up to 30-35 degrees still maintains a margin of safety over the increasing stall speed. In exchange, more altitude will be saved during the turn than if glide speed was increased proportionally. For banks ranging between 35 and 45 degrees, adding 5 units (knots or mph) to Vbg will keep it ahead of the rising stall speed while holding the altitude loss down.

Whenever appropriate, perform medium banked, gliding turns to conserve altitude. Hold glide speed constant up to 30 degrees of bank, then add 5 units for banks of 35 to 45 degrees. Avoid steeply banked turns, unless you're prepared to push simultaneously for extra airspeed if needed, and unless you're willing to accept the accompanying high rates of descent and altitude loss. It makes more sense to work within your normal range of bank angles during an emergency. If you're uncomfortable banked beyond 30 degrees, for example, perform gliding turns up to 25 degrees of bank. This will conserve the most altitude relative to **YOUR** operating envelope.

Best glide speed isn't affected greatly within the usual operating ranges of weight, wind, and bank angle. For the most part, varying best glide speed plus-or-minus 5 units (knots or mph) is all that's needed to enhance our glide performance. Correcting Vbg for weight, wind, and turns is summarised in Table 10-2.

WEIGHT	BANK ANGLE	HEADWIND		TAILWIND	
		LIGHT (0-10MPH)	HEAVY (10-20MPH)	LIGHT (0-10MPH)	HEAVY (10-20MPH)
LIGHT	LEVEL	-5	0	-5	10
	5° - 30°	-5	0	-5	-5
	35° - 45°	0	+5	0	0
HEAVY	LEVEL	0	+5	0	-5
	5° - 30°	0	+5	0	0
	35° - 45°	+5	+10	+5	+5

Table 10-2: Summary of Correction Factors for Best Glide Speed

Airplane Configuration

Energy conservation is important in any glide, since added Drag increases the rate of descent, steepens the glide slope, and ultimately reduces the glide range. Minimising Drag helps optimise glide performance. How we manage airspeed, adverse yaw, flaps, landing gear, and the powerplant influence the glide. As a rule, you'll get the most from a glide if you keep it clean and keep it simple. Fluctuating airspeed, for instance, continually alters the glide ratio, needlessly consuming energy and shortening glide distance. The resulting descent profile varies as well, adversely impacting our ability to judge the glide accurately. Don't allow the airspeed to wander. Properly managing Speed is the cornerstone of a successful forced landing.

Uncoordinated flight also reduces turn efficiency and consumes extra altitude. Deploying flaps and extending landing gear add Drag and reduce glide distance. Each of these whittles away altitude that could be used to get somewhere. Keep the wings level unless you intend to turn. Exercise proper rudder coordination. And leave the flaps and gear up until you're absolutely sure the landing site is made, and you're sure you need to use them.

If the amount of fuel remaining is ever in doubt, configuring the airplane for level flight at Vbg plus 5-10 (knots or mph) strikes an acceptable compromise between aerodynamic (wing L/D) and mechanical (prop/engine) efficiencies. Slowing down reduces the rate of fuel consumption. It also cleans up the airplane in terms of L/D; consequently, you'll cover more ground prior to fuel exhaustion. Rocking the wings as fuel starvation occurs may slosh normally unusable fuel into the fuel lines, allowing additional distance to be covered before commencing a glide. Slow to Vbg once the powerplant is eliminated from the range equation.

A windmilling propeller creates more Drag during a glide than if it was stopped, especially at low blade angles. The potential altitude saved after stopping the propeller, though, must be weighed against two other factors: the altitude consumed in order to stop the prop, and the increased demands on the pilot during the process. The airplane must be slowed close to its 1-g stall speed for the prop to stop turning. Once stopped, speed must be increased back to best glide. The airplane experiences higher rates of descent, more Drag, and an attendant rise in altitude loss throughout this manoeuvre. Proficiency in stalls is required as well; otherwise, the pilot might be hesitant about slowing down sufficiently to stop the propeller. Considerably more altitude could be lost during the attempt to stop the prop than will be saved in the ensuing glide.

All things considered, it's better to forgo stopping the propeller. Accept this Drag penalty in favor of maintaining positive control of the airplane. The time and altitude that would be needed to stop the prop is better spent preparing for the forced landing. Also, if you've never stopped a prop before, why try it for the first time while under the duress of an emergency? More pressing items need our attention. With a constant speed propeller, Drag can often be reduced by pulling the prop control all the way back to the high pitch/low rpm position during the glide.

Judging Glide Distance

We've seen how weight, wind, turning flight, and airplane configuration affect glide speed and performance. Their net impact on airspeed is within 5 units (knots or mph) of Vbg in the typical gliding environment. Employing medium banks (20-45 degrees) when turning conserves more altitude. Minimising Drag penalties improves glide range. Even so, reaching a particular landing site depends on judging how far the airplane will glide, and what type of manoeuvring will be needed.

Maximum glide range in zero wind is achieved at Vbg with the wings level, flaps and gear up, and **NO** manoeuvring. A straight line gliding approach to touchdown is all that's possible. The glide ratio at (L/D)max defines our minimum glide angle, which is independent of altitude. This angle, formed between our glide path and the ground, is the same angle formed between the glide path and the horizon. If we look below the horizon at this angle and project our glide path earthward, we automatically combine height-to-distance into one convenient line. Sighting along this line defines glide range limits more precisely than estimating ground distance, especially at higher altitudes.

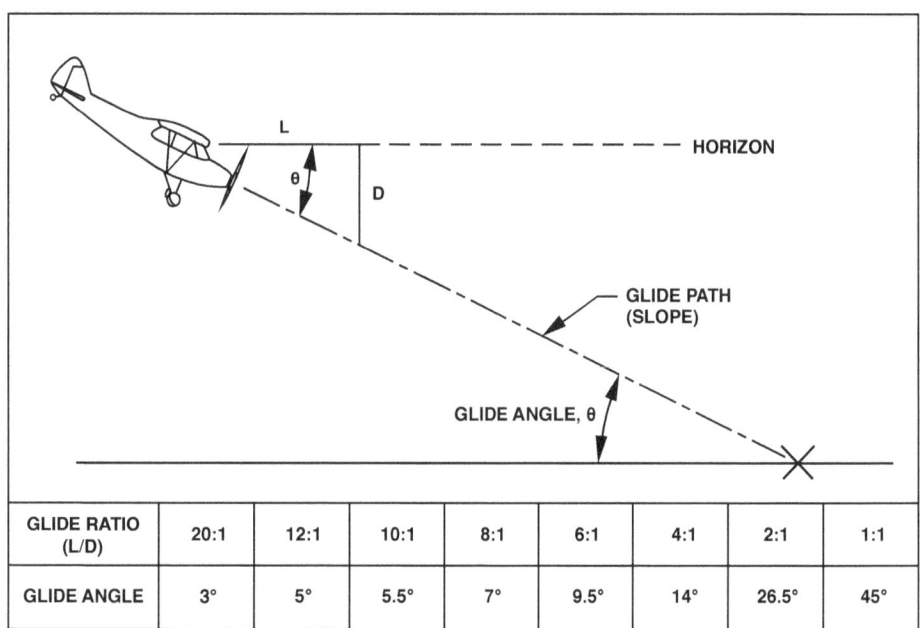

Figure 10-7: Converting Glide Ratio into Glide Angle

If the airplane's glide ratio is 8:1, for example, the glide angle is close to 7 degrees. The maximum glide point will be on a line 7 degrees below the horizon, no matter how high you are. On the other hand, estimating distance becomes more difficult with altitude. At 1000 feet and 8:1, the maximum glide point is 1-1/2 statute miles ahead, but at 8,000 feet, the point is 12 miles ahead. The apparent length of a mile from the cockpit, however, shrinks as we gain altitude, reducing judgment accuracy.

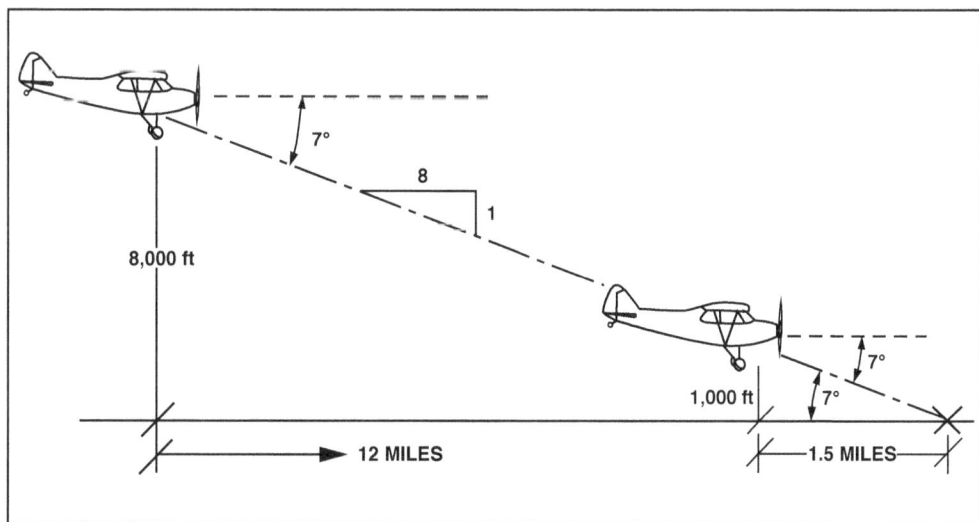

Figure 10-8: Judging Glide Distance using Glide Angle

Visualising the minimum descent angle represents our first estimate of glide range. Fine tuning this estimate entails continuous scrutiny of our progress during the glide. Good airspeed management, coupled with a correct interpretation of perceived changes in the glide picture, are the keys to judging glides accurately. Our attention during a forced landing should be on the interaction between Speed and Spot variables.

Maintaining a constant airspeed cannot be overemphasised. Unchecked variations in speed thwart all attempts to determine glide distance and to judge the landing spot. This is why our first priority following an engine failure must be Speed control. If we turn this into a fixed quantity, we'll have more precise information with which to evaluate our options. Let's observe the changes occurring during a glide and learn how to read the clues presented.

What happens when gliding along the 7 degree slope discussed earlier, assuming we hold the airspeed constant at Vbg? Studying the relative motion of various landmarks over the nose, we'll notice several things: Landmarks beyond our glide slope seem to slide up the wind-screen, toward the horizon. Landmarks inside of our glide slope drop toward the bottom of the wind-screen, eventually sliding underneath the nose, away from the horizon. The point on the ground representing maximum glide range displays no relative motion in the wind-screen, other than growing larger as we get closer.

With airspeed constant, the stationary point represents maximum glide range. Landmarks moving up the wind-screen, toward the horizon, must be beyond our reach. Those moving down the wind-screen, away from the horizon, must be within glide range. We judge these same exact movements subconsciously every time we land. When landing on the first third of the runway, for example, the numbers at the far end move up in our field of vision, while the numbers on the approach end move below our visual field. The actual touchdown point, somewhere in between, does not move.

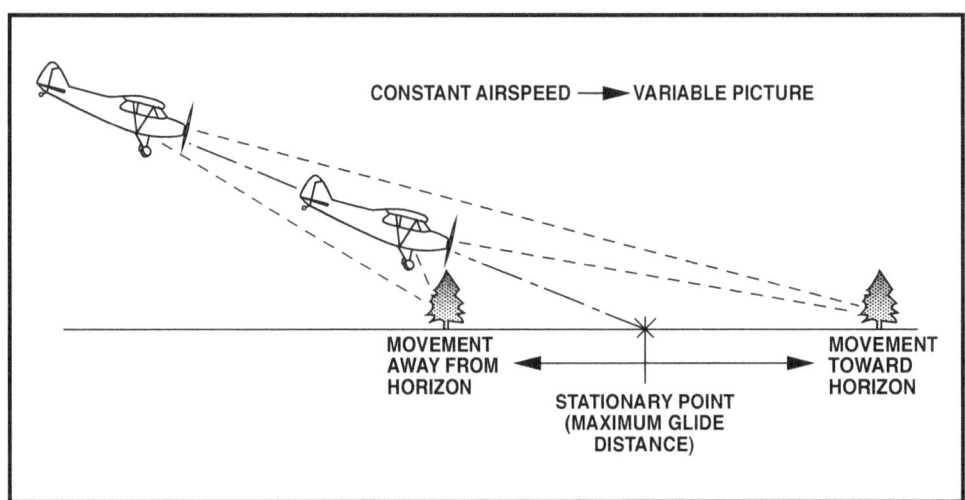

Figure 10-9: Judging Glide Distance by Observing Landmark Trends

Strong headwinds steepen the glide angle and reduce glide range. Strong tailwinds shallow the glide angle and increase glide range. These effects alter the location of the furthest point reachable in a glide, but they don't affect the relative movement of landmarks on the wind-screen. Their motion will be wind-corrected already, revealing what's within range and what isn't as long as airspeed is held constant. Objects sliding up to meet the horizon simply are unreachable, regardless of the wind.

Let's try gliding along the 7 degree slope again, this time holding the location of various landmarks constant in the wind-screen. To keep points from sliding up the wind-screen, we must now pull the nose toward the horizon. Airspeed begins to decrease, steepening the glide slope. A vicious cycle develops: As the glide slope steepens, the landmarks move faster toward the horizon, requiring more pull to keep them fixed in your field of vision. This results in even less speed, which further steepens the glide slope, and so on. If allowed to continue, either the wing will stall, or the airplane will contact the ground with a high rate of descent. Either way, the airplane falls short of the maximum glide spot.

The above demonstration illustrates a classic principle concerning glides: Never attempt to stretch a glide by pulling on the elevator control! In fact, attempting to reach a spot that's beyond glide range quickly places other potential landing sites out of range. If airspeed displays a downward trend while gliding to a selected site, **YOU WILL NOT REACH IT**. Abandon the chosen spot immediately, no matter how inviting. Resume best glide speed and find someplace closer.

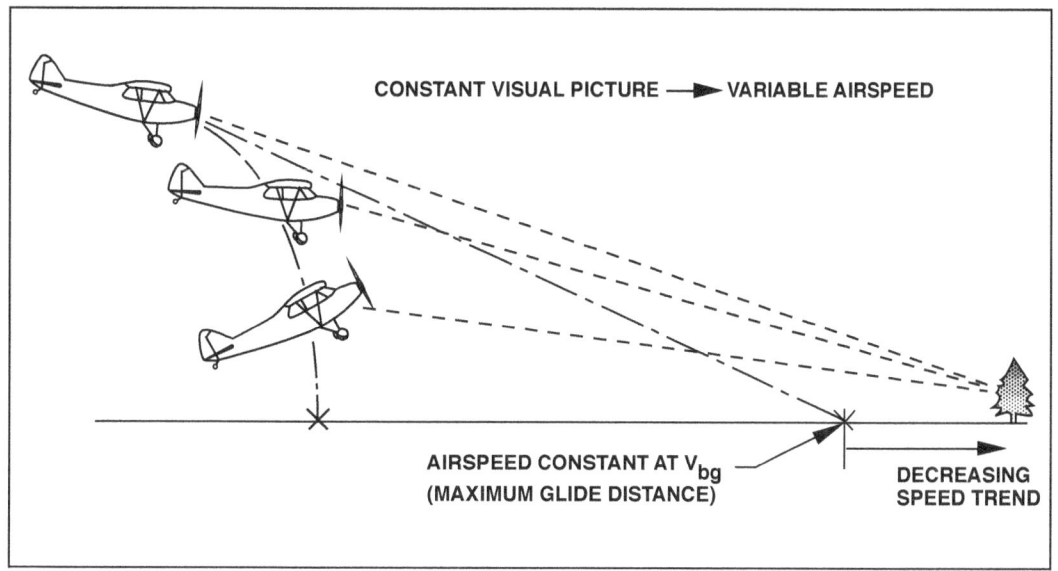

Figure 10-10: Attempting to Stretch a Glide by Maintaining a Constant Visual Picture

A similar combination of events occurs in the evolution of the dangerous low-and-slow final approach, especially if the approach started below the normal glide slope. Instead of maintaining a constant airspeed and correcting to the proper glide slope by adding power, the pilot attempts to freeze the approach end of the runway in the wind-screen. The airplane only gets lower and slower, and considerably more power is needed to drive to the runway. If airspeed is decreasing, and if power is not available to arrest the descent, the airplane **WILL NOT** reach the intended spot. Focus on airspeed control first, and don't fixate on the landing spot.

Landmarks within glide range moved down and away from the horizon when airspeed was held constant. To keep these points from moving now, we must push the nose away from the horizon. Airspeed increases above Vbg as we dive toward the ground. The glide slope steepens as well. Carried to its conclusion, the airplane either exceeds Vne, or contacts the ground nose low at high speed right on the desired spot.

We've all probably experienced or at least witnessed a similar situation arising from a high landing approach. The pilot locks onto the desired landing spot, which is now well short of the true touchdown point corresponding to the high approach. Rather than managing the airspeed, the pilot tries to maintain the normal visual picture by diving toward the intended mark. The only way to hit this spot using this technique is to drive the prop spinner through it at high speed.

In the majority of cases, the pilot eventually raises the nose to flare. The airplane might balloon, but it absolutely, positively does not land on the intended spot. It floats until the extra speed gained in the dive bleeds off. Touchdown actually occurs closer to the original spot corresponding to the high approach profile, in spite of the pilot's attempt to hit a shorter mark. Diving at a closer spot on the runway does not culminate in a shorter landing. Instead, it only creates more work for the pilot just to end up landing long anyway.

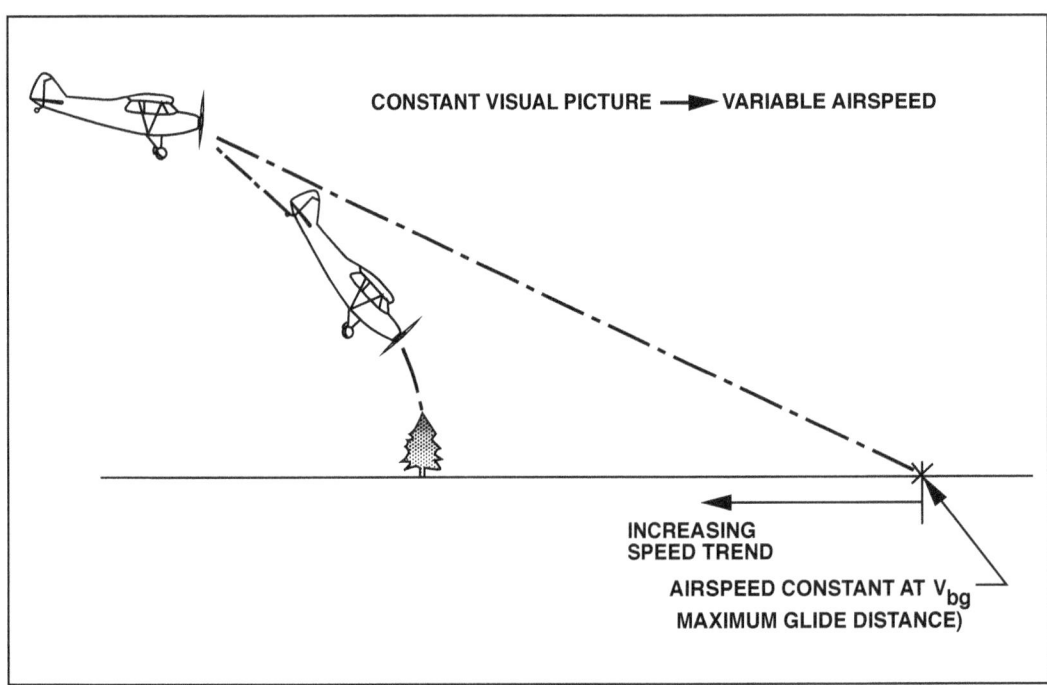

Figure 10-11: Attempting to Shorten a Glide by Maintaining a Constant Visual Picture

If airspeed displays an upward trend while gliding toward a selected site, it's within glide range. We'll have altitude to spare upon arrival, as long as we resume best glide speed. The altitude left over can be used for manoeuvring. Don't rush, and don't fixate on the landing site, either. Control your speed. Gravity will make sure you get to the ground in due time.

The Glide Envelope

As we saw earlier, the maximum glide spot did not exhibit any relative movement when airspeed was held constant; therefore, no elevator inputs are needed now to keep this spot constant in the wind-screen. Likewise, no change in airspeed will be observed either. **BOTH** Speed and Spot variables remain constant for landmarks at maximum glide range. Perceiving changes in these parameters, coupled with visualization of the glide slope, lend important insight into our progress during the glide.

It's generally impractical to glide to a spot at the end of your glide range. Most glides will be influenced by the wind. They'll usually require some manoeuvring, and we should allow for imperfect technique. Also, unfavorable ground features may not be discernible until it's too late if the farthest field is selected. Identifying the maximum glide distance, however, shapes our glide envelope. It gives us a starting point for field selection. Choose the landing site well within this envelope, even if it appears less desirable than a field near the edge of your glide range. More time will be available to evaluate terrain, obstacles, and the approach by choosing the closer site. The altitude saved could come in handy when manoeuvring for the best landing possible.

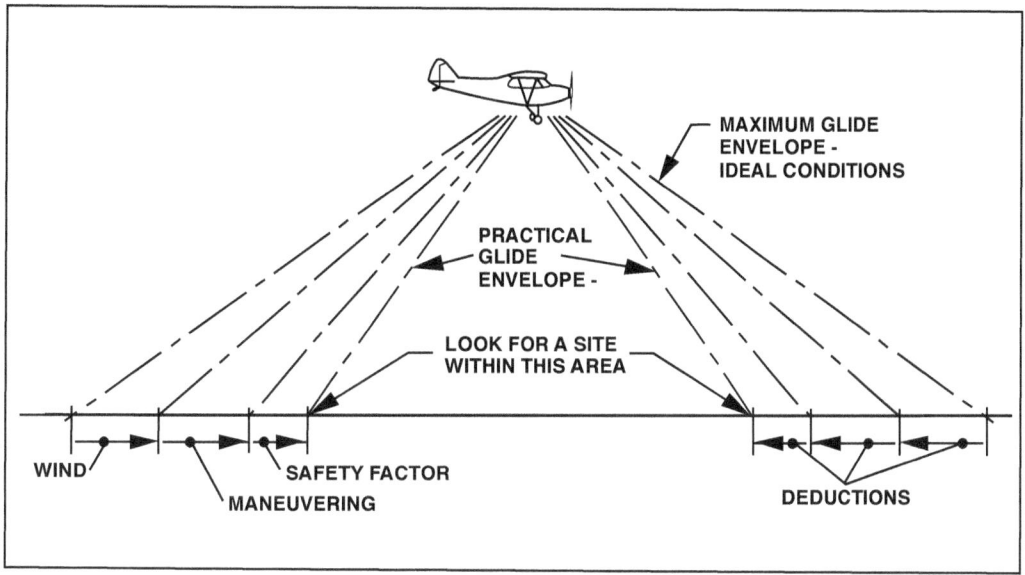

Figure 10-12: Visualizing the Glide Envelope

We should try to incorporate glide techniques into our normal flight routine whenever possible. Consciously visualise your glide slope and control the airspeed precisely during each landing. This will increase your proficiency and will improve the chances of arriving on the chosen spot in the event of a forced landing. Unpracticed skills will be less reliable in a crisis, so make it a habit to practice. Keep in mind that your glide range in a totally unpowered descent, with a windmilling prop, will likely be less than when practicing gliding approaches at idle power.

Glides are an integral part of the topics discussed in the next two chapters. First, we'll discuss Powerplant Failures from low altitude, as in the traffic pattern around an airport. Following that, we'll look at Off-Airport Landings initiated from the higher altitudes typical of cross country flights.

11
Powerplant Failures

Engines and propellers are designed to give us reliable, long-term control over our altitude, as demonstrated in Chapter 4—Pitch and Power. The most critical phase of powered flight occurs at low altitude, usually around an airport. Here, we rely on power to climb on the upwind leg, to hold traffic pattern altitude on the downwind leg, and to control rate of descent on base and final. Powerplants, however, are not infallible. They do fail occasionally, taking our altitude control with them.

Without power, airplanes revert to gliders. All gliders ultimately do one thing; they travel earthward, powered by the relentless pull of gravity. Our first priority in any emergency is to **FLY THE AIRPLANE**. Proper energy management becomes paramount during the inevitable exchange of altitude for airspeed following an engine failure.

It's not the forced landing that presents a hazard after an engine failure, but rather how we force the airplane to land. Our attitude, speed, and control over the airplane is more significant, in terms of landing survivability, than the type of terrain encountered. This chapter highlights some strategies for coping with powerplant problems, particularly those occurring when operating around an airport. Let's categorise powerplant problems into two types: Power Loss, which could be either total or partial, and Loss of Power Control, such as a broken or jammed throttle linkage.

Power Loss

Should the engine suddenly lose power, don't be startled into pulling on the elevator control. This reaction literally pulls the airplane toward stalled flight, often spelling disaster close to the ground. Only power can keep us in the air. Without it, airplanes descend. All of the aft elevator in the world won't hold us "up". Instead, efficient use of the elevator is needed to achieve an optimum blend of airspeed, angle of attack, g-load, and turning flight before reaching the ground.

Should the engine balk during the takeoff roll, simply close the throttle. This prevents the engine from roaring back to life unexpectedly. Maintain directional control, apply firm, even braking, and raise the flaps, if deployed. In many light tailwheel airplanes, holding the elevator control fully aft improves directional stability. In tricycle gear airplanes, some back elevator pressure can improve braking action by focusing more Weight on the main wheels, where the brakes are located.

An aborted takeoff might demand maximum deceleration. Aerodynamic Drag can be effective in slowing the airplane, but it's significant only during the brief, initial phase of a high speed rollout. Our principal stopping power comes through the airplane's brakes, especially as speed decays. We can adopt several simple strategies that will maximise the effectiveness of our brakes, thereby reducing our stopping distance:

1. Taxi at slow speeds, using minimal power. Plan your turns and stops in advance. Avoid riding the brakes during taxi as well. This simple act reduces unnecessary preheating of the brakes, yielding cooler, more effective brakes

in the event of an aborted takeoff.

2. Upon aborting the takeoff, apply the brakes firmly, smoothly, and evenly. Don't pump the brake pedals when striving for maximum deceleration. Instead, push the brakes right up to the point of skidding the tyres. Modulate your pedal pressure just enough to prevent skidding. The same applies on wet or icy surfaces, only you'll certainly need to modulate brake pressure more gingerly.

   We don't want the wheels to lock-up for several reasons: first, surface friction decreases when skidding, thus it'll take longer to stop if the tyres slide across the ground; second, skidding could cause the tyres to fail; third, it's more difficult to maintain directional control while skidding, especially if the tyres blow out! Keep the tyres rolling.

3. Raising the flaps during rollout improves braking by reducing the amount of Lift generated by the wing. Dumping Lift from the wing transfers more Weight onto the wheels, improving traction between the tyres and the ground.

4. In tricycle gear airplanes, pushing forward on the elevator control during rollout diminishes braking effectiveness by shifting Weight off the mains, onto the nosewheel. Holding the nosewheel off the ground, on the other hand, generates excess Lift on the wing, which also relieves Weight from the mains. Keep as much Weight on the mains as possible by easing the elevator control progressively aft as speed dissipates, without pulling the nosewheel off the ground.

An aborted takeoff or even a routine landing on a rain-soaked runway could result in the airplane sliding across the ground as though it was on a banana peel. This phenomenon, called dynamic hydroplaning, happens when tyres lose contact with the surface and ride on a film of water instead. Virtually all braking action disappears. The possibility of hydroplaning, and its detrimental impact on directional control and stopping ability, should be considered whenever standing water rests on the runway.

The speed at which dynamic hydroplaning begins depends on the condition of the tyre and its pressure. It also varies during takeoff, where tyres are rolling already, and landing, where tyres initially have no rotation. A new tyre maintained at 30 psi, for example, could hydroplane during takeoff above 57 mph. Near its service limit, the same tyre could start hydroplaning as slow as 44 mph. Tyres near their service limit, usually with 1/32-inch or less of tread remaining, could blow out during hydroplaning. (If you place a penny in the tyre groove and can see the top of Lincoln's head, it's probably time to replace the tyre.)

CONDITIONS	TYRE PRESSURE				
	20 psi	25 psi	30 psi	35 psi	40 psi
TAKE-OFF, NEW TYRES	46/40	52/45	57/49	61/53	65/57
TAKE-OFF, WORN TYRES	36/31	40/35	44/38	48/41	51/44
LANDING, NEW TYRES	40/34	44/38	48/42	52/46	56/49

Table 11-1: Dynamic Hydroplane Speed (mph/kts) vs. Tyre Pressure

If the airplane is going to roll off the end of the runway, pop the door open, pull the mixture to idle cut-off, turn the mags and the fuel off, keep working the brakes, and hold the elevator control aft. Rather than hitting obstacles at high speed, it may be more desirable in some cases to induce a ground loop. Apply full rudder and brake simultaneously on one side to try to swing your path from a straight line into a circle.

Dealing effectively with any emergency requires the implementation of a prioritised sequence of events. Once airborne, coping with a loss of power consists of managing one, two, or all three key elements associated with any impending landing: Speed, Spot, and Set-up. We balance these variables on each landing we make, normal or otherwise. It just so happens that during normal approaches, we fly at specified traffic pattern airspeeds, our spot is somewhere on a nicely groomed runway, and we set-up (i.e.: configure) the airplane for landing according to the airplane's flight manual.

Since altitude is limited in the pattern, we may not have time to address each of these steps during a power failure. Our overall plan, though, still follows the Speed-Spot-Set-up hierarchy. Give Speed control top priority. If it's all you can do to fly the airplane at the appropriate airspeed, focus on that task alone. It's vital to maintain positive control of the airplane through the touchdown. (To maintain control during an engine failure in twins, be prepared to reduce power on the good engine if necessary.)

Don't add Spot to the juggling act if it means dropping the ball on Speed control. Select and manoeuvre toward a landing Spot **ONLY** if Speed control will not be compromised. Set-up for landing **ONLY** if neither Speed control, nor Spot manoeuvring, will suffer. Manage these parameters one at a time. Keep cycling through the list, concentrating on Speed control. Sacrifice your landing Spot to hold your Speed, and sacrifice Set-up to manoeuvre to your Spot.

Figure 11-1: Give Speed Control Top Priority over Other Actions

Speed

Good airspeed management forms the foundation upon which all controlled landings are built. Also, since altitude is at a premium in the pattern, strive to conserve every precious foot of it. On departure, for example, adopt a strategy to maximise altitude gain. It's important during the early phase of flight to put distance between you and the ground. The optimum climb speed on departure is best rate, Vy. This speed gains more altitude per second of flight time than any other airspeed.

Although obstacles may require initially climbing at best angle, Vx, accelerate to Vy as soon thereafter as practical. Power failures during climbs require quick, coordinated reflexes to transition into a descent at best glide speed. The steep attitudes associated with climbs at Vx require greater forward pitch changes than shallower climbs. In addition, forward elevator inputs push the airplane away from the 1-g stall speed, which may be perilously close to your best angle speed.

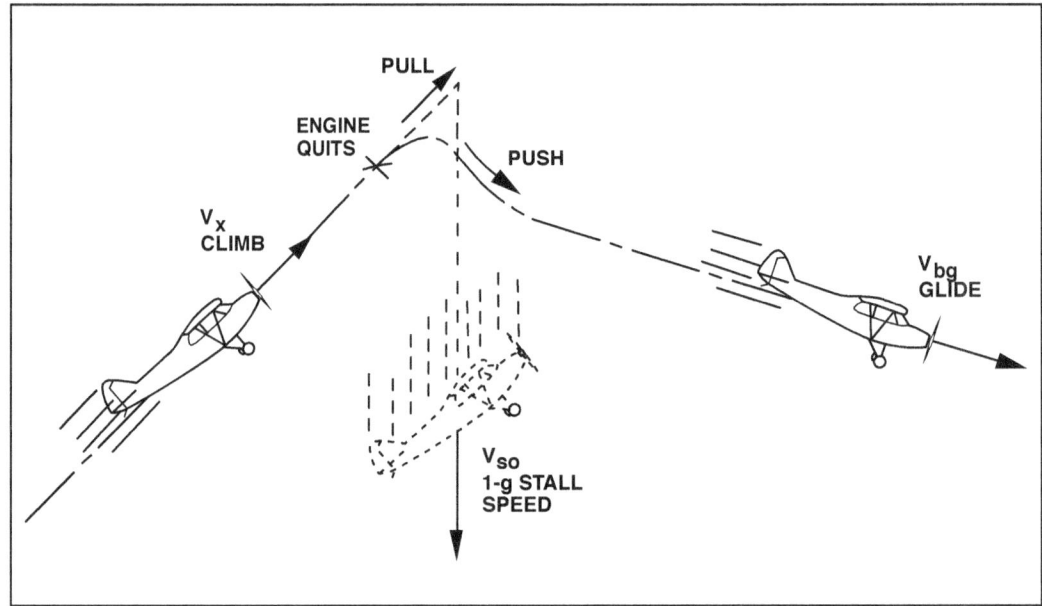

Figure 11-2: Engine Failure During a Climb at Vx

Mentally condition yourself to respond with a **PUSH** should the engine sputter in flight. Accept the fact that a significant amount of altitude may be consumed during the transition to best glide. The exchange of altitude for airspeed is necessary for better control prior to touchdown. Although climbing at Vx may be impressive in some airplanes, the flight path following an engine failure at Vx definitely will turn heads! Climb at Vy, unless circumstances dictate otherwise. Think **PUSH** if the engine quits.

Similar to the departure phase, we should adopt a strategy to minimise altitude loss during the final approach phase. It's important to conserve altitude until the runway can be reached without power. Avoid making power reductions by rote in the pattern, particularly on the base and final legs. Judge your position and height above the runway first. Evaluate wind effects, other traffic, and the size of the pattern. Retard the throttle only to lose excess altitude. "Excess altitude" is altitude that would not be required to glide to the runway with the power off. If the airplane will not reach the runway with a lower power setting, **DON'T REDUCE THE THROTTLE**.

The optimum approach speed for landing is best glide speed, Vbg. Power off flight at Vbg often defines your minimum acceptable glide slope. Approaches flown above this line at Vbg require a gradual power reduction to land on the desired spot. We're not dependent on the engine to reach the runway. Approaches flown below this line force us to drive toward the runway, relying solely on power. Such approaches can evolve into the potentially dangerous low-and-slow energy combination, placing us in the Region of Reversed Command (review Chapter 4—Pitch and Power). The airplane will land short of the intended mark if the engine quits.

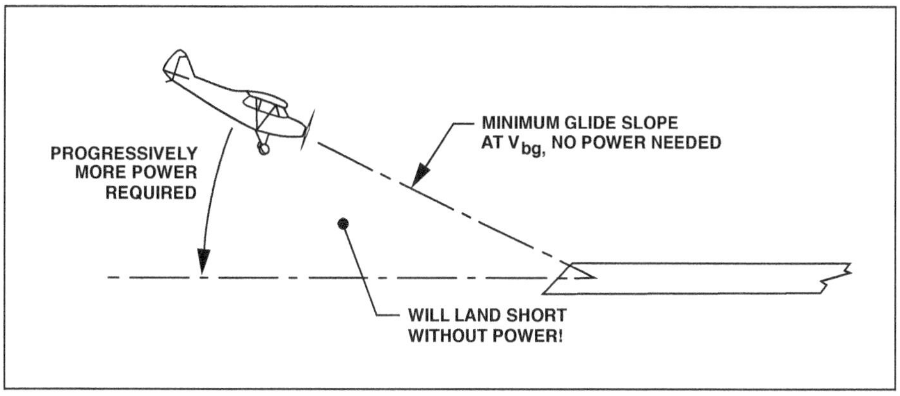

Figure 11-3: Relying on Power during Low Approaches

This brings up an important point concerning single engine operations at airports equipped with VASI systems. The standard VASI projects a 3 degree glide slope, which translates to a glide ratio of about 20:1 in zero wind. The typical light single has a glide ratio down in the range of 10:1, with glide slopes in the neighborhood of 5-1/2 degrees or more. Unless you're in a motor-glider, flying a 3 degree approach requires power to reach the runway. This is not to say that single engine pilots—who have no redundancy in the event of engine failure—shouldn't fly along a VASI slope. Just recognise, however, that if the engine does fail on final, you'll probably land short of the runway. React within the confines of this limitation and don't try to stretch the glide without power.

Obstacles may require short field approach and landing techniques, which are predicated on the continuous use of power to control rate of descent precisely at critically low airspeeds. As with climbs at Vx, be ready to react swiftly with a slight **PUSH** on the elevator control should the engine falter. Resist the urge to pull. Instead, reach **FORWARD** for best glide speed. Move away from the 1-g stall speed. Be willing to sacrifice some of the remaining altitude for enhanced control over the impending landing. Unless pressing considerations demand otherwise, fly your approaches at Vbg, and stay at or above the airplane's best glide slope.

Again, forward elevator is the first reaction to an unexpected loss of power when in slow flight. Push for best glide airspeed. Once Speed is under control, our next objective is to select and manoeuvre toward a landing Spot.

Spot

Obviously, the runway is the preferred landing spot when flying in the traffic pattern. Landing on a runway is a routine part of flying under normal conditions. It's so routine, in fact, that many pilots become complacent in the pattern, heaving a sigh of relief once the airport is in sight. The nature of operating near an airport, however, commands heightened awareness and concentration. manoeuvring at low altitude, low airspeed, and high angle of attack requires precisely coordinated control inputs, on top of the added work load imposed by other airplanes, wind, and air traffic control.

View the airport as **ONE** landing site, not necessarily **THE** landing site. Given the effects of wind, the physical size of the traffic pattern, altitude, and the type of airplane, the airport becomes a viable landing option only when it's within power-off gliding distance. Avoid fixating on the runway. Look around, and remain aware of your position relative to the runway at all times. When beyond glide range from the airport, pick and choose alternate landing spots in case the engine lets you down.

Fly defensively in the pattern as well. Don't surrender any altitude unless you can do without it in an emergency. Study the terrain around the airport, too. Look for additional landing sites on the various legs. Formulate an alternate plan of action in case of engine problems. View the runway as the eventual goal, not the sole landing option. Knowing how you'll respond to problems beforehand reduces indecision, improves reaction time, and minimises the likelihood of falling prey to two dangerous traffic pattern scenarios: attempting to stretch the glide on final approach, and turning back to the runway shortly after departure.

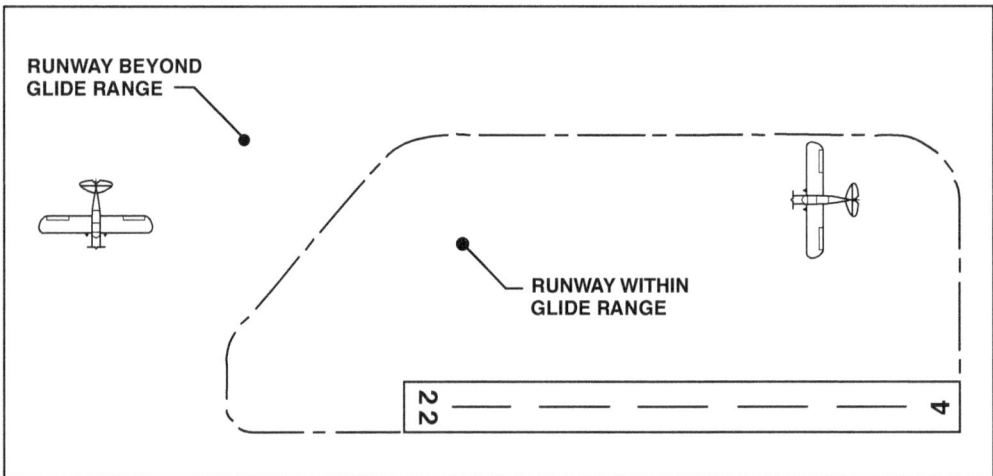

Figure 11-4: Visualising the Glide Envelope in the Traffic Pattern

The lure of a nice runway surrounded by flat ground certainly is strong when the engine falls silent. Like the sirens of Greek mythology, the airport beckons to pilots in distress, feigning safe haven from the emergency. Unfortunately, like those ancient mariners who couldn't resist the sirens' enticing song, many pilots have met their fate trying to make it to the runway. Attempting to turn back to the runway after an engine failure on departure offers a vivid example of this often fatal attraction.

In spite of volumes of aviation accident reports testifying to its futility, recurring articles in aviation publications warning against it, and theoretical calculations and empirical observations demonstrating the marginal ability to return to the runway with less than 1,000 feet of net altitude, even under ideal conditions, pilots still attempt to turn back rather than proceeding straight ahead. Turning back without power or sufficient altitude is a perilous act; resist the temptation.

Turning back to the runway tosses too many variables into the air at a time when pilot work load and anxiety are high. Just to line up for a downwind landing requires a minimum of two turns, totalling 270 degrees: a 225 degree turn and a 45 degree turn. As discussed earlier, g-load, angle of attack, stall speed, and Induced Drag all increase during turns, thus limiting our control options. A gliding turn with 45 degrees of bank, for example, doubles our Induced Drag, increases our stall speed almost 20 percent, causes an increase in rate of descent, and could drive us into an undesirable corner of our operating envelope. The increased stall speed in the turn may coincide with our best glide speed, resulting in an accelerated stall close to the ground.

To turn around, the pilot must pull the airplane to the edge of its aerodynamic operating limit as the ground races up to meet the airplane. Perfect coordination, a light control touch, flawless execution, and a dose of good luck are crucial. Since altitude dissipates much faster in turns, it's likely that this limited resource will be depleted in the midst of turning around. Contacting the ground in a bank, rather than wings level, greatly reduces the probability of survival.

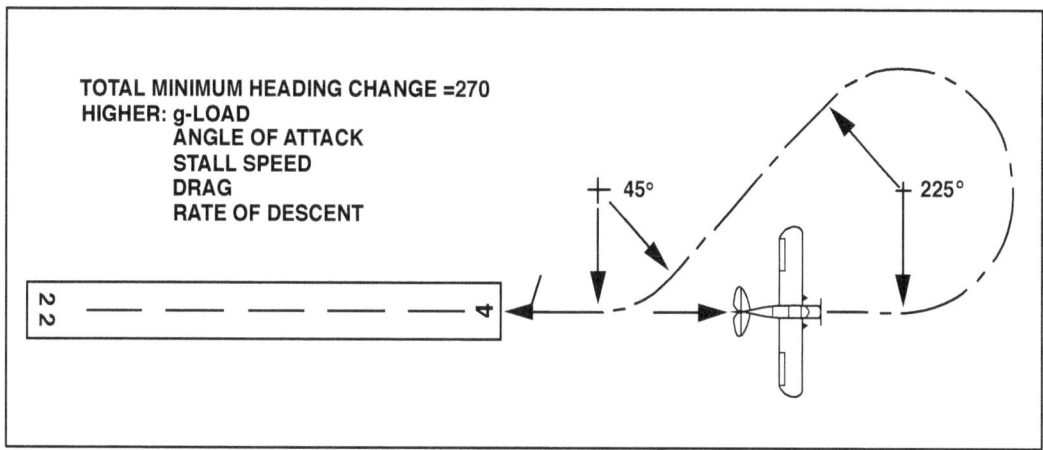

Figure 11-5: Factors Involved when Turning Back to the Runway

Few cases warrant turning around at low altitude. Too many variables are stacked against the pilot. Confusing an increase in groundspeed as increasing airspeed as the airplane turns downwind further complicates matters. Extra aft elevator applied to slow the ground rush reduces airspeed, increases g-load, and moves us toward critical angle of attack and an accelerated stall instead. If that wasn't enough, we may then have to cope with a downwind landing **AND** opposing traffic on the runway.

It's far more survivable to contact obstacles on the departure end of the runway while slow, controlled, and in the landing attitude (wings level). Cartwheeling across the open space of an airport, or stalling, spinning, or rolling to inverted and pulling into the ground often lead to serious injury. Accident reports confirm this over and over again. As soon as an airplane ventures outside of its glide window in an emergency, the chances of survival drop almost to zero.

Should power totally fail on the upwind leg just after takeoff, **PUSH** to establish best glide Speed. Don't look back. Envision a window, diverging at 45 degree angles on both sides of your heading. Scan this area out front for your landing Spot, regardless of the terrain. Make small, coordinated heading adjustments within this area prior to landing with the wings level. Avoid the roughest terrain and the largest obstacles if possible. Fly the airplane all the way to the ground. Try to treat the forced landing as though it was a normal landing.

Use this same "window" technique should power fail on final approach, too. If the approach is flown below the no power, best glide slope discussed earlier, resign yourself to landing short of the runway. Fly the airplane accordingly. Don't try to stretch the glide. Aft elevator pressure will not improve glide performance, but it will pull you to slower speeds, higher angles of attack, increased g's, increased Drag, and greater rates of descent. Push for speed instead, and control the airplane through touchdown.

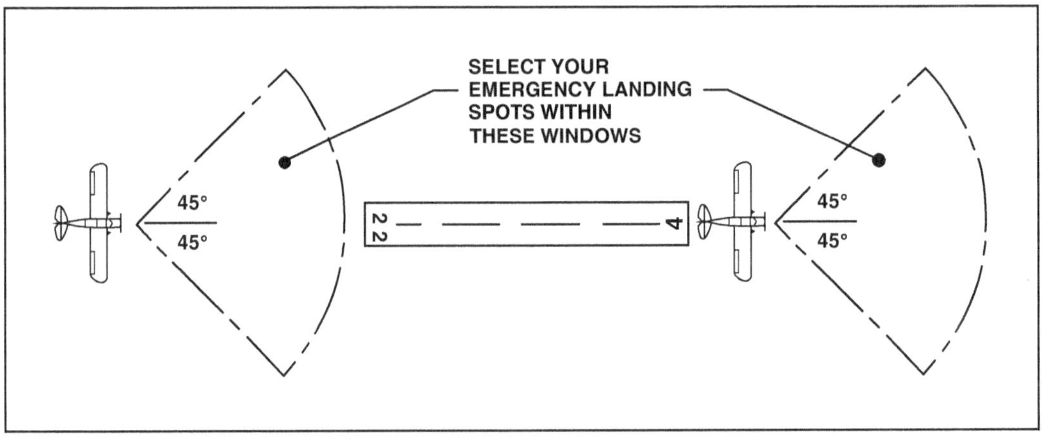

Figure 11-6: Visualising the Glide Window on Departure and on Approach

Pitch for best glide Speed whenever the airplane loses power unexpectedly, then head toward a landing Spot. If the engine is still producing some power, but you cannot hold altitude at best glide speed, manoeuvre for landing as though you have a total power failure. The engine could stop completely at any moment. Pick the same spot you would if you had no power and manoeuvre accordingly. Right after takeoff or on final approach, establish best glide speed and land within the recommended glide windows.

Even if sufficient power remains to hold altitude at best glide speed, don't assume the airplane will be able to hobble back to the runway. Plan on the engine quitting completely at any moment. With this in mind, head toward the first landing site reachable in a power-off glide. If enough power is available to climb during the process, then climb. Continue manoeuvring from one potential landing site to another. Work your way toward the airport whenever feasible. Proceed from site to site until power output ceases altogether, or until the next landing site within glide range is a runway. This is an emergency; take charge and do whatever is necessary for your own safety.

For instance, assume you're practicing touch and go's at a controlled field with a single runway. You've been flying a right-hand pattern that overflies a busy freeway, hilly terrain, and housing developments. The left-hand pattern is in use simultaneously, and it overflies flat, agricultural land (e.g.: Camarillo airport in California). The engine suffers a partial power failure during one of your climb-outs. Since the left-hand pattern offers more favorable landing sites, don't hesitate to break from your right-hand pattern. Establish best glide Speed first, then select a Spot on the left side of your glide "window". If you can hold altitude at best glide speed, fly from one landing site to another, approximating a left downwind back toward the runway. With Speed and Spot variables firmly under control, let the controllers know you have a problem and prepare the airplane for landing.

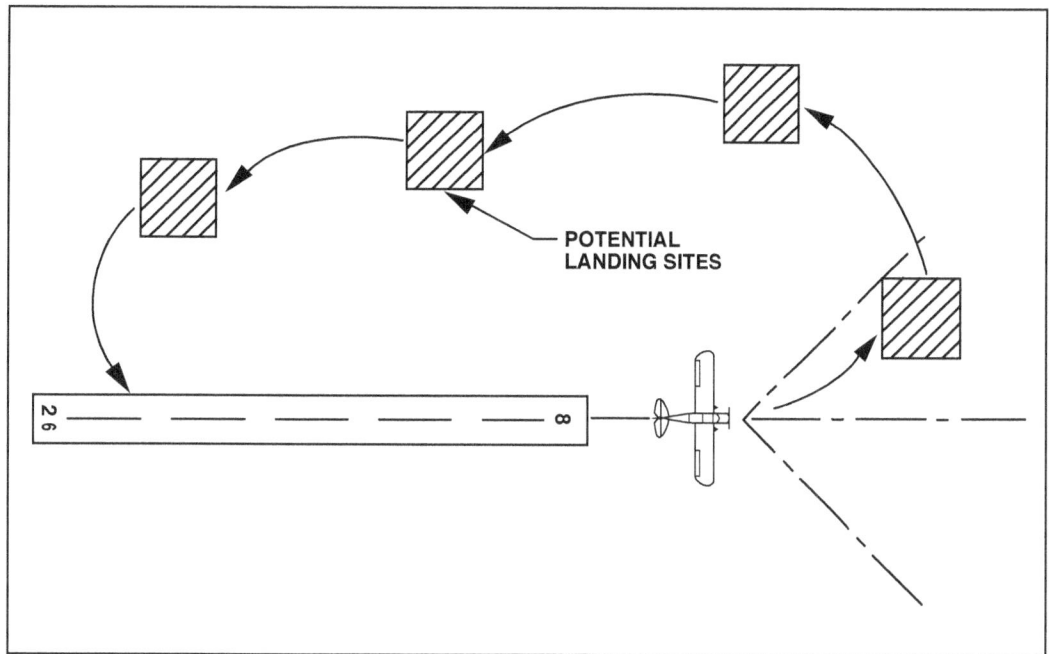

Figure 11-7: Leapfrogging between Landing Sites after a Partial Power Failure

Set-up

An engine failure at low altitude may not afford ample time to configure the airplane for the forced landing. Managing higher priority Speed and Spot elements may require our undivided attention. If altitude and our own ability permit, however, we can perform additional tasks to enhance the probability of post-impact survival. Other actions taken prior to touchdown include leveling the wings, shutting down the powerplant, reducing the risk of fire, configuring flaps and landing gear, and preparing to evacuate the airplane. Exact preparatory procedures are outlined in most flight manuals. Review them, before you need them! In general, such procedures include the following items, which are divided here into related sub-tasks:

1. Engine Shut Down/Reduce Fire Hazard:
   Throttle—Closed
   Fuel—Off
   Mixture—Idle cut-off
   Mags—Off

2. Gear & Flap Management:
   Gear—Position as appropriate
   Flaps—Deploy as needed, when needed
   Master Switch—Off

3. Pilot & Passenger Preparation:
   Prepare Egress—Unlatch doors and windows
   Seat belts—Tighten

As many of these tasks as possible should be addressed before landing once Speed is firmly under control and the Spot is chosen. Given the proximity to the ground when operating in the pattern, adequate time generally is not available to initiate engine restart procedures. Little time may be left to prepare for landing by the time Speed and Spot have been addressed, so don't waste precious altitude trying to restart the engine. Fly the airplane, and set yourself up to survive the landing.

Consider the position of retractable landing gear only if you have time to change it. Unless the airplane flight manual specifically recommends otherwise, leave the gear up unless sufficient altitude remains to extend it fully before impact **AND** the intended Spot is hard packed. Leave the gear down unless the Spot is quite rugged **AND** enough altitude exists to raise it completely before impact. The proximity of landing gear to fuel tanks in many low wing airplanes can make its position critical during a forced landing.

Lower airspeeds are possible with deployed flaps, thus reducing the amount of energy to be dissipated during the landing. Adding flaps, however, reduces gliding distance, so don't lower them unless a landing on the intended Spot is guaranteed. Compensate for secondary pitch changes as the flaps move into position to control your airspeed. If the flaps are already deployed when the engine fails, **DO NOT RETRACT THEM**. First establish best glide Speed and head toward a landing Spot. In cases where sufficient partial power remains to hold altitude at Vbg, raise the flaps incrementally to reduce Drag as you move between potential landing sites.

Egress is an important, yet often overlooked item when preparing for a forced landing. Doors and canopies may be jammed shut if the fuselage bends on impact, so it's a good idea to unlatch them prior to touchdown. If you only have time to do one Set-up task, **MAKE IT THIS ONE!** Also, it's our responsibility as pilots in command to brief our passengers on emergency egress procedures. This includes how to unlatch the door when directed (especially if the airplane only has one door, and it's on their side) and how to unfasten the seat belts.

Loss Of Power Control

Although the most common type of powerplant failure is a sudden drop in power, another scenario is possible wherein precise control over the power setting is lost. A failed throttle linkage, for example, removes our direct line of communication with the engine. Consequently, power is frozen at one particular setting. We can influence power indirectly, though, by tapping the effects various engine accessories have on power output. Applying carburetor heat, for instance, reduces engine rpm. So does shutting off one of the magnetos. Pulling the mixture to idle cut-off reduces power output to zero. By pulling handles, turning knobs, and flipping switches that effectively steal power away from the propeller, we can exercise limited power control.

Our alternate means of controlling power can be classified under two headings: incremental power reductions and total power reductions. Each produces a different net effect on power output. The cumulative effect of incremental power reductions may drop engine output 100-500 rpm. Diluting power incrementally allows a commensurate reduction in airspeed without climbing. If airspeed can be slowed below maximum gear and/or flap extension speeds, the additional Drag from landing gear and deployed flaps could help to reduce speed further before landing. Incremental power reduction techniques include the following actions:

1. Carburetor Heat (or Alternate Air)—On
2. Magnetos—Set to left or to right mag only
3. Mixture—Lean until rpm drops slightly
4. Electrical Switches—On
5. Constant Speed Propellers—Pull out to increase pitch/decrease rpm slightly

On the other hand, total power reduction techniques allow us to remove all remaining power instantaneously. Depending on the situation, we could implement at least one, if not both, total power reduction techniques at some point during the landing process:

1. Magnetos—Off
2. Mixture—Idle cut-off

Before airplane engines were equipped with throttles and mixtures, power was controlled by turning the magnetos off and on. With power stuck "on", cycling the mags results in better control over the landing approach than merely pulling the mixture to idle cut-off and gliding to touchdown. An extra bonus when using the mags is the ability to add a momentary burst of power late in the approach, should it be needed to make an adjustment or to go around.

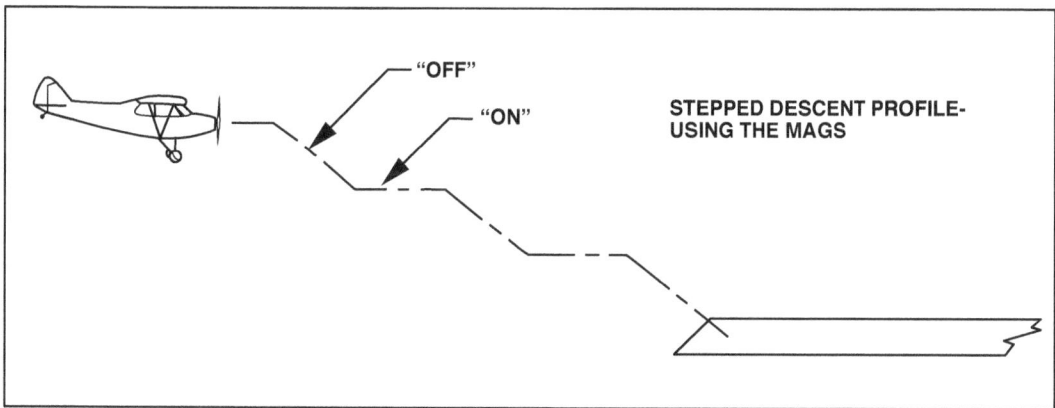

Figure 11-8: Cycling the Magnetos on Final Approach

Proper airspeed control may require anticipating the need for additional forward elevator pressure when turning the mags "on", and slight back elevator pressure when turning the mags "off". Such rapid power changes may be accompanied by loud backfiring as well, but don't let this distract you from controlling the airplane. Once you're committed to land, turn the mags off.

The same Speed-Spot-Set-up hierarchy discussed for Power Loss still applies during Loss of Power Control. Should the throttle linkage fail at a low power setting in the pattern, with insufficient power remaining to hold altitude at best glide speed, react the same as in any engine failure: Establish and maintain best glide Speed, manoeuvre toward a suitable landing Spot reachable within the applicable glide "window", and if time permits, Set-up for the landing.

Even though glide range is enhanced with partial power stuck "on", resist the urge to try to stretch the glide farther by pulling the elevator control aft. Choose a Spot within glide range at Vbg, which may or may not be the runway. Also, be prepared to turn the mags off, and/or to pull the mixture to idle cut-off, to avoid overshooting the intended landing site.

Should the throttle linkage fail at a high power setting in the pattern, climb to a safe altitude and orbit over, or near the airport. Take time to evaluate your options. See what power and airspeed combinations are possible using incremental power reduction techniques. Divert to a nearby airport with a longer runway and fewer obstacles on the approach end, if necessary. Address these questions before rushing to the surface: Will the approach be fast, or will enough power be reduced to fly at best glide speed in the pattern? How will the airplane be configured prior to landing? What flap setting will be used? Which total power reduction technique will be employed: cycle the mags on final, or pull the mixture to idle cut-off and glide to touchdown?

Once you've mapped out a strategy and have visualised the approach, proceed to land. Use incremental power reductions to permit slower airspeeds without climbing. Adjust your final descent profile and compensate for errors in judgment by cycling the mags. Fly the airplane all the way to the surface with smooth, coordinated control inputs. Plan ahead and stay ahead of the situation.

This chapter focused on powerplant problems, particularly those occurring at low altitude around an airport. It should come as no surprise that many of the strategies discussed here also come into play during off-airport landings from higher altitudes, as we'll see in the next chapter.

12
Off-Airport Landings

We developed the Speed-Spot-Set-up hierarchy in the previous chapter as part of forced landings from the low altitude, low airspeed operations typical around airports. We'll expand on this sequence to include forced landings from higher altitudes, like those associated with cross-country flying. Proper glide management, interrelated with Speed and Spot variables, is always critical following an engine failure. Given sufficient altitude, we also can address field selection and obstacle parameters as they relate to the Set-up for landing.

When faced with the prospect of an off-airport landing, we need to analyse our options quickly and begin the landing process. Our priorities are Speed-Spot-Set-up: Establish best glide Speed first, without delay. If the airspeed is near cruise speed, initiate a shallow climb to gain extra altitude while slowing to best glide. Next, select a Spot and head the airplane toward it. Postpone attempts to restart the engine until the airplane is on its way to a potential landing site. Choose the closest suitable site to your present location, even if it looks less desirable than a field near the end of your glide range. Selecting the closer site improves the accuracy of our judgments. Also, any spare altitude can be used to weigh approach options while circling overhead and could come in handy while manoeuvring into position for landing.

Evaluate your progress by monitoring the interaction between Speed and Spot during the glide. Recall from Chapter 10—Glides that if your Spot moves up the wind-screen, or if you note a decreasing trend in Speed, the chosen site is **BEYOND GLIDE RANGE**. Pick a closer field. On the other hand, if your Spot slides down the wind-screen, or if you observe an increasing trend in Speed, the chosen site is **WITHIN GLIDE RANGE**. Fly at best glide Speed and continue toward the Spot.

Engine Restart

Work load and altitude permitting, implement engine restart procedures en route to the landing site, before securing the powerplant for landing. Restart procedures attempt to troubleshoot some of the more common causes for engine failure, which include fuel starvation or contamination, carburetor or induction system icing, and ignition system failure or interruption. Restart actions provide continuity checks of systems furnishing the three elements essential for internal combustion: Fuel, Air, and Sparks.

The main components of the fuel system are the fuel tanks and an engine-mounted carburetor or fuel injection unit. These are interconnected by a series of fuel lines. Several pilot-controllable accessories are often integrated into the system, including fuel selector and/or shut-off valves, electric fuel pumps, manual primers, and mixture controls. We want to make sure that fuel, if it's available, can flow from the tanks to the engine unimpeded by these accessories.

Configure the fuel system for restart by switching the selector valve to another fuel tank. Verify that the shut-off valve is "on", turn the electric boost pump "on", and make sure the primer is in and locked. Adjust the mixture accordingly: full rich at density altitudes below 5,000 feet, especially if the mixture control is leaned out and the engine quit while descending; lean it slightly at higher density altitudes if the mixture control is all the way in. Suspect fuel system problems whenever the engine quits abruptly, without making any other sounds.

The air intake system isn't as intricate as the fuel system. Outside air for combustion usually comes from two independent sources close to the engine. The primary air source passes through an air filter prior to mixing with fuel. The back-up air source, though unfiltered, is preheated by the engine before it's mixed with fuel. This may be done by passing it through a heater muff or shroud around the exhaust muffler, or by taking warm air directly from the engine compartment. Both air sources are ducted to an air box mounted on the carburetor or injection unit. The position of carburetor heat or alternate air controls determines which air source is being tapped.

The engine failure could be related to a lack of sufficient air for combustion, perhaps caused by a clogged or disintegrating air filter or the formation of induction ice. In either event, switching to the secondary air source could alleviate the problem and provide enough air to keep the engine running. Configure the air intake system for restart by applying carburetor heat, or switching to alternate air. If power fades gradually, suspect air intake problems and change the air source.

Once sufficient quantities of fuel and air reach the cylinders, a spark is needed for combustion. Sparks are provided by the ignition system, which is comprised of an engine-driven magneto, spark plugs, ignition leads (wires), and an on/off switch. Two complete ignition systems are provided for the engine. Under normal operation, they function simultaneously for increased efficiency and power output. Should components of one system fail, however, combustion will still occur as long as the other system is operational.

The reliability inherent in redundant ignition systems greatly reduces the probability of a total failure in our ability to generate sparks. It's possible, though, to interrupt these systems by inadvertently turning their switches off. Configure the ignition systems for restart by first verifying that the magneto switches are on "both". If the propeller is windmilling, it'll drive the magnetos, which in turn will presumably produce sparks. If the prop has stopped, verify that the master switch is also "on" and engage the starter. Even though exact restart procedures may be included in your airplane's operating handbook, look for these common elements:

FUEL	AIR	SPARKS
SELECTOR VALVE—SWITCH TANKS	CARBURETTOR HEAT—ON	MAGNETOS—ON "BOTH"
SHUT-OFF VALVE—ON	—or—	—if prop is stopped—
FUEL PUMP—ON	ALTERNATE AIR—ON	MASTER SWITCH—ON
PRIMER—IN & LOCKED		
MIXTURE—FULL RICH BELOW 5,000		
—LEAN ABOVE 5,000		

Table 12-1: Typical Elements of Engine Restart Procedures

The prop must turn in order to drive the magnetos, otherwise no sparks can be generated. Suppose the prop has stopped, though, and the airplane is not equipped with a starter, or the battery is too weak to crank the engine. Two options may be available: we might consider diving the airplane until enough speed is gained to windmill the propeller, or we could shelve the restart procedure and concentrate on the forced landing.

Diving for speed to turn the prop sacrifices altitude and glide range. Also, it's uncertain that the engine will start again anyway. If you cannot pinpoint and then correct the cause of the engine failure, it doesn't make sense to gamble away altitude on an unknown quantity. Furthermore, unless you're directly over a suitable landing site, with an abundance of reserve altitude, and unless you're committed to pushing the nose over forcefully until the prop turns, why compound the emergency with this distraction?

Limiting the number of extraneous variables acting on the pilot during an emergency increases the probability of a successful outcome. Avoid one-of-a-kind bits of fancy flying. Keep your actions simple, straightforward, and as routine as possible. Although diving for speed may be an option at high altitude, it usually makes more sense to take advantage of the improved glide performance with the prop stopped while focusing ahead on the landing.

Should attempts to restart the engine fail, continue toward your landing site at best glide speed. Reduce propeller Drag by pulling the prop control into the high pitch/low rpm position on controllable pitch propellers. Your duties will now be divided between controlling Speed, evaluating the terrain around the landing Spot, and working through the emergency procedures outlined in the airplane's operating handbook to Set-up for an approach.

If you reach the field with altitude to spare, perform a moderate spiral and circle overhead. Determine wind direction and strength by observing the spiral's movement over the ground while holding airspeed and bank angle constant. Your flight path will creep downwind. Once wind direction is known, modify the spiral or fly an oval pattern to compensate for wind effects. Don't let the wind push the airplane downwind, away from the field. Orbit the landing site, favoring the upwind side.

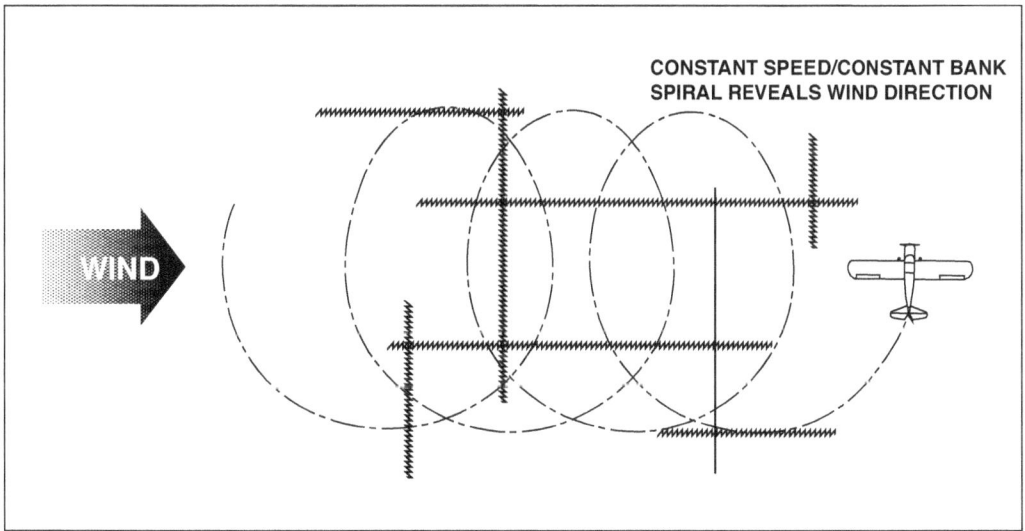

Figure 12-1: Determining Wind Direction Based on Ground Track

Evaluating Your Options

Throughout this process, we must weigh wind, terrain, and obstacle variables to select an appropriate landing strategy. Wind direction and strength should be one of the first considerations. Although landing into the wind is preferable, it may be inadvisable, or even impossible given the terrain or our height above the ground. For crosswind landings, plan an approach that results in a headwind component on base leg whenever possible.

A tailwind component could cause you to overshoot the turn to final, increasing the tendency to perform a dangerous, skidding turn. Also, misinterpreting the attendant rise in groundspeed from a tailwind as increased airspeed can result in excessive back elevator pressure, higher angles of attack, and critically low airspeeds.

Obstacles surrounding a landing site reduce our usable altitude and the length of the field available for rollout. Approaching over the lowest obstacles increases the effective altitude and field length available to us. Whenever possible, land facing the higher obstacles. For instance, suppose the selected site has a row of 10 foot trees on one end, 50 foot trees on the other, and wind is not a factor in our decision. The best direction in which to land is over the lower obstacles, heading toward the higher ones.

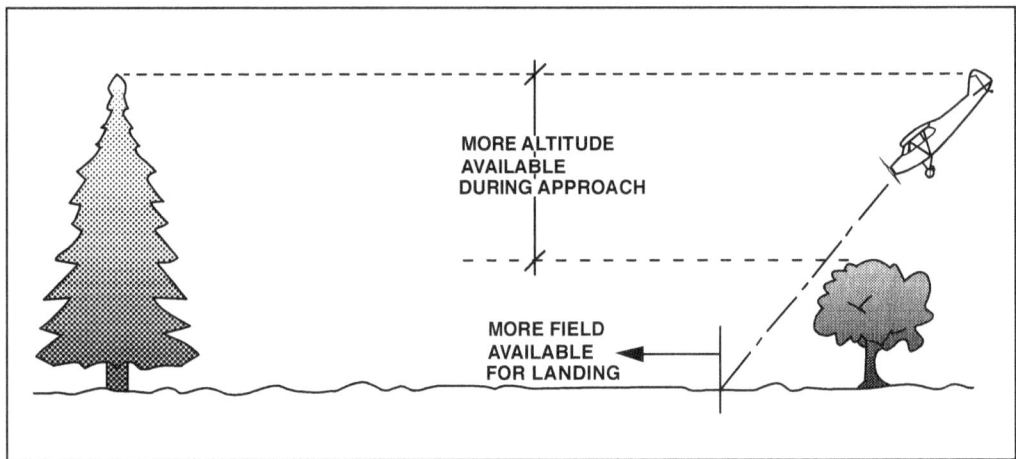

Figure 12-2: Increasing the Effective Altitude and Field Length

If the long side of the field has tall obstacles on each end and the short side is too narrow for a landing, consider turning your base leg inside of the tall obstacles, rather than attempting the approach over them. Misjudging low and hitting the tops of the obstacles may cause you to lose control of the airplane too high above the ground. Even if turning inside of these obstacles causes you to overshoot the field, you are in position to contact obstacles at the far end while low, slow, and in the landing attitude. More importantly, it will be a **CONTROLLED** impact. Approaching over lower obstacles and landing diagonally across such a field may be another possibility.

When over rugged terrain, be wary of isolated service roads or cut-outs in the trees. They may indicate the presence of high tension power lines, which could be invisible against the terrain. It's often easier to see towers, poles, and other supporting structures than power lines themselves, so scan the ground for these telltale signs. Should high tension lines loom in the wind-screen, resist the urge to stretch the glide over the top of them, particularly if airspeed is below best glide. **PUSH** on the elevator control and dive **UNDER** them! This is a better option than clipping high tension lines and losing control of the airplane altogether, or becoming entangled in the wires. Flying beneath the wires may cause you to overshoot the intended field, but you'll be closer to the ground and under control upon impact.

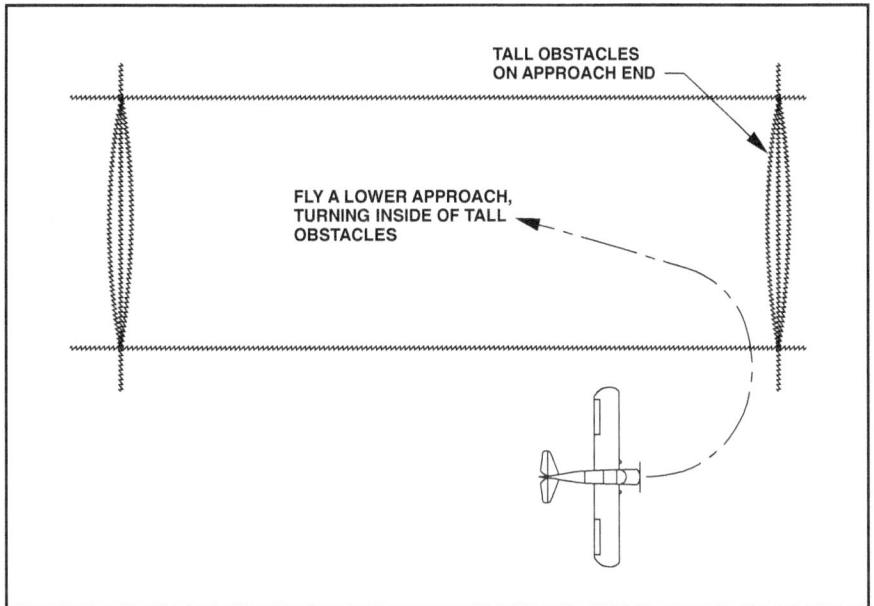

Figure 12-3: Turning Inside Tall Obstacles on the Approach End

We certainly have fewer options in hilly terrain. Even so, we remain in charge of how we will land. Maintain precise control over the airplane all the way to touchdown. Landing uphill will decelerate the airplane quicker, even with a tailwind, than travelling downhill. Gravity acts like Drag when rolling uphill, reducing landing distance. On the other hand, it acts like Thrust when rolling downhill, lengthening the rollout and making it difficult to stop. In steep terrain, landing diagonally uphill reduces the likelihood of rolling backwards after touchdown.

Terrain features influence our landing decisions as well. For example, it's usually better to land parallel to furrows and to accept a crosswind than it is to land perpendicular to them, into the wind. Clumps of low brush, or darker-colored patches on the ground often signify softer, wetter terrain. Whenever possible, aim for more barren, lighter-colored areas.

With wind, terrain, and obstacles considered, adjust your pattern over the site to arrive at the first key position for final approach. This position is normally downwind, abeam the intended landing spot, and represents the start of an 180 degree power-off approach. You must arrive at this point with adequate altitude to cover not only the linear distances along the base and final legs, but also extra altitude for the turns onto these legs, other corrective manoeuvres, and wind effects. Flying farther from the landing site demands greater height above the ground at the key position. Try to achieve the familiar look and feel of similar approaches flown at your home airport, and be conservative with your judgments.

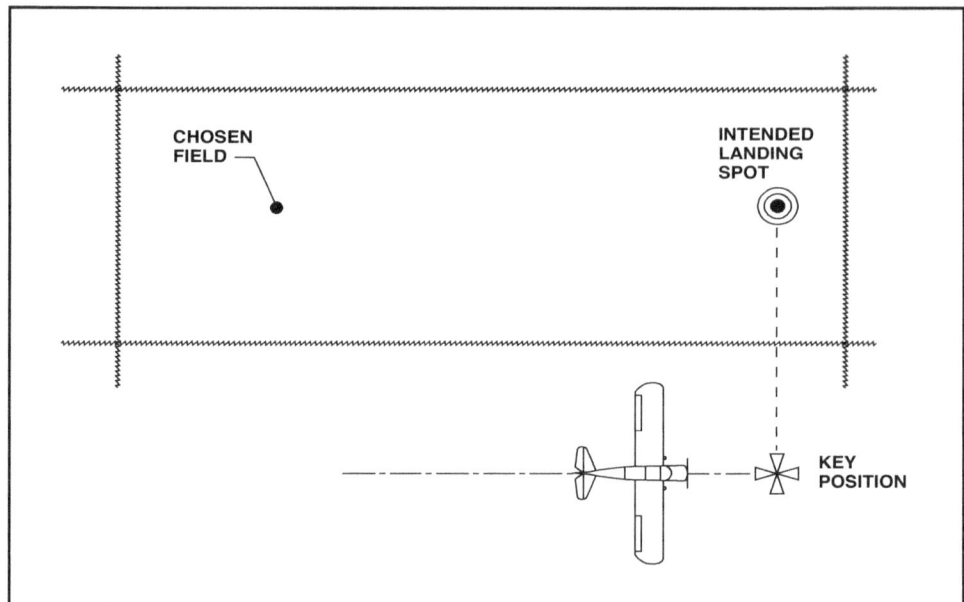

Figure 12-4: Visualising the Key Position and the Intended Landing Spot

Devote any spare time to preparing the airplane for landing. Secure all loose objects and follow the Set-up procedures outlined in the last chapter, Powerplant Failures. To prevent the engine from roaring back to life unexpectedly during the flare—and to minimise fire hazards—close the throttle, close the fuel valve, pull the mixture to idle cut-off, and turn off the mags. Unless otherwise recommended in the airplane's flight manual, consider leaving retractable gear up if the landing area is rugged, especially in low wing airplanes. Landing gear torn from, or forced through the wings could rupture fuel tanks, increasing the risk of fire. If you choose to extend the gear, plan to do so upon reaching the key position. Be sure to account for diminished glide performance with the gear down, too.

Reserve flap deployment for later in the approach. Use your flaps to dissipate excess altitude on final and to help slow the airplane prior to touchdown. Be certain you will reach your Spot if the flaps are lowered. Tighten your seat belts and unlatch the door(s) or the canopy. Lock the door latch open after undoing it, or wedge a sectional chart or other object between the doorjamb and the fuselage to provide an exit in case the fuselage is deformed on landing.

Flying the Approach

It's critical to stay ahead of the airplane from the key position down to landing. Increase your situational awareness another notch. Control the airspeed with small corrections. Remember, we're balancing Speed and Spot, so keep tight reigns on your position relative to the landing site. Track a flight path that either parallels, or converges on, the landing site. Don't diverge from it. The only way to know exactly where you are, how the approach is progressing, and what type of manoeuvring is needed is to look at your Spot. Make a conscious effort to view the site **AS MUCH AS POSSIBLE** from here on down.

Manoeuvring from the key position onto base and final consumes additional altitude; therefore, you must have altitude to spare before initiating these turns. Whenever possible, choose a touchdown Spot that allows you to compress or stretch the base leg to compensate for misjudged height. Also, avoid the tendency to manoeuvre tentatively from the key position onto the base leg. This is the single most important manoeuvre between the key position and touchdown. Proper execution is crucial. Timid, indecisive actions here often snowball into larger corrections later in the approach, while precariously close to the ground.

For example, a simulated, 180 degree power-off approach in the training environment typically goes something like this: After passing the key downwind position, the pilot's eyes fixate straight ahead. The airplane continues downwind, often diverging away from the Spot at the same time. A tentative, shallow turn is initiated sometime later, based on some internal cadence. The manoeuvre occurs without establishing a definite bank, without considering wind effects, and without thinking about a final heading. The bank angle wanders back to wings level during the process as the airplane drifts away from the landing site. Three factors drive this drifting tendency:

1. The inherent stability of the airplane in a shallow bank tends to return the wings to level.

2. A crosswind on the base leg tries to roll the wings level while pushing the airplane farther downwind.

3. Rather than positively controlling the airplane to reach the site, the pilot allows the above detrimental effects to go unchallenged. In fact, the pilot may compound matters by inadvertently applying aileron opposite to the direction of the turn. Also, the pilot is reluctant to look at the landing Spot, making it difficult to evaluate the situation accurately.

The turn to final progresses with a similar lack of conviction. As the site moves into the pilot's forward field of vision, the airplane is perceived to be low, too far from the site, and usually not lined up for landing. It's now too late in the approach to correct the errors that have accumulated since passing the key position. Had the pilot maintained visual contact with the site and vigorously pursued it right from the start, the airplane would be in a better position to reach the chosen Spot.

Fly the approach such that progressively smaller corrections are needed as you get closer to the ground. Make your gross corrections early, when you have the most altitude. Fine tune the approach thereafter. Keep the site within glide range at all times, and don't let the wind push the airplane away from it. Remember, no strategies exist to reclaim altitude once it has been lost. Several strategies are available, however, to dissipate excess altitude if we misjudge on the high side. These include varying the position and length of the base leg, slipping turns, slipping on final, lowering flaps, and slowing down slightly below best glide speed.

Our objective is to reach the intended Spot. A minimum heading change of 90 degrees is required to achieve this from a downwind position. In fact, a downwind-to-base turn should continue **BEYOND** 90 degrees to compensate for wind and judgment errors. Turning through 90 degrees and pointing the nose at your Spot automatically builds in a crab angle against any headwind. It also gets us moving toward our destination while minimising the stretching effects of the wind.

When you decide to turn toward the site, establish an appropriate angle of bank and bend the flight path around until the nose points at your Spot. If turning from a downwind position, the steepest bank always occurs right at the start of the turn, perhaps then shallowing as the airplane swings around upwind. Remember that shallower banks and descending turns may require a small amount of aileron held in the direction of the turn. Set the bank, and don't let it vary unless you command it to change. Maintain best glide speed throughout, stay coordinated, and look at the site. Forge ahead until the nose is locked onto your Spot.

Modify the approach as the nose comes around to the landing site. If altitude is marginal, maintain the bank and keep turning. The resulting flight path will be a continuous curve from the key position onto final. If you have too much altitude, reduce the bank and square off the approach. Stretch the base leg to dissipate some of the excess altitude before turning onto final. If the altitude is about right, the airplane will follow a somewhat segmented flight path while continually heading toward the desired site.

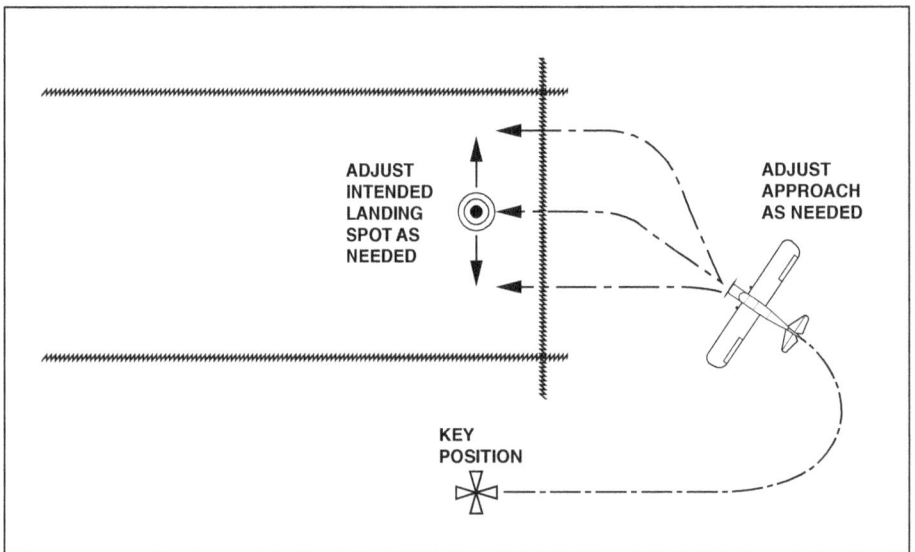

Figure 12-5: Modifying the Final Approach Path

We must make corrections during the approach based on the steady-state consequences of our inputs, not their transient effects on our descent profile. The typical response to a high approach, for instance, is to dive the airplane at the aim point. Diving appears to solve the problem initially, but it paints a deceiving picture. The steady-state result is too much speed and excessive float, with the airplane overshooting the aim point anyway. Conversely, pulling back to stretch a glide during a low approach momentarily balloons the airplane upward. This appears to yield the desired result; however, once we're done ballooning, the airplane settles into a steeper descent and lands even shorter. Again, you cannot stretch a glide by allowing the speed to drop below best glide.

Should the aim point slide toward you on final, you're high. Don't dive the airplane at the ground. Extra speed will only shorten the length of field available for rollout. Instead, steepen the descent by deploying a notch of flaps, executing a controlled slip, slowing down three to five units (knots or mph) below best glide, or a combination of these. Don't be swayed by the transient effects of these corrections. Make small adjustments first, and give the airplane a chance to stabilise before correcting further.

Should you perceive the Spot moving away from you on final, and if obstacles on the approach end begin looming above the horizon line in your wind-screen, you're too low. We cannot climb back to the desired glide slope. Attempting to stretch the glide by pulling is futile. Maintain your Speed, even if it means nudging the stick or wheel forward a bit. In fact, if the approach end is relatively obstruction-free, increasing your speed three to five units above best glide may allow you to float toward the intended

Spot in ground effect. Accept, however, that the airplane will land short of the mark, and don't allow the speed to dip below best glide.

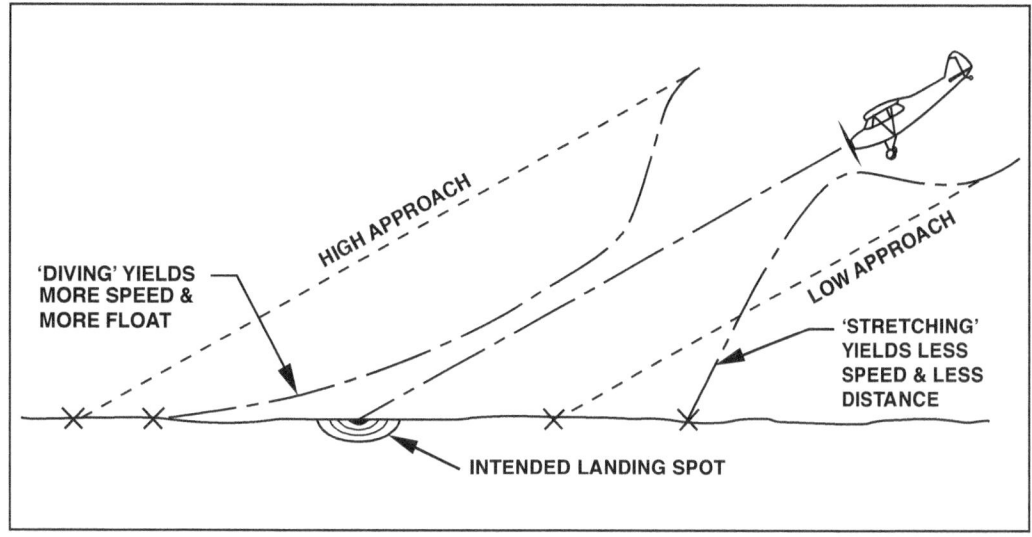

Figure 12-6: Steady State Consequences of Incorrect Reactions to High & Low Approaches

Resist the urge to rush earthward during the final stage of the approach. Exercise positive control over the airplane through the touchdown. Fly a stabilised approach, continue to scan the landing site, and make small, controlled corrections as you near the ground. If the approach has been planned and executed properly, you should have a touch of altitude to spare on short final. Extending some flaps, performing a shallow slip, or reducing the approach speed slightly below best glide should be all that's needed to dissipate any excess altitude.

Avoid fixating on obstacles on the approach end to the exclusion of Speed control and Spot judgment. Only those obstructions protruding through the horizon line, or whose tops are sliding up your wind-screen, are of concern. Provided airspeed remains at best glide, trees and other obstacles that don't creep up toward the horizon will be under your flight path; so, ignore these particular objects. Fly the Speed and judge the Spot.

The Touchdown

Suppress feelings of anxiety by focusing on positively controlling the airplane. Don't brace for impact by freezing on the controls prematurely. Control your attitude and airspeed as long as possible. Actively bleeding off speed in the flare will shrink your overall stopping distance and lessen impact forces. Consider that each additional 10 percent reduction in airspeed before impact will reduce destructive energy required to stop the airplane by 19 percent. Excess speed, on the other hand, compounds destructive energy by 21 percent for each 10 percent increase in speed. Manage your airspeed, and slow down in the flare.

The modern light airplane's structure is designed to protect occupants during a controlled emergency landing. For example, with seats and restraint systems properly adjusted, occupants must be protected to at least the following static loads: 9.0 g's in the forward direction, 3.0 g's upward (4.5 g's in the Acrobatic category), and 1.5 g's sideways. Dynamic load test criteria include a 26 g deceleration in 0.05 seconds or less without seat or restraint system failures. Emergency landing survivability, therefore, can be improved simply by taking advantage of the crashworthiness designed into your airplane.

Position yourself to contact obstacles low, slow, in the landing attitude (wings level).

Configure the airplane to minimise the probability of serious injury: keep it straight, and try to spread the deceleration out over time. Point the nose between trees and other obstacles wherever possible. Use the airplane like a shield. Allow the wings, landing gear, and other disposable parts of the airframe to absorb the brunt of the impact. Try to maintain the integrity of the cockpit/cabin area to protect the occupants. Sacrifice the airplane to save yourself and your passengers.

Statistically, surviving an emergency off-airport landing has surprisingly little to do with the type of terrain and obstacles encountered. The airplane's speed and attitude at the time of ground contact, coupled with the degree of control exercised by the pilot, are far more significant. It would be easy to succumb to normal anxieties over the impending forced landing, but our focus must remain on flying the airplane as long as possible.

Don't deny that you have an emergency, either. Accept it, recognising that the airplane is going to return to the Earth. Acknowledge that the airplane may necessarily sustain damage so as to protect its occupants. Relinquish any false sense of control over the why or the where of the situation. Shift your attention, instead, to the **HOW** of it. As the pilot, you remain in charge of the type of forced landing to be executed. Choose the controlled landing option. Concentrate on the Speed-Spot-Set-up hierarchy, beginning and ending with an emphasis on Speed control.

13

The Pilot In Command

Emergency manoeuvre training is about helping the pilot remain in control. So far, we've focused on the three dimensional language of flight from the pilot's perspective. We've explored the aerodynamic limitations of our equipment and the continual interaction between the pilot and the airplane. It's now time to examine the awesome responsibility we assume when we climb into the cockpit as pilots in command (PIC's). We'll also consider the influence our psychological make-up has on our capacity to cope with the demands of the flight environment. Let's start by reviewing some of the definitions pertaining to the PIC listed in Subchapter A, Part 1, Section 1.1 of the FAR's:

"Air traffic control" [ATC] means a service operated by appropriate authority to promote the safe, orderly, and expeditious flow of air traffic.

"Pilot in command" means the pilot who is responsible for the operation and safety of an aircraft during flight time.

"Flight time" means the time from the moment the aircraft first moves under its own power....

The FAR's clearly delineate the roles of the pilot and ATC. By definition, ATC does not assume responsibility for our safety; it only enhances our ability to fly safely. Before we perform a preflight or plot a cross-country, we must understand the responsibility we accept when we choose to fly. Realise that the aviation system in which we operate exists only to provide information to help us make better judgments; the ultimate responsibility for aeronautical decision-making is ours alone. Moreover, the PIC's absolute authority is established in Subchapter F, Part 91, Section 91.3:

(a) The pilot in command of an aircraft is directly responsible for, and is the final authority as to, the operation of that aircraft.

(b) In an in-flight emergency requiring immediate action, the pilot in command may deviate from any rule of this part to the extent required to meet that emergency.

The PIC must always determine what the safest course of action is, even if it seems contrary to FAA regulations, guidelines, or instructions. The objective is survival, especially in an emergency—no one can be responsible for your well-being but **you**! The PIC shoulders this solemn burden alone; it cannot be shared with anyone else. Acting as PIC requires transforming knowledge and skill into good judgment. Along with this, the PIC must develop and maintain a high degree of situational awareness.

Arrogance, rebellion, and recklessness certainly are not traits of pilots in command. Instead, PIC's display a courteous and professional attitude toward flying. They are decisive, they fly with confidence, and they manage stress well. PIC's recognise their human aptitude to commit errors, but strive to minimise their consequences. Positive qualities associated with model PIC's include the ability to lead, to establish priorities, to access and use available information, and to maintain open channels of communication with others in the flight environment.

The PIC is the active ingredient in the flight process, not a passenger along for the ride. Leadership in the cockpit manifests itself as the capacity to admit when a problem exists, then to take appropriate steps to address it. When necessary, the PIC must be willing to delegate certain duties to passengers or to ATC. A PIC also accepts information from a variety of sources, verifies its accuracy through a series of independent checks and balances, and makes decisions based on its validity.

Although denial, hesitation, and confusion are normal first reactions to an in-flight emergency, prioritising your needs minimises mental down time. The popular *"aviate, navigate, communicate"* strategy is an ideal example of prioritised actions designed to improve a pilot's odds during an emergency. The pilot must fly the airplane first (aviate) to have any chance of surviving. Navigational duties are next in line, added in once positive control is re-established. Talking on the radio occupies the lowest rung on this crisis management ladder.

Conflict resolution requires the PIC to access information from sources inside and outside of the cockpit. An impressive—and sometimes intimidating—network has evolved to help pilots assess various situations and flight conditions. This network includes the national airspace system, Federal Aviation Regulations (FAR's), air traffic control (ATC), Flight Service Stations (FSS's), fixed-base operators (FBO's), aircraft manufacturers, navigational charts, flight instructors, aircraft equipment and instruments, airports and facilities, checklists, books, and videos. Even passengers can be a valuable source of information. It's important to remember, though, that this information network exists to serve the PIC, not vice versa.

A PIC must never be afraid or embarrassed to ask questions, or to ask for clarification of any ATC instruction. You are the key to safe flight. Lives depend on your ability to fly the airplane, so remain vigilant even when under air traffic control. Although ATC specialists are highly skilled in their profession, they are subject to the same human failings as the rest of us. Use ATC as a resource; don't simply follow instructions without considering their ramifications. Maintain an open dialogue with your passengers as well. They might spot traffic or a discrepancy that you don't see. And don't ignore your own senses. Pay attention if the little voice in the back of your head has something to say.

Situational Awareness

Much of this book focuses on the mechanical aspects of flying an airplane and dealing with in-flight emergencies. Although a complete understanding of the interaction between the pilot and the airplane is important, safe flight ultimately involves three mental processes: reflexive, reflective, and repeated reviewing. The reflexive process is purely instinctive, involving automatic reactions learned by the pilot. Small control inputs made to maintain heading and altitude in cruise flight represent one example of reflexive actions.

The reflective process, on the other hand, is a conscious, systematic thought process aimed at problem solving. Performing an in-flight groundspeed calculation, plotting a course to an alternate landing site, or evaluating landing options following an engine failure illustrate the reflective process. Closely tied to this process, repeated reviewing involves intelligence gathering in which the pilot looks for changes in the flight environment that might impact the safety of the flight. Examples include comparing engine instruments with the sound and feel of the engine, matching several landmarks on the ground with those shown on a sectional chart, and keeping track of other airplanes in the pattern.

Situational awareness arises from these mental processes. A knowledgeable, well-trained, experienced, and proficient pilot generally develops a broad base of reflexive responses. More mental energy is then available for reflective and repeated reviewing processes, thus improving the pilot's situational awareness. By contrast, a poorly-trained, inexperienced pilot who only flies one hour a year may possess few truly reflexive skills. An inordinate amount of energy may have to be diverted from cognitive processes to perform what should be reflexive functions. Situational awareness is often compromised as a result.

A good example of a situationally aware pilot-in-command places an experienced and proficient instrument-rated individual in solid instrument meteorological conditions (IMC). ATC errantly gives the pilot a vector that could result in contact with a mountain. Rather than being complacent under the "control" of ATC, and because this pilot has maintained sharp instrument skills (reflexive), this PIC is able to cross reference the instruction with aeronautical charts (repeated reviewing). The pilot notes the conflict, advises ATC, receives and complies with an amended clearance, and avoids the mountain (reflective process).

But what if the pilot had zero instrument training and flew into IMC? How much reflexive flying could the pilot do in this unfamiliar environment? Would sufficient mental faculties be available to work with ATC? The odds are stacked solidly against such a pilot. Statistically, this pilot will last just two minutes in IMC before losing control. In spite of this revelation, non-instrument rated pilots continue to flirt with flight into IMC.

Judgment

Since an overwhelming majority of accidents are driven by a pilot error component, a considerable amount of research has focused on human factors during flight. A simple model has been developed that fits the elements of the flight environment together like pieces of a puzzle. These elements are labelled Software, Hardware, Environment, and Liveware: Software includes such things as checklists and standard operating procedures; Hardware includes the airplane, its systems, and the physical layout of the cockpit; Environmental components include the weather as well as ambient noise, lighting, and temperature levels; Liveware includes passengers, ATC, and other pilots. The PIC, also a Liveware element, is placed at the heart of the human factors model.

The interaction of these elements greatly influences the mental processes that characterise situational awareness. Proper interfacing between elements is crucial in order for the pilot to make good judgments. Judgment itself is an intangible; however, it leads to actions that have tangible consequences. Judgment is the art of problem resolution. It involves making choices about an uncertain future based on a review of known or perceived quantities. Evaluations are made, risk is assessed, decisions are reached, and actions are taken continuously. Time constraints and stress imposed by one or more elements in the human factors model are usually thrown into the mix as well. In the end, good judgments culminate in a safe flight; poor judgments, in an accident.

Figure 13-1: The Human Factors "SHELL" Model

For example, suppose we're en route VFR to an important business meeting. Headwinds are stronger than forecasted and the weather at the destination is deteriorating rapidly. We must make a judgment whether to press on or to divert to a nearby alternate. Time limitations imposed by at least three elements now come into play: Will we make it **IN TIME**—before the airport goes IFR (Environmental)? before we run out of fuel (Hardware)? at the appointed meeting hour (Liveware)? These constraints also add a stress component, which can taint our assessment of risk: diverting sure would be inconvenient; we could lose the contract if we miss the meeting. What will our client think about us? Will we be able to cope with flight into IMC?

Good judgment requires a certain amount of objectivity throughout the decision making process. Don't lose sight of the primary goal of every flight—to return safely to the Earth. All else is secondary to this fundamental principle. Of course, good judgment is developed through experience, which is gained through an ongoing commitment to improve our flying skills and to expand our knowledge. Equally important is recognising factors that degrade or impair our ability to make good judgments.

Poor planning tends to be the father of poor judgment. Denial of an emergency, an undue concern about personal injury, and a desire to save the airplane are a few examples of internal factors that often lead to errors in judgment. Lack of familiarity with the airplane, the flight environment, operating procedures, the route of flight, and the destination airport contribute to bad decisions as well. Minor deficiencies may seem inconsequential when viewed one at a time, but it's their cumulative effect that generates momentum in favor of an accident.

Unfortunately, bad decisions tend to foster more bad decisions. False information from poor judgment negatively influences judgments that follow, setting up a chain of events that can snowball into a full blown emergency. The number of safe alternatives also dwindles rapidly as the links in the error chain multiply. Eventually, situational awareness collapses into tunnel vision.

Hazardous Attitudes

Objective, rational judgments require us to weed out our own biases from the decision-making process. The FAA has identified five attitudes that cloud a pilot's ability to make sound judgments: Anti-authority, a nobody-can-tell-me-what-to-do attitude; Invulnerability, an everything-is-wonderful-and-nothing-bad-can-happen-to-me attitude; Impulsivity, an it's-better-to-do-something—anything—right-away attitude; Macho, an I-can-handle-anything attitude; Resignation, a what's-the-use-I-give-up attitude. We all have a natural propensity toward these hazardous attitudes. It's part of the human condition. However, by being cognisant of them and their detrimental effects, we can modify our behavior so as to diminish their impact on aeronautical decisions.

The easiest way to alleviate the influence of hazardous attitudes is first to acknowledge which ones are most prevalent at a given time. Examine your state of mind before each flight: Do you feel compelled to make the flight? If so, why? Is your life worth the risk inherent in the particular flight? Be honest. The best strategy is to climb into the cockpit with a clear head and a clear plan of action. Avoid situations where you're pre-stressed with anger, resentment, get-there-itis, fatigue, or peer pressure. Once airborne, look for the warning signs indicative of shifts in your temperament that might feed an error chain.

Suppose, for instance, that you undertake a long cross country. You're fully refreshed as the flight begins, without any pre-flight stress. Initially, your skills are razor sharp. Your mind is crystal clear. As the flight continues, unanticipated turbulence and strong headwinds increase your work load. You have to change course several times to skirt around rapidly building cumulus, and you feel your energy being sapped.

The first sign of imbalance creeps in as a loss in proficiency. Discrepancies appear between targeted headings and altitudes and those actually flown. Time pressure mounts as the turbulence and frequency of diversions increase—how much fuel remains? will the weather get any worse? will I reach my destination before dark? In spite of increasing uncertainty, you now feel a sense of euphoria (Invulnerability). You've reached the second stage in the error chain.

Stage three begins. You're annoyed by the worsening developments. You blame your predicament on the weather briefer, on the FBO for delaying your departure, and maybe even on your spouse. You suddenly dislike anything ATC has to offer (Anti-authority). Annoyance becomes hostility by the fourth stage. You vent your frustrations by making erratic, abrupt control inputs (Macho and Impulsivity attitudes combined). Lastly, you exhibit irrational behavior, not caring what happens next. You feel panicky (Resignation). The stage is set for an accident. It's possible to reach this dangerous state of mind sooner by climbing into the cockpit already annoyed, or at some other unacceptable level of pre-flight stress.

Most pilots have experienced one or more of these behaviors in an airplane. The key is to recognise what's happening and to take actions to break the chain. When you note a hazardous attitude, simply stop what you're doing. Identify the attitude out loud, calling it by name. Then shake it off, relax, and regain control of the situation one piece at a time. The earlier you snap yourself out of the accident cycle, the greater the chances are that you'll maintain your composure and improve your decision-making.

Be vigilant for other indications of an error chain as well. Feeling confused or withdrawing from active participation in the flight process should raise red warning flags. Not looking outside the cockpit or fixating on one item to the exclusion of others point to a breakdown in situational awareness. Failing to meet targets (e.g.: heading, altitude, fuel consumption), violating weather minimums, exceeding operating limitations, and departing from standard operating procedures should trigger alarm bells in your head.

Stressors

The continual interaction of human factors elements deplete a pilot's mental and physical energies. Events in our lives and in the cockpit that affect our equilibrium, whether they are good or bad, are called stressors. Stress is the body's reaction to the myriad of internal and external stimuli relentlessly bombarding us. It's a necessary part of life. In fact, stress often motivates people to excel. Stress over time, though, ultimately expresses itself as fatigue. Its symptoms include daydreaming, sloppy flying, a lazy instrument scan, and slurred speech. Fatigue makes it easier to succumb to hazardous thought patterns and poor decisions.

Physical, emotional, and sociological stressors that cause fatigue are funneled to the pilot by elements in the human factors model. Physical stressors, for example, are introduced through Environmental factors like noise, vibration, turbulence, temperature and humidity extremes, and variations in breathable oxygen. They can be imposed by Hardware through unusually heavy control forces or poor panel layouts. Or they can come from such pilot (Liveware) deficiencies as illness, hunger, dehydration, an unsynchronised circadian rhythm, and lack of rest.

Boredom, self-imposed demands, and lack of physical activity generate emotional stressors that wear us down. Increases in mental work load from such Software problems as ambiguous procedures and congested aeronautical charts can also create emotional stressors. Liveware can induce sociological stressors in the form of job and peer pressures, marital problems, or traumatic events like a recent death or an upcoming wedding in the family. A sudden in-flight emergency piles physical and emotional stressors on top of these other forms of stress.

Identifying and managing stress is an important skill for the PIC to master. Interestingly, studies have found that performance degrades when people are subjected to too much stress, or too little. Peak performance occurs when under moderate amounts of stress. This may partially explain why pilots at all experience levels fall prey to so many similar accident scenarios. The important factor may not necessarily be experience, but rather performance as a function of stress.

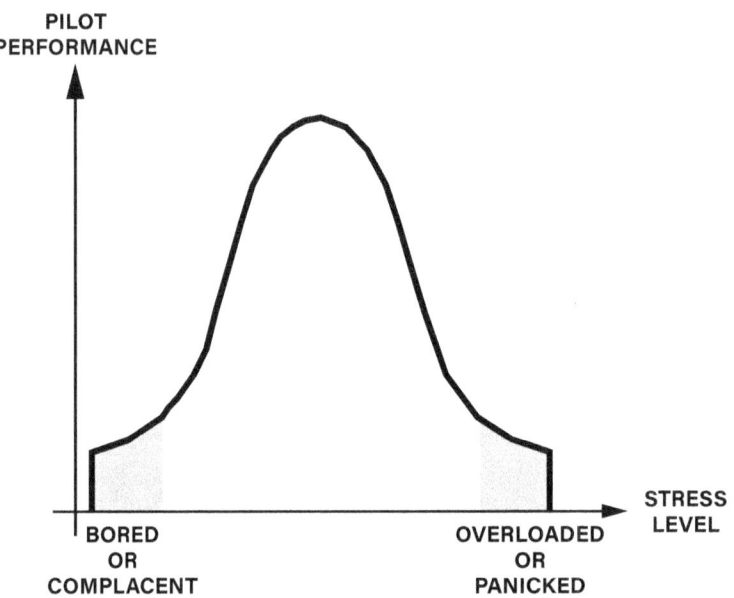

Figure 13-2: Pilot Performance as a Function of Stress

For example, one might expect an experienced pilot to be better equipped to avoid accidents than an inexperienced pilot. Complacency, however, is often a negative side effect associated with experience. The experienced pilot may be under-stimulated, whereas the inexperienced pilot may be flying on the edge, easily over-stimulated. The resulting diminished performance is the same for each, but for different reasons: the experienced pilot may be lulled into the error chain whereas the inexperienced pilot may be thrust into it by panic.

How we cope with stress varies from one individual to the next. Our physiological reactions to it, however, are identical: heart rate, blood pressure, respiration, and perspiration all rise. The degree to which these functions increase depends on our level of awareness, the impression left from similar past experiences, and the recency of those experiences. Stress imposed by an in-flight emergency will elicit a basic fight or flee response. If we have the necessary knowledge and skill, we'll initiate actions that will enhance the likelihood of a successful resolution (fight response). Otherwise, we'll either aggravate the emergency with improper inputs, or we'll become immobilised by panic (flee response).

Certainly, the better prepared we are for a crisis, the higher the probability is that we'll act instinctively to correct it. Physically practicing procedures for various scenarios develops a kinesthetic memory (like learning to ride a bicycle) that can give you a critical edge in an emergency. Familiarity also allows you to suppress the urge to panic. Your head must stay with the airplane, no matter how dire the circumstances. Many of the strategies discussed in this book strive to break emergency actions into smaller, pinpointed tasks. Using the PARE spin recovery procedure is one example. Implementing the Speed-Spot-Set-up hierarchy following an engine failure is another. By focusing on specific reactions, we reduce the likelihood of stress overload.

As stated repeatedly throughout this book, avoidance is our most powerful emergency strategy. Heed the warning signs of a growing error chain and break it early. If you find things slipping out of control, stop what you're doing. Slow down. Relax for a few moments. Take some deep breaths. If you're feeling tense, loosen your grip on the controls. Shake out your limbs and consciously let your jaw go slack. Loosen up your shoulders and neck. If you're feeling fatigued, open the air vents. Try to keep your mind active, too. Realise, though, that these are only temporary stress-reduction techniques. It may be advisable to cut the flight short so you can adequately address the stressor, perhaps by getting something to eat, or taking a nap, or allowing the weather to clear.

One of the best ways to reduce pilot work load is to plan your flight thoroughly beforehand. Proficiency is important as well. So is maintaining an organised cockpit, with easy access to maps, checklists, and other necessities. Review pertinent emergency procedures often. Be flexible, and keep your options open. If you do encounter an emergency, talk yourself through the appropriate actions. Verbalising checklist items or the strategies outlined in this book, for instance, will help your mind and body work in concert to resolve the conflict.

A margin of safety exists whenever our capability exceeds the demands placed upon us. This margin fluctuates throughout the course of a normal flight, typically shrinking to a minimum during the landing phase. In terms of routine operations, landing imposes the greatest requirements on the pilot. Here, the airplane is manoeuvred at critically low speeds and altitudes, at high angles of attack, in close proximity to other aircraft, while trying to converge on a single point on the runway. At the same time, fatigue has been chipping away at our own capability since takeoff.

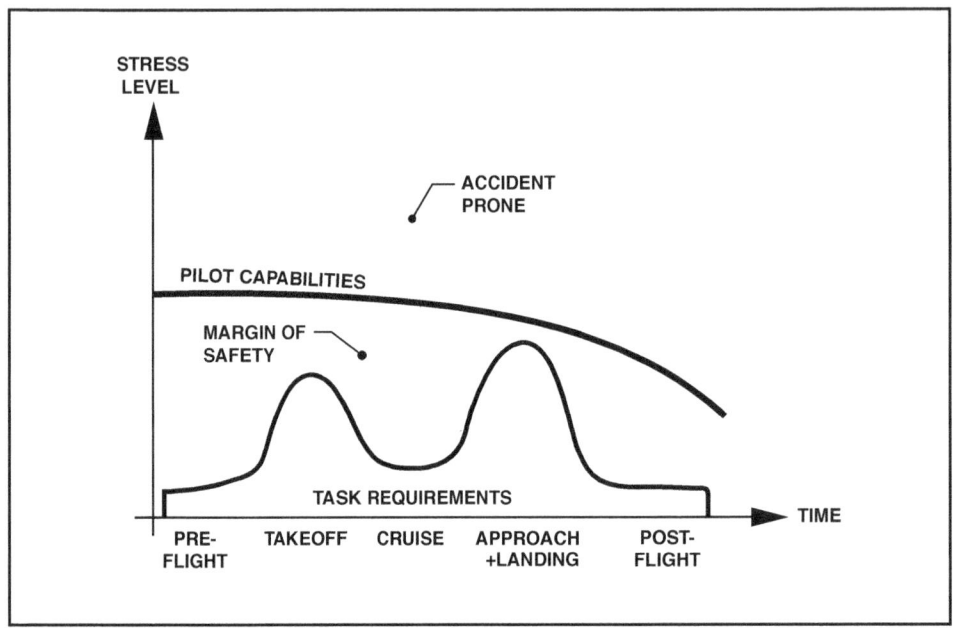

Figure 13-3: Pilot Capability vs. Task Requirements during a Routine Flight

A routine takeoff also places a high work load on the pilot, although it often isn't as demanding as landing. Furthermore, since takeoffs obviously occur before landings, our relative capability is greater. This typically results in a larger margin of safety during takeoff than during landing. Interestingly, research has shown that while task requirements are lower during takeoff than landing, takeoffs tend to be more stressful. Although this may seem counterintuitive, the start of a flight is fraught with far more uncertainty than the end.

A cross country, for instance, begins with many unanswered questions: will the engine quit on climb out? will anything go wrong en route? will I remain on course? will fuel consumption be as estimated? will I get lost? Upon arriving at the destination, most of these questions have been answered. The runway is in sight, and everything has gone according to plan so far. Although the landing will be the most demanding part of the flight, the initial stress created from all of the uncertainty now manifests itself as fatigue.

We can maintain a suitable margin of safety by engaging only in flight activities where our capability exceeds task requirements. All of the influencing elements discussed in this Chapter must be considered when evaluating the safety factor for a particular operation. Flying fatigued or pre-stressed reduces your margin of safety. Encountering situations in which neither you nor your airplane are equipped to handle also reduces your margin of safety. Once task requirements overshadow capability, an accident is likely.

As the pilot in command, establish a set of personal operating limitations. They should be flexible, and should factor in your recency of experience, your current state of mind and body, and common sense. Incorporate the limitations published for your airplane into your personal limitations as well. And don't be influenced by the credos of other pilots—do only what's comfortable for you! Also, keep in mind that the FAR's establish **minimum** acceptable operating standards. Challenge yourself to conduct your flight operations to higher standards.

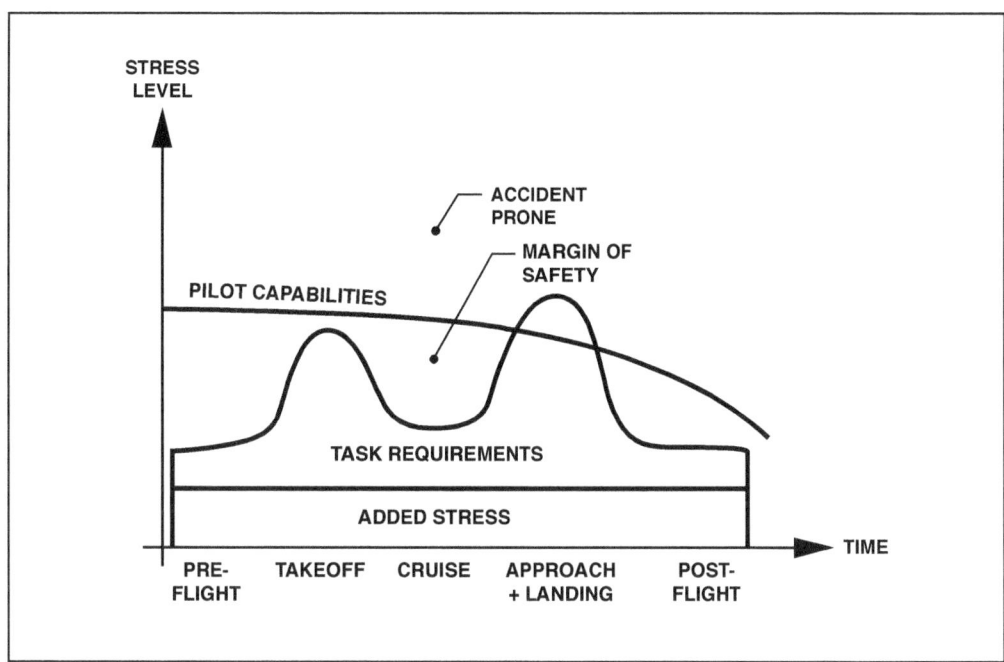

Figure 13-4: Pilot Capability vs. Task Requirements with an Added Stress Component

See And Be Seen

A fundamental responsibility of the PIC is to minimise the threat of mid-air collisions. As one might expect, this threat is greatest within five miles of an airport. Most mid-airs occur in broad daylight under VFR conditions. The PIC, therefore, must be vigilant scanning for potential conflicts, especially in and around the traffic pattern. We should always scrutinise as much of the sky as possible, but our most immediate threats are those appearing within a sector from our 9 o'clock to our 3 o'clock position, within 1,000 feet of our altitude.

Of course, we must be looking outside of the cockpit for the see-and-avoid concept to be effective. If you fly VFR and choose to fixate on the instruments, YOU are responsible for increasing your chances of a midair. If ATC directs you into the path of another aircraft in the pattern, YOU are still responsible for seeing and avoiding. Remember, ATC is generally provided where higher concentrations of air traffic and greater chances for conflicts exist—hardly the environment in which to bury your head in the cockpit.

Our piloting skills must be advanced enough to maintain airspeed and altitude almost reflexively in the pattern. Only then can we spend adequate time spotting other traffic and sequencing safely into the loop. Situational awareness means not only knowing what's going on in front of you, but also what's going on behind you and on the surface. Form a good mental picture of the traffic flow before plunging headlong into the pattern. Take inventory of airplanes in the vicinity, and keep track of their progress relative to you. Make adjustments in your flight path as needed.

We can lessen our exposure to a mid-air by planning ahead. As PIC, you're required to ascertain all of the pertinent information regarding your destination. This includes radio frequencies, traffic pattern altitudes and directions, recommended operating procedures, and runway lengths and conditions. You may have to reference several sources, like sectional charts, Airport/Facility Directories, and NOTAMS to collect the necessary data. Also, a phone call to an FBO at an unfamiliar airport could give you important insight into pattern procedures there.

En route, monitor the correct radio frequency to get a feel for the runway in use and the traffic in the pattern. Configure your airplane for a smooth transition into the flow of the pattern. Establish the proper altitude and airspeed early. Don't enter the pattern from an unexpected position, or at high speed, or at an unusual altitude. When unsure about the flow of traffic at a non-tower airport, overfly the field at least 500 feet above the recommended pattern altitude. Study the segmented circle and wind indicators, look for traffic, then blend yourself into the pattern.

Give other pilots an opportunity to see and avoid you, too. Be conspicuous in the air—turn on your lights, rock your wings once in a while, and perform an occasional S-turn. Give accurate position reports, especially around non-tower airports. Reporting "over the golf course", for instance, should mean that it's directly under your seat as you speak, not that you can see it over the nose and you'll be there in a minute or two. An erroneous position report can divert another pilot's attention to an empty piece of sky, away from your true position. Be literal when you speak.

You may even want to modify your radio calls at non-tower fields to help other pilots spot your airplane. For example, if you're one of a half dozen airplanes in the pattern, identifying yourself as the "red and white Cessna", or the "yellow Biplane", conveys more useful information than merely stating your N-number. Transmitting "blue Piper turning left downwind, Runway 22" when profiled in a bank will get you recognised far more easily than stating, "Piper 12345, left downwind, Runway 22".

Know where you're vulnerable as well. Low wing airplanes are blind to traffic underneath; high wing airplanes, to traffic above. Biplanes have blind spots above and below. Slow airplanes are vulnerable to fast traffic behind them (look over your shoulder now and then if that's you). A nose high attitude in slow flight can create a blind spot straight ahead. Even the bill on a baseball cap can restrict your vision. Clear those blind areas ahead, above, and below with coordinated S-turns. Occasionally lean forward as you look around, too. When rolling onto base leg, be sure to look for potential conflicts on an opposing base leg or on a long, low final.

It's Up To You

The confidence required to act as a pilot in command is built on education, experience, and an understanding of the flight environment. Inadequate training, misinformation, and a lack of understanding, on the other hand, increase pilot passivity, foster insecurity and lack of control, and cloud the judgment process. How can we navigate, communicate, and deal with in flight situations efficiently if we doubt our basic knowledge and skill?

The solution begins with accepting your role as the pilot in command. Be committed to honing your skills each time you fly. Concentrate on specific tasks, be it slow flight in the pattern, or smooth and coordinated turns, or precise altitude and airspeed control. Pay attention to details. Don't simply drive the airplane from point A to point B.

On your next cross-country, for example, try a VOR cross-fix to locate your position on the sectional chart, or calculate the time, distance, and fuel to an alternate landing site, or perform a no flap landing at your destination. Treat yourself to an hour or two of dual instruction each year. Get involved with the FAA's Pilot Proficiency Award (Wings) Program. Take the opportunity to learn something new as part of your next Flight Review. Better yet, consider enrolling in an emergency manoeuvre training program.

Continued training improves our ability to divide our attention between several tasks, to see and avoid potential conflicts, to react to the effects of the wind, and to control an airplane smoothly and safely. Ultimately, training and practice transform rote manipulation of the controls into reflexive responses. Don't continue to fly with unaddressed concerns, especially when some competent instruction can dissolve your apprehension. Take control of your airplane, don't let it control you.

And above all, please—**BE SAFE!**

Appendix 1—For More Information

If you're interested in receiving hands-on training in the subjects discussed in this book, a number of flight schools and books specialising in some form of spin, aerobatic, or emergency manoeuvre training can be found in Australia. Please use the following list to advance your education:

Rich Stowell Consulting
Meridian, ID U.S.A.
www.RichStowell.com, Rich@RichStowell.com, +1 (805) 218-0161

Brett Anderson at Anderson Aviation
Riddells Creek, Victoria
www.andersonaviation.com.au

Edge Aviation
edgeaviation@yahoo.com

Strike Aviation Training
www.strikeaviationtraining.com

Stall Spin Awareness by Rich Stowell
www.pilottrain.com.au

David Pilkington's Aerobatics Down Under Series
www.ozaeros.net.au

Aerobatics by David Robson
www.aviationtheory.net.au

Flight Tests by Jim Davis
www.jimdavis.com.au

Before signing up for hands-on training, be sure to interview a few flight schools and ask plenty of questions. Minimum specifications should include: a qualified flight instructor specialising in the training sought, an airplane approved for the manoeuvres to be flown, two current parachutes (periodically inspected and repacked per the FAR's), and a logical course outline that includes in-depth ground instruction before each flight.

Inquire about the instructor's background and experience, especially with the manoeuvres to be performed. Will the instructor work at **YOUR** pace? Does the instructor appear confident, but not pretentious? Do the instructor's answers make sense to you? Don't be afraid to ask about the potential for motion sickness, too; conscientious instructors will be sensitive to your physiological make-up.

This type of training also demands a lot from an airplane, so closely inspect it inside and out. Ask about the practice area, training altitudes, and potential landing sites in the event of an emergency. It's wise to review the CASRs pertaining to aerobatic flight, parachutes, and parachuting as well, which are contained in Part 61, 91 and 105. Does the school have or need an aerobatic waiver to perform the manoeuvres outlined? If so, what are the provisions on the waiver?

Make sure the flight school can provide the service that your time and dollars command. More importantly, the interview must instill the confidence to place your life into the hands of the instructor and the equipment. If it doesn't, keep looking.

Appendix 2—EMT® Program Syllabus

The following pages contain the 1993 copyrighted version of the EMT® Program syllabus. The complete program encompasses three building-block Modules. Each specialised Module consists of three hours of ground instruction and three hours of flight instruction, spread over four separate lessons. This version was approved under Federal Aviation Regulations Part 141—Pilot Refresher Course, (March of 1994) in the United States of America.

Here are just a few comments received from EMT® Program students over the years:

Rigorous, challenging, and exciting... perhaps the best training I have yet had. —Bill Gruber, AOPA PILOT magazine

Emergency Maneuver Training is the best kind of life insurance; it helps you avoid having an accident. —Murry Rozanski, Sport Pilot's Hot Kits & Homebuilts magazine

an educating and eye-opening experience with applications to real life situations. —Amy Laboda, Sport Pilot magazine

The most rewarding and exciting experience I have encountered. —John Bizal

I have highly recommended it to all of the pilots I know! —Linda Schad

It truly was the pinnacle of my student pilot training. —Loni Miller

The dynamics of control inputs were more complicated than I had thought. —Jim Cunningham

spread the word ... "real training is back!" —Jim Houston

I learned more comparatively in one week than many other years combined. —Rick Johnston

MODULE I

Stall/Spin Awareness

Lesson 1

1. Climbing Dutch Rolls
2. Turns & Slow Flight
3. Stalls—Power On & Power Off
4. Rudder Stall Exercise
5. Introduce One-Turn Spin

Lesson 2

1. Review
2. One-Turn Spins Left & Right
3. Two-Turn Spins Left & Right
4. Spin Orientation
5. 180 Degree Power Off Approach to Land

Lesson 3

1. Review Spins
2. Spin Dynamics
3. Selected Aggravated Spin Modes
4. Unusual Attitudes—Spin Recoveries
5. 180 Degree Power off Approach to Land

Lesson 4

1. Incipient Spin Entries
2. Skidding Turns
3. Critical Flight Operations
4. Spirals
5. 180 Degree Power Off Approach to Land
6. Optional—Introduction to Rolls

MODULE II

In-Flight Emergencies

Lesson 1

1. Review Dutch Rolls & Spins
2. Aileron Rolls Left & Right
3. Half Aileron Rolls Left & Right
4. Inverted Flight
5. 180 Degree Power Off Approach to Land

Lesson 2

1. Review Spins
2. Rolls & Half Rolls Left & Right
3. Unusual Attitudes—Overbanked Recoveries
4. Aerobatic-Style Turns
5. 180 Degree Power Off Approach to Land

Lesson 3

1. Review Spins & Rolls
2. Slips Left & Right
3. Slipping Turns Left & Right
4. Turning Dutch Rolls
5. Slip to Land on Final Approach

Lesson 4

1. Review Spins & Rolls
2. Simulated Control Loss Practice
3. Simulated Off-Airport Landings
4. 180 Degree Power Off Approach to Land
5. Optional—Introduction to Loops

MODULE III

Basic Aerobatics

Lesson 1
1. Review Spins & Rolls
2. Half Loops
3. Full Loops
4. Immelmanns

Lesson 2
1. Review Loops, Spins, & Rolls
2. Half Cuban Eights
3. Reverse Half Cuban Eights
4. Hammerhead Turns

Lesson 3
1. Review All Manoeuvres
2. Design & Fly an Aerobatic Sequence

Lesson 4
1. Review All Manoeuvres
2. Inverted Turns
3. Inverted Dutch Rolls
4. Inverted Spins Left & Right

Bibliography

AOPA Air Safety Foundation. "To Spin Or Not To Spin." Flight Instructor's Safety Report, 17, No. 4 (October 1991), pp. 1-8.

Beggs, Gene. "Out Spinning with Gene Beggs." Sport Aerobatics, February 1984, pp. 14-17.

Beggs, Gene. "Out Spinning with Gene Beggs, Part II." Undated manuscript.

Bramson, Alan. "Parke's Dive and All That." Flyer, February 1994, pp. 41-44.

Burk, Sanger M., Jr., James S. Bowman, Jr., and William L. White. "Spin-Tunnel Investigation of the Spinning Characteristics of Typical Single-Engine General Aviation Airplane Designs." NASA Technical Paper 1009. NASA-Langley, 1977.

Cessna. Spin Characteristics of Cessna Models 150, A150, 152, A152, 172, R172 & 177. Wichita, KS: Cessna Aircraft Company, 1981.

Chambers, Joseph R., and H. Paul Stough, III. "Summary of NASA Stall/Spin Research for General Aviation Configurations." AIAA Paper No. 86-2597, September 1986.

Cole, Duane. Roll Around a Point. Milwaukee: Ken Cook Company, 1976.

Cox, Jack. "Velocity ... Solving a Deep Stall Riddle." Sport Aviation, July 1991, pp. 53-59.

Czaplyski, Vincent. "Improving Pilot Performance." Aviation Safety, 12, No. 16 (15 August 1992), pp. 6-7.

DeLacerda, Fred, Ph.D. "CRM For The Single Pilot." Flight Training, October 1992, pp. 26-30.

DeLacerda, Fred. Surviving Spins. Ames: Iowa State University Press, 1989.

DiCarlo, D.J., et al. "Development of Spin Resistance Criteria for Light General Aviation Airplanes." AIAA Paper No. 86-9812. Hampton, VA: Langley Research Center, 1986.

Douglas, Andrew B. "Fatigue in the Cockpit." Aviation Safety, 1 & 15 December 1990, pp. 9-11.

Douglas, Andrew. "Fear, Panic Can Wreck Pilot Ability." Aviation Safety's 1990 Pilot's Safety Handbook, pp. 25-29.

FAA. "Aeronautical Decision Making." Advisory Circular 60-22. 13 December 1991.

FAA. "Aircraft Wake Turbulence." Advisory Circular 90-23E. 1 October 1991.

FAA. "Anatomy of a Landing, Cue by Cue." Accident Prevention Program, FAA-P-8740-26.

FAA. "Flight Training Handbook." Advisory Circular 61-21A. Oklahoma City: U.S. Department of Transportation, Federal Aviation Administration, rev. 1980.

FAA. "Hydroplaning and the Pilot." <u>AFS Examiner Update</u>, 5, No. 1 (January 1993), p. 2.

FAA. "Impossible Turn." <u>Accident Prevention Program, FAA-P-8740-44</u>.

FAA. "Introduction to Pilot Judgment." <u>Accident Prevention Program, FAA-P-8740-53</u>.

FAA. "On Landings Part I." <u>Accident Prevention Program, FAA-P-8740-48</u>.

FAA. "On Landings Part II." <u>Accident Prevention Program, FAA-P-8740-49</u>.

FAA. "On Landings Part III." <u>Accident Prevention Program, FAA-P-8740-50</u>.

FAA. <u>Pilot's Handbook of Aeronautical Knowledge</u>. Basin, WY: Aviation Maintenance Publishers, rev. 1980.

FAA. "Stall and Spin Awareness." <u>General Aviation News</u>, September-October 1979, Reprint.

FAA. "Stall and Spin Awareness Training." <u>Advisory Circular 61-67B</u>. 17 May 1991.

FAA. "To Spin or not to Spin, Part I." <u>Aviation News</u>, 31, No. 3 (May-June 1992), pp. 11-14.

FAA. "To Spin or not to Spin, Part II." <u>Aviation News</u>, 31, No. 4 (July-August 1992), pp. 16-18.

FAA. "Torque, What It Means To The Pilot." <u>Accident Prevention Program, 1978-785-810</u>.

FAR Part 23. <u>Code of Federal Regulations—Airworthiness Standards: Normal, Utility, Acrobatic, and Commuter Category Airplanes</u>. Washington, DC: U.S. Government Printing Office, 1990.

Fried, Howard J. "Conscious Pursuit of Safety." <u>Aviation Safety</u>, 15 February 1993, pp. 6-7.

Garrison, Peter. "Deep, Deep Stall." <u>Flying</u>, January 1992, pp. 102-103.

Garrison, Peter. "Turnbacks: For Paper Airplanes?" <u>Flying</u>, January 1991, pp. 91-92.

Gless, Richard D., and Paul Bray. <u>Avoiding the Stall/Spin Accident</u>. Frederick, MD: AOPA Air Safety Foundation, 1988.

Heitman, William P. "Managing Stress." <u>Aviation Safety</u>, 1 & 15 December 1990, pp. 12-13.

Hoffman, William C., and Walter M. Hollister. "General Aviation Pilot Stall Awareness Training Study." <u>Report No. FAA-RD-77-26</u>. U.S. Department of Transportation, Federal Aviation Administration, September 1976.

Holmes, Harold. <u>"Cockpit Classroom"—Aviation Training Articles From EAA's Sport Aviation Magazine</u>. Palatine, IL: Haldon Books, Inc., 1987.

Hurt, H.H., Jr. <u>Aerodynamics for Naval Aviators</u>. Office of the Chief of Naval Operations Aviation Training Division, rev. 1965.

Jacobson, Brian M. "Handling Slick Runways." Aviation Safety, 12, No. 19 (1 October 1992), pp. 7-8.

Jacobson, Brian M. "Poor Judgment Is a Killer." Aviation Safety, 15 March 1993, pp. 8-10.

Jones, Barry E. "Deep Stall ... Continued!" Sport Aviation, September 1991, p. 55.

Katz, Peter. Emergency Landing Techniques. Peter Katz Productions, 1991.

Kelly, Bill. "Beyond the Basics of Icing." Aviation Safety, 13, No. 22 (15 November 1993), pp. 1-6.

Kelly, Bill. "Deep Stall." Aviation Safety, 1 March 1990, pp. 4-6.

Kelly, Bill. "Surviving a Power Loss on Takeoff." Aviation Safety, 10, No. 20 (15 October 1990), pp. 1-5.

Kelly, Bill. "The Perils of Turning Back." Aviation Safety, 10, No. 20 (15 October 1990), p. 6.

Kershner, William K. The Basic Aerobatic Manual. Ames: Iowa State University Press, 1987.

Kershner, William K. The Flight Instructor's Manual. Ames: Iowa State University Press, 3rd ed. 1993.

Langewiesche, Wolfgang. Stick and Rudder. New York: McGraw-Hill Book Company, 1972.

Lindemann, F.A., H. Glauert, and R.G. Harris. "The Experimental and Mathematical Investigation of Spinning." Advisory Committee for Aeronautics Reports and Memoranda, No. 411. London: Sir Joseph Causton & Sons, Ltd., March 1918.

Lowery, John. Anatomy of a Spin: A Complete Study of the Stall/Spin Phenomena. Long Beach, CA: Airguide Publications, Inc., 1981.

Manuel, G.S., et al. "Investigations of Modifications to Improve the Spin Resistance of a High-Wing, Single-Engine, Light Airplane." SAE Technical Paper Series: No. 891039. Warrendale, PA: Society of Automotive Engineers, Inc., 1989.

Mason, Sammy. Stalls, Spins, and Safety. New York: Macmillan Publishing Company, 1982.

McAvoy, W. H. "Piloting Technique for Recovery from Spins." NACA Technical Note No. 555, 16 January 1936.

Medore, Art. Primary Aerobatic Flight Training. Dover, NJ: Ardot Enterprises, Inc., 1970.

Merkt, Juan R. "The Power Curve's Other Side." Flight Training, January 1992, pp. 26-33.

Müller, Eric. "The Spin—Myth and Reality." Sport Aerobatics, November 1981, pp. 16-17.

Müller, Eric, and Annette Carson. Flight Unlimited. Great Britain: The Eastern Press Ltd., 1983.

Neihouse, Anshal I., Walter J. Klinar, and Stanley H. Scher. "Status of Spin Research for Recent Airplane Designs." NASA Technical Report R-57. Langley Field, VA:

Langley Research Center, 1960.

NTSB. "Special Study—General Aviation Stall/Spin Accidents, 1967-1969." <u>NTSB Report Number: NTSB-AAS-72-8</u>. Washington, DC: National Transportation Safety Board, 1972.

Patiky, Mark. "Averting Disaster." <u>Aviation Safety</u>, 11, No. 22 (15 November 1991), pp. 1-4.

Patton, James M., Jr. "A Status Report on NASA General Aviation Stall/Spin Flight Testing." <u>S.E.T.P. Technical Review</u>, 15, No. 1 (1980), pp. 36-49.

Patton, James M., Jr., H. Paul Stough, III, and Daniel J. DiCarlo. "Spin Flight Research Summary." <u>SAE Technical Paper Series: No. 790565</u>. Warrendale, PA: Society of Automotive Engineers, Inc., April 1979.

Schiff, Barry. "A Judgment Call." <u>AOPA Pilot</u>, November 1993, p. 112.

Schiff, Barry. "Deep Stalls." <u>AOPA Pilot</u>, September 1993, pp. T29-T32.

Seldes, George. <u>The Great Thoughts</u>. New York: Ballantine Books (a division of Random House, Inc.), 1985, p. 460.

Smith, H.C. "Skip". <u>The Illustrated Guide to Aerodynamics</u>. Blue Ridge Summit, PA: TAB Books, 1992.

Smith, Robert T. <u>Advanced Flight Maneuvers and Aerobatics</u>. Blue Ridge Summit, PA: Tab Books, 1980.

Stough, H. Paul, III, Daniel J. DiCarlo, and James M. Patton, Jr. "Flight Investigation of Stall, Spin, and Recovery Characteristics of a Low-Wing, Single-Engine, T-Tail Light Airplane." <u>NASA Technical Paper 2427</u>, May 1985.

Stowell, Rich. <u>PARE™ - The Emergency Spin Recovery Procedure</u>. Ventura, CA: Loren Educational Services, 1991.

Taylor, Richard L. <u>Fair-Weather Flying</u>. New York: MacMillan Publishing Company, 1974.

Thomas, Bill. <u>Fly for Fun</u>. Ed. Hank Foley and Joye Thomas. 1985.

Thomas, Kas. <u>Fly the Engine</u>. Old Greenwich, CT: TBO Advisor Books, 1993.

Veillette, Patrick R., and Rand Decker, Ph.D. "Handling Horizontal Tornados." <u>Aviation Safety</u>, 13, Nos. 13-14 (July 1993), pp. 3-9.

Waldock, William D. "Surviving a Forced Landing." <u>Aviation Safety</u>, 11, No. 2 (15 January 1991), pp. 1-4.

Williams, Neil. <u>Aerobatics</u>. New York: St. Martin's Press, first published in the United States in 1979.

www.ingramcontent.com/pod-product-compliance
Lightning Source LLC
Chambersburg PA
CBHW081418300426
44109CB00019BA/2338